Montgomery in the Good War

MONTGOMERY
in the GOOD WAR

Portrait of a Southern City • 1939–1946

WESLEY PHILLIPS NEWTON

Introduction by ALLEN CRONENBERG

THE UNIVERSITY OF ALABAMA PRESS

Tuscaloosa and London

Copyright © 2000
The University of Alabama Press
Tuscaloosa, Alabama 35487-0380
All rights reserved
Manufactured in the United States of America

2 3 4 5 6 7 8 9 . 08 07 06 05 04 03 02 01 00

Designer: Michele Myatt Quinn
Typeface: Granjon

∞

The paper on which this book is printed meets the
minimum requirements of American National Standard for
Information Science–Permanence of Paper for Printed Library
Materials, ANSI Z39.48–1984.

Newton, Wesley Phillips.
    Montgomery in the good war: portrait of a Southern city,
    1939–1946 / Wesley Phillips Newton; introduction by Allen
    Cronenberg.
            p. cm.
    Includes bibliographical references and index.
      ISBN 0-8173-1043-6 (alk. paper)
    1. World War, 1939–1945—Alabama—Montgomery. 2.
    World War, 1939–1945—Social aspects—Alabama—
    Montgomery.   3. Montgomery (Ala.)—History—20th
    century. 4. Montgomery (Ala.)—Social conditions—20th
    century. 5. Montgomery (Ala.) I. Title.
    D769.85.A21 M665 2000
    940.53'76147—dc21

00-008741

British Library Cataloguing-in-Publication Data available

To
Peggy Penton Cravey, who represented in ways both
graceful and spirited that wartime generation,
and
Georgia Lin Bartels-Newton and any other of my
grandchildren who may be born in the future

Contents

Illustrations

Acknowledgments

Two persons were vital to completion of the manuscript that became this book. Merlin Owen Newton, my wife, has played a key role in the creation of every book I have published. A fine historian with a prize-winning book of her own, Merlin read the manuscript chapter by chapter and did not let our relationship stand in the way of trenchant commentary on the substance and themes of the work. I have her to thank, too, for exacting copyediting of the writing itself. Without her the book would never have achieved the dignity of print.

Stephen L. McFarland, a friend, with me the coauthor of several worthwhile works, a former colleague and associate dean of the graduate school at Auburn University, and one of the foremost historians of airpower, evaluated the manuscript. Steve did not let friendship stand in the way of frank criticisms. Among other cogent observations, he noted that the epilogue was lacking and that it failed to analyze changes in Montgomery that had been brought about by the war. As a result of Steve's comments I headed back into the trenches.

My bright and accomplished children, Linda, Alan, and Brent Newton, have always shown an interest in their parents' scholarship. Many times I found the energy to plow ahead by anticipating their reactions. Robert Newton, my brother, a World War II veteran, offered encouragement.

Veterans of the home front and the war fronts who granted me interviews and provided photographs, letters, and other documents have given this book much life and substance, flesh and blood; my gratitude is boundless to those whose names are found in the text, notes, and bibliography. My memory contained only a fragment of

Montgomery's wartime experience. My gratitude extends to relatives of certain deceased veterans who graciously shared documents and photographs regarding their loved ones. The names of these people appear in the sources.

I am grateful to Allen Cronenberg for his introduction to the book. He is director of the Arts and Humanities Center at Auburn University and author of the definitive history of Alabama in World War II.

The Alabama State Department of Archives and History was the major repository for records used in researching the manuscript. Director Ed Bridges has an excellent and patient staff. Nancy Dupree, Albert LaBlanc, Willie Maryland, and Frazine Taylor made labor easier in the microfilm reading room and helped me get copies of articles from newspapers and other sources. Rickie Louise Brunner, John Hardin, Norwood Kerr, and Ken Tilley were models of professionalism in helping me find documentation and photographs.

At Auburn University in Montgomery, history department head John Fair and reference librarian Debbie West together expedited my review of microfilm copies of the *Montgomery Advertiser* on interlibrary loan from Auburn's main campus. They arranged to let me use the microfilm reader usually reserved for regular faculty in the AUM Library and thereby saved me countless hours of research.

In the office of the Montgomery city clerk, Brenda Blalock readily located volumes of the minutes from the meetings of the Montgomery City Commission. She also provided me with work space out of the way of those with business in the clerk's office.

At Landmarks, where she was the director, Mary Ann Neeley arranged to have me present a version of the section describing Montgomery's reaction to Pearl Harbor. She also cosponsored, with Bert Hitchcock, then director of Auburn University's Arts and Humanities Center, my overview of Montgomery in World War II, which was also presented at Landmarks. Lew Nyman, program chairman of the local chapter of the Retired Officers Association, asked me to speak about Montgomery's reaction to the Battle of the Bulge at a chapter meeting at Maxwell Air Force Base. I appreciated the recognition of my work that came thanks to these individuals; it greatly lifted my morale.

Jerome Ennels, director of the Air University Office of History and coauthor with me of a history of Maxwell Air Force Base, was a cheerleader and provided some valuable photographs. Joe Caver of the Historical Research Agency at Maxwell provided some valuable documentation. Starr Smith, a fine photographer and travel writer, volunteered to take the photograph of me with the historic Fountain in the Square and Winter Building in the background that appears on the dust jacket. He was a constant source of encouragement. Bill Brown, associate editor of the *Advertiser,* and that paper's former publisher Dick Amberg, also encouraged me in various ways.

Nicole Mitchell, director of the University of Alabama Press, and her able staff, particularly Kathy Swain, Michelle Sellers, and Mindy Wilson, held me to the grindstone. As a result of their efforts, the project is far better than it was when I submitted it. The two prepublication readers of the manuscript, selected by the press, made evaluations that I found right on target. Marcia Brubeck, an independent copyeditor, made the book more readable.

Earlier versions of certain parts of the book appeared in various places. My discussion of Montgomery's role in and reaction to the invasion of Normandy and the Battle of the Bulge, and reactions to V-E Day and V-J Day, originally appeared in the *Advertiser.* I first traced the early history of the Blue-Gray game in *Montgomery Living.* Sketches of the Montgomery chapter of the Red Cross in World War II and the tornado of February 1945 first appeared in the *Herald* of the Montgomery County Historical Society. Shorter versions of parts of the history of Maxwell and Gunter Fields originally saw print in *The Wisdom of Eagles,* coauthored by Jerome Ennels and me.

For permission to quote from Randall Williams's interview with E. D. Nixon, prepared for a radio history of the civil rights movement entitled "Will the Circle Be Unbroken," I thank the Southern Regional Council, Atlanta, Georgia.

For helpful criticism of the section on social class and caste in Chapter 1, I thank Sarah Woolfolk Wiggins and J. Mills Thornton III, natives of Montgomery as well as distinguished scholars, and friends and acquaintances who lived in Montgomery at the outset of World War II, including Mary Louise (Caton) Weed, Dorothy Ghent, Robert Lawrence, Ralph Loeb, Jr., my brother, Robert Newton, John Sawyer, and Idessa (Taylor) Redden.

For permission to reproduce photographs, I thank: the Alabama State Department of Archives and History, Stanley Paulger Studio/ Tommy Giles Photographic Service, the estate of Horace Perry, the Air University Office of History, Martin Epsman, Mrs. Charles W. Davis, Albert Krause Studio/Tommy Giles Photographic Services, Joanna B. Crane, Catherine Cobb, William Howard, Paul Robinson, Dorothy Sams, Dorothy Ghent Moore, Penton Cook, Fred Burks, Ralph Loeb, Jr., Silas and Jean Nettles, Idessa Redden, John Sawyer, Marguerite Sherlock, Robert Sternenberg, Robert Young, and Laurens W. Pierce.

I alone remain responsible for any misrepresentations, faulty analysis, and errors.

Introduction

Allen Cronenberg

World War II had a profound impact on America, including Alabama and the rest of the American South, and perhaps shaped society even more than the Civil War. Such was the view cautiously advanced a little more than a decade ago by Morton Sosna.[1] More recently, a probing collection of essays by Sosna, James C. Cobb, and Clarence L. Mohr, among others, in *Remaking Dixie: The Impact of World War II on the American South,* edited by Neil R. McMillen, suggests that World War II produced dramatic changes that ultimately led to the modern Sunbelt South.[2]

While they do not deny the Civil War's significance—most importantly with respect to the preservation of the union and the abolition of slavery—some of these historians maintain that it produced little fundamental long-term change. The South remained overwhelmingly rural, still dependent on cotton and on the industry of the North. The planter class, in alliance with a small industrial, financial, and commercial class, retained most of its power, if not its wealth. Sharecropping and tenancy took the place of slavery. Jim Crow laws robbed African Americans of the elusive promise of equality under the law. The patriarchal social order at home and in the community was still intact. Because of poll taxes, poor whites were as disenfranchised as blacks.

On the other hand, some of the most important developments that radically altered Alabama and the American South in the second half of the twentieth century originated in World War II. Although Gerald Nash has written quite convincingly about the role that World War II played in transforming the American West, especially California, into the booming juggernaut of modern American society, no comparable study exists for the American South. By almost any measure, however—significant industrial and commercial growth; revolutionary changes in race relations and civil rights; remaking of gender relations and family structures; vast expansion of governmental authority, especially federal; demographic shifts, especially urbanization and the influx of nonsoutherners into the region; erosion of the Democratic Party's primacy and the emergence of a genuine two-party political system; and greatly expanded and more democratic access to higher education—World War II clearly marked the start of a comparable transformation in the American South.

In contrast to the seemingly endless stream of books and articles on the Civil War and its aftermath, only a few modern studies or anecdotal histories—on Alabama, Louisiana, Arkansas, Georgia, North Carolina, Texas, and Florida—examine the profound impact of World War II on southern states and assess their contributions to the war effort.[3] Even fewer accounts of the impact of World War II on southern cities have been written. A notable exception is Robert Spinney's splendid and recently published study of Nashville, Tennessee, during World War II.[4] Nashville lacked the booming defense industry or a huge, newly established military facility on the scale of comparable medium-sized towns such as Mobile, Norfolk, or San Diego, which almost overnight became heavily impacted metropolitan areas. Nonetheless, Spinney argues, Nashville experienced a decisive rupture with its past. He argues that, in addition to the war's influence on the future of race relations and the role of women in American society—arguably two of the defining issues in southern history, and indeed in American history, in the second half of the twentieth century—World War II further broke down resistance to the growth of the power and scope of the state, especially the federal government, which assumed ballooning responsibilities in subsequent decades. Even in the South, Spinney argues, traditional opposition to the expansion of state power eroded when political and economic leaders were confronted with demands for improved public works, better jobs, and, after World War II, access to higher education and improved health care.

Now Wes Newton's book on Montgomery provides another important case study of the impact of World War II on a major southern city. This is the first important study of an Alabama city—and its people—in World War II. Newton describes the enormous contributions that Montgomery and its people made to the war and considers how the war served as a catalyst for future change while also reinforcing many traditional values, beliefs, and practices. This book is, in many ways, a personal memoir. Wes Newton's perceptions of events are shaped by his own memories and experiences. Newton came of age in Montgomery during the early 1940s, graduated from Sidney Lanier High School, fought in the European theater, and was captured by the Germans and held in a prisoner-of-war camp until his liberation in the spring of 1945. Like many returning veterans, he took full advantage of the educational opportunities provided by the GI Bill of Rights. Later, as a distinguished professor at Auburn University and an authority on the history of airpower, Newton combined scholarly thoroughness and a fondness for narrative history. He possesses a keen eye and ear for anecdotes. Not surprisingly, he interviewed dozens of Montgomerians about their experiences on the battlefield or the home front. His unprecedented efforts to locate and interview African Americans from Montgomery who served in World War II set the standard for the study of any southern city—or state—in World War II. Newton also diligently discovered and interviewed women from Montgomery about their service in auxiliary military units or wartime volunteer activities. Only in the case of Mobile—thanks to the pioneering research of Mary Martha Thomas—do we know more about the roles of Alabama women in World War II.[5] Newton's book successfully combines historical authenticity and human drama.

Montgomery's major contribution to the war effort—apart from sending its own men and women into the military services or its contributions to the volunteerism on the home front—was, of course, Maxwell Field. Because so many flyers trained there, it was often said that "the road to Tokyo ran through Montgomery." This study, however, provides only a succinct summary of Maxwell Field's impact on

Montgomery and its role in fighting the wars in Europe and the Pacific. A detailed account of Maxwell Field's role in the war has been provided by Newton and Jerome Ennels.[6]

Even before the United States became a combatant in World War II, Alabama and the rest of the United States had felt the effects of wartime preparations. In the Far East, Japan's expansionist policies—launched by an invasion of China in 1937—threatened not only the people of Asia but the economic interests of Europe and the United States. In September 1939, World War II erupted in Europe when German troops invaded Poland. By mid-1940, after the collapse of French resistance, the situation in Europe was grave. Prodded by the prospect of German and Italian domination of Europe and of northern Africa, President Franklin Roosevelt and a few military and political leaders urged a reluctant Congress to build up America's military and economic preparedness for possible war against the Axis nations. As news from the battlefronts grew ever more grim, Congress appropriated funds to activate divisions of the National Guard, to create a peacetime draft, to build bases necessary for the military training of millions of young men and women, and to provide the armed services with badly needed planes, tanks, ships, guns, bombs, and ammunition.

New or expanded military bases and defense plants came to Alabama in part because land was cheap and the climate was relatively temperate. More important, Alabama's wartime congressional delegation—the most influential nationally in the state's history—was energetic, powerful, and well connected to the Roosevelt administration and in Congress. This delegation included Senators Lister Hill of Montgomery and John Bankhead of Jasper, Congressmen Frank Boykin of Mobile, Sam Hobbs of Selma, and Henry Steagall of Ozark, and, until his death in 1940, Speaker of the House Will Bankhead. Although Alabama's governor Frank Dixon was an ardent opponent of Roosevelt and a champion of states' rights, he strongly supported efforts to expand the state's industrial base. To this end, Dixon took the highly unusual step of sending a lobbyist to Washington to win defense contracts for Alabama businesses.

Alabama was extraordinarily successful in acquiring new military bases, expanding existing bases, and winning defense contracts. Alabama led the South in major war supply contracts during the war.[7] Mobile alone had $522 million in contracts for combat equipment, or half the state's total. The state ranked seventeenth in the nation and second in the Southeast—only behind Tennessee—in new defense-related industrial growth down through 1943, when investment peaked.

Existing military posts, including Maxwell Field in Montgomery and Fort McClellan in Anniston, expanded to train aviators and infantrymen. The army built Camp Rucker in the Ozark area for infantry training and Camp Sibert near Gadsden for chemical warfare exercises. New army airfields arose at Selma (Craig Field), Tuskegee (Tuskegee Army Air Field), Dothan (Napier Field), and Montgomery (Gunter Field) and in Lawrence County (Courtland Field) to instruct American and Allied pilots and navigators. Brookley Field near Mobile became the major army air forces supply base for the southeastern United States and the Caribbean and also served as a modification and repair center for military aircraft. The Bechtel-McCone plant at the Birmingham airport was another major aircraft modification facility.

Steel mills in the Birmingham area received millions of dollars in contracts for defense-related products such as bombs, helmets, and steel for shipbuilding. Alabama also played a critically important role in the production of aluminum, which, because it is both strong and light, was the ideal material for military aircraft. Alcoa Aluminum had a plant at the Alabama State Docks in Mobile, and Reynolds Metals had a facility in the Tennessee River valley. Alabama's textile mills, including a few small operations in Montgomery, spun and wove furiously to produce fabric for uniforms. The state's timber industry, already ranked third in the nation, boomed as a result of wartime demand for construction materials and paper products.

Alabama emerged as a major manufacturer of munitions during World War II. This entirely new industry was by 1944 the sixth largest industry in the state. More than 20,000 workers flooded into the

Coosa River valley to build and operate two munitions plants. The Alabama Ordnance Plant at Childersburg made smokeless gunpowder and TNT. In nearby Talladega, a plant bagged gunpowder for artillery. Two munition plants were built in Huntsville in the early 1940s. The Huntsville Arsenal and the Redstone Arsenal, later better known for its role in the nation's space program, produced not only conventional bombs but also incendiary bombs, including napalm and chemical ordnance such as mustard gas. Fortunately, chemical weapons were never used by or against American troops in World War II.

Alabama played a crucial role in the war at sea. Mobile was home port for two important ship lines. Freighters operated by Waterman Steamship Company transported valuable wartime cargoes throughout the world. Alcoa Aluminum Company operated its own fleet of ships to transport bauxite—the ore from which aluminum is made—from South America to the company's refinery in Mobile. Waterman lost twenty-seven ships and 313 seamen's lives during World War II; Alcoa lost eight ships and 67 sailors as well as thirteen chartered bauxite carriers. The war came close to Alabama's shores in the spring and summer of 1942 and again briefly in 1943, when twenty-four German U-boats, or submarines, sank nearly fifty Allied ships in the Gulf of Mexico.

Thanks to the efforts of local congressman Frank Boykin, Mobile's two shipyards won contracts to build desperately needed merchant vessels and warships. At the height of the war, ship construction was the second largest component of Alabama's total industrial production. Alabama Drydocks and Shipbuilding (ADDSCO) built freighters and tankers. Gulf Shipbuilding, a subsidiary of Waterman Shipping, constructed destroyers and minesweepers. Mobile boomed as a result of wartime production. At the height of the war, the two shipyards and Brookley Field employed nearly 60,000 people. Only cities such as San Diego, California, and Norfolk, Virginia, experienced comparable population explosions and accompanying strains on housing, education, and public utilities.

In 1946 there were 46 percent more industrial and commercial jobs in Alabama than had existed in 1939. Wage payments tripled during that time. In the postwar world, the state was poised to lead the South in industrial production and continued prosperity. Alabama failed to capitalize on its head start, however, and relinquished leadership to other southern states that elected New South governors and moved energetically in the 1950s and 1960s to lure industries and to create hospitable environments for business expansion. These states led the South into the post–World War II Sunbelt.

Aided by the automobile, World War II produced a more mobile civilian society. Millions of Americans moved in search of new, better-paying jobs. Although the largest and best-known population shifts were to the industrial heartlands of the North and to the new aviation and shipbuilding industries in the West, monumental migrations of people, especially sharecroppers, occurred in Alabama. In Alabama, 10 percent of whites and a staggering 27 percent of blacks moved from the countryside to towns and cities—or out of the state altogether—in search of higher-paying jobs and a better way of life. Alabama's urban population grew by 57 percent during the war.

Mobile's experience was especially traumatic. Lured by jobs in the shipyards and at Brookley Field, nearly 90,000 people—briefly including a young musician named Hank Williams—descended upon Mobile, causing the city's population to increase by 60 percent. In comparison, Birmingham's population increased by 2.3 percent between 1940 and 1943, and Montgomery's rose by 3.4 percent in the same period. Newton points out, however, that Montgomery's population had already doubled—from 40,000 to 78,000—in the two decades prior to World War II.

Although Montgomery's recovery from the depression was fueled by the expansion of Maxwell Field in 1940, signs of a rebounding economy and growing public confidence, feebly prompted by the New Deal, were already visible. By 1939, retail sales, automobile sales, and housing starts were noticeably rising, and as Newton notes, Montgomery's moving companies were once again enjoying a brisk business.

Emerging scholarship and a great deal of anecdotal evidence indicate that the modern South acceded, however unwillingly, to an expanding role for the federal government. This shift had begun in earnest with the dramatic, if not always productive, proliferation of New Deal programs. By the early 1940s the race to prepare for war, and, after 1941, the waging of essentially two wars against Japanese expansion in the Far East and the aggression of Germany and Italy in Europe and North Africa, required, on an unprecedented scale, the management of manpower, regulation of the economy at home, and the coordination of war effort with our wartime allies. Many Americans found that the successful battles against depression at home and dictators abroad outweighed their misgivings about an expanded role for government in American society. By the end of the century, the pendulum had swung back, and momentum had grown for the downsizing of government, but during the three or four decades following World War II, most Americans, including many southerners, seemed willing to tolerate an expanded role for government.

Newton shows that, on the eve of World War II, Montgomery's leaders welcomed assistance from the federal government to make local improvements and to meet critical housing needs. Federal funds enabled Montgomery to build a housing project for blacks and another for whites on the eve of World War II. Federal monies also paid for the expansion of Cramton Bowl to provide a more suitable stadium for collegiate football's all-star Blue-Gray game. The transfer of the municipal airport to the army and its transformation into Gunter Field led to the construction of a new city airport—paid for by the Civil Aeronautics Authority—on the Selma highway. Earlier, Mayor Gunter and other commissioners had emulated the pump-priming policies of Franklin Delano Roosevelt and the New Deal by putting hundreds of people on city payrolls during the height of the depression.

Also, with the hindsight of half a century, we see that World War II served as a catalyst for the modern civil rights and women's movements. These liberating developments also produced social and political tensions of their own that continued to play out in the political life of Alabama and the nation in the second half of the twentieth century.

The war brought unique employment opportunities and dramatically improved economic conditions for women and African Americans, who were hired to do jobs formerly open only to white men. With 15 million American men in uniform, including one-third of Alabama's 900,000 draft-age men, industry and commerce desperately pleaded with women to leave the schoolroom or their housework to contribute to the defense effort. Toward the end of World War II, females held between one-fourth and one-half of all defense-related jobs. Approximately 10 percent of the 40,000 workers at Mobile's two shipyards were women. Nearly 50 percent of the 17,000 jobs at Brookley Field were held by women. At the arsenals and gunpowder plants in Huntsville, Childersburg, and Talladega, women workers comprised 20 to 60 percent of the labor force. African Americans held 22 percent of the jobs at the Huntsville Arsenal. Women who had once worked as teachers, earning an annual salary that started in those years at $800, found jobs as assembly line workers in the Huntsville Arsenal at $1,400 or as welders in the Mobile shipyards at $3,600 a year. Although Montgomery offered few opportunities for highly paid female industrial workers, many women entered retail trades and other jobs that had often been vacated by servicemen. Montgomery women, several of them interviewed by Newton, also joined one of the auxiliary military forces or served as military nurses and experienced what some of them regarded as the most exciting and perhaps rewarding times of their lives.

Alabama women who stayed at home played important roles during the war as well. Many volunteered for Red Cross work, manned canteens at train and bus stations for traveling military personnel, worked in civilian defense posts, participated in scrap drives and war bond campaigns, and staffed USO centers. Montgomery, in fact, was one of the earliest cities in the country to open a USO club. More important, women ran households and farms in the absence of husbands, fathers, brothers, and sons. It was generally left to women to understand and handle ration books. Responsible wartime duties and employment—often paying good wages and providing previously unknown personal independence—convinced many women that they could find satisfaction in the peacetime economy without returning to a life devoted solely to domestic work.

After the war, most women in Alabama returned—at least temporarily—to more traditional roles. Many women left the labor force in the postwar world because they lost their job to a returning serviceman or because companies laid off workers as demand for war products declined. Some women who had worked mainly from a belief that it was their patriotic duty to do so willingly gave up their jobs at war's end. Other women quit the factory or retail store to rejoin their husbands or to marry wartime sweethearts. Nonetheless, the greater independence of women in the war years did much to foster a movement for gender equality in future years.[8]

A less patient and more strident struggle for civil rights for African Americans that began in earnest in the 1950s also had its origins in World War II. The war plainly revealed the yawning disparity between the ideals of American society, with its wartime rhetoric of freedom and democracy, and the reality of racial inequality that most African Americans experienced at home and even in military service.

Although Alabama did not experience the most violent episodes of racial conflict—such as those that rocked Los Angeles, Detroit, Harlem, and Beaumont, Texas—the state saw several racial confrontations. At the ADDSCO shipyard in Mobile, an attempt by management to integrate black and white workers resulted in a white-led attack on black workers that left several persons injured. Crowded city buses in the South, where municipal ordinances and local custom required black riders to sit or stand at the rear, incited racial tensions that erupted into conflict in Montgomery, Nashville, Tennessee, and other places. Because some cities, including Mobile and Montgomery, allowed bus drivers to carry guns, the potential for disaster was ever present. One lethal episode occurred on a Mobile bus when a black serviceman who had the nerve to complain about the treatment of black riders was shot to death by the driver. Another episode on a Montgomery bus in July 1942 led to the shooting and subsequent arrest of a black serviceman by the police. Racial tensions flared in 1943 when a white Maxwell military policeman shot and killed a black enlisted man and wounded a civilian outside a black dance hall for allegedly disturbing the peace. Although army officials in Montgomery, including the commander of Maxwell Field, urged the city to respect black servicemen and accord them equal treatment under the law, the city acted, according to Newton, with "virtually unchecked brutality against hapless blacks."

Voter registration drives of later decades were also foreshadowed during the war. In 1943, attorney Arthur Madison, the first African American to practice law in Montgomery, organized two attempts to get blacks registered. Although Madison was arrested on flimsy charges and subsequently moved his law practice to New York, registrars reluctantly added several prominent African American leaders to the voting list.

In Montgomery there emerged during the war years a group of black leaders who would play a prominent role in the civil rights struggle in the 1950s and afterward. They included E. D. Nixon, Rosa Parks, Idessa Redden, Rufus A. Lewis, and Johnnie Carr. Newton tells how these individuals honed their organizational skills in war bond and scrap drives and as volunteer workers at the black USO club. In addition, some black leaders served on an advisory committee—one of the few created by cities in the state—to help African Americans register for selective service.

For most African Americans, World War II was a struggle against racism abroad and racial inequality at home. They had demonstrated their competence to fly and maintain warplanes in the Ninety-ninth Pursuit Squadron trained at Tuskegee, to build ships as efficiently as any crew on the Gulf coast, to supply Allied armies with provisions on the Normandy shores, and to carve the Ledo Road through some of Asia's most rugged mountain and jungle terrain under the command of General Lewis Pick of Alabama. They, too, sacrificed young sons, bought war bonds, and proved themselves loyal Americans. Having demonstrated their patriotism in the fight against aggression and totalitarianism, African Americans—especially the veterans—were never again going to submit willingly to racism and a segregated society. The wartime rhetoric of democracy, justice, and freedom that underlay the titanic struggles against dictatorship and territorial aggression in Europe and Asia became the standard by which they measured their own status in American society.

The stimulus that the war gave to the civil rights movement, however, produced a backlash among many white Alabamians, who preferred the status quo and who particularly resented the intrusion of the federal government in local matters and in labor relations. These whites particularly objected to what they regarded as the preferential treatment accorded blacks and women by such measures as President Roosevelt's Fair Employment Practices Committee. In many ways, the racial politics that dominated the scene in Alabama in later decades—culminating in defiant stances against federal court orders to integrate schools and public facilities—were born in World War II. The ardent defense of states' rights by Alabama governor Frank Dixon, his rejection of the national Democratic Party, and his repudiation of FDR and, especially, the president's wife—which he muted for the sake of national unity during the war—found an echo in the platform of the breakaway Dixiecrat movement in the postwar years. George Wallace's subsequent denunciation of the federal government and its pointy-headed bureaucrats was just a more populist, and some would say demagogic, version of Dixon's more restrained, thoughtful, and elitist views.

Despite the persistence of sectional rivalries in the relatively harmless guise of Yankee jokes and Blue-Gray football games, World War II—accompanied by a wave of patriotism and a sense of moral duty that swept the nation—repaired some of the sectional division that had ripped the country apart in the Civil War and the subsequent Reconstruction. Military service forced millions of Americans to come to know and, in combat, to trust with their lives, people of other places, other backgrounds, other races, and even the other gender. Hundreds of thousands of young men and some women from all parts of the country and from all walks of life poured into Alabama for military training in new or expanded bases. Many letters written by servicemen who trained in Montgomery or visited one of the USO clubs attest to their gratitude for the hospitality of most residents of Montgomery.

When the war ended, many people from different states—some who had worked in defense industries and others who had done some of their military training here—remained in Alabama or returned to the state. Wartime romances blossomed into marriages, producing record numbers of households and children, resulting in a major baby boom. Wartime savings caused by the scarcity of consumer goods and a patriotic duty to purchase war bonds fueled a postwar spending binge in Alabama and the rest of the country to satisfy pent-up demands for housing, automobiles, and home appliances. Many veterans came out of the service determined to take advantage of new educational and employment opportunities. In a state in which only 7 percent of the population had any college education and only 22 percent of its young people had advanced beyond the eighth grade, the GI Bill of Rights provided unparalleled opportunities and more democratic access to higher education and skilled jobs. Thanks to the leadership of Senator Lister Hill, the postwar years brought improved health care and greater access to medical treatment. These factors contributed to the emergence of a more diverse, mobile, and prosperous Montgomery and Alabama.

NOTES

1. Morton Sosna, "More Important than the Civil War? The Impact of World War II on the South," in James C. Cobb and Charles R. Wilson, eds., *Perspectives on the American South: An Annual Review of Society, Politics, and Culture,* vol. 4 (New York: Gordon and Breach Science, 1987), 145–61. A decade earlier, James R. Skates, Jr., wrote a tentative, almost apologetic essay calling attention to the important influence of World War II on the South. See his "World War II as a Watershed in Mississippi History," *Journal of Mississippi History* 37 (May 1975): 131–42.

2. Neil R. McMillen, ed., *Remaking Dixie: The Impact of World War II on the American South* (Jackson: University Press of Mississippi, 1997).

3. Allen Cronenberg, *Forth to the Mighty Conflict: Alabama and World*

War II (Tuscaloosa: University of Alabama Press, 1995); Jerry Purvis Sanson, *Louisiana During World War II: Politics and Society, 1939–1945* (Baton Rouge: Louisiana State University Press, 1999); Lamar Q. Bell, *Georgia in World War II: A Study of the Military and Civilian Effort* (N.P., 1946); Sarah M. Lemmon, *North Carolina's Role in World War II* (Raleigh: North Carolina State Department of Archives and History, 1964); C. Calvin Smith, *War and Wartime Changes: The Transformation of Arkansas, 1940–1945* (Fayetteville: University of Arkansas Press, 1986); Kay B. Hall, ed., *World War II: From the Battle Front to the Home Front: Arkansans Tell their Stories* (Fayetteville: University of Arkansas Press, 1995); James W. Lee, Carolyn N. Barnes, and Kent A. Bowman, eds., *1941: Texas Goes to War* (Denton: Center for Texas Studies and University of North Texas Press, 1991); Joseph Freitus and Anne Freitus, *Florida: The War Years, 1938–1945* (Niceville, Fla.: Wind Canyon Publishing, 1998).

4. Robert G. Spinney, *World War II in Nashville: Transformation of the Homefront* (Knoxville: University of Tennessee Press, 1998).

5. Mary Martha Thomas, *Riveting and Rationing in Dixie: Alabama Women and the Second World War* (Tuscaloosa: University of Alabama Press, 1987); Mary Martha Thomas, "The Mobile Homefront During the Second World War," *Gulf Coast Historical Review* 1 (Spring 1986): 55–75; Mary Martha Thomas, "Rosie the Alabama Riveter," *Alabama Review* 39 (July 1986): 196–212; Mary Martha Thomas, "Alabama Women on the Homefront, World War II," *Alabama Heritage* 19 (Winter 1991): 2–23. Also see Patricia G. Harrison, "Riveters, Volunteers, and WACs: Women in Mobile During World War II," *Gulf Coast Historical Review* 1 (Spring 1986):33–54.

6. Jerome A. Ennels and Wesley Phillips Newton, *The Wisdom of Eagles: A History of Maxwell Air Force Base* (Montgomery: Black Belt Press, 1997).

7. Alabama received $1.1 billion in war contracts for combat equipment between June 1940 and September 1945, slightly more than Virginia. Georgia, Florida, North Carolina, South Carolina, Tennessee, and Mississippi had less than $1 million each in contracts for combat equipment. Only Virginia topped Alabama among southern states in expenditures on projects for major war facilities.

8. There has been much debate over the impact of World War II on the emergence of the women's movement of the late twentieth century. Some

historians have argued that because women were last hired, and first fired, and because so many returned to traditional roles, the war's effects were minimal. William Chafe's groundbreaking study, *The American Woman: Her Changing Social, Economic, and Political Roles, 1920–1970* (New York: Oxford University Press, 1972), viewed the war as a catalyst for change. See, more recently, Judy Barrett Litoff, "Southern Women in a World at War," in McMillen, *Remaking Dixie,* 56–69. In other publications Litoff and David C. Smith have amassed, edited, published, and commented on thousands of letters written by women during World War II. Other scholars have viewed World War II as less important, placing it in a continuum of change. For this more cautious view, see, among many writers, Susan M. Hartmann, *The Homefront and Beyond: American Women in the 1940s* (Boston: Twayne, 1982); D'Ann Campbell, *Women at War with America: Private Lives in a Patriotic Era* (Cambridge, Mass.: Harvard University Press, 1984).

1

The City at the Start of the War

Court Square, leading into Commerce Street, in 1941. *Courtesy of Stanley Paulger Studio/Tommy Giles Photographic Services.*

The *Advertiser* headline of September 1 struck the reader with explosive force: " HITLER UNLEASHES 'WAR DOGS' ON POLAND; GUNS ROAR ON THE BORDER."[1] The event that triggered the twentieth century's second world war had taken place at 5:30 A.M. European time, or 10:30 P.M. on Thursday night Montgomery time. Bicycling paper boys threw the news onto lawns and porches as September 1 dawned in Montgomery.

City residents with particular reason to fear the turn of events in

Europe included Selma Wampold, the German-born wife of Charles Wampold, Sr., an insurance agent, and their son, members of Montgomery's Jewish community. Selma's parents had moved to Montgomery in early 1939, after SS thugs had trashed their home in the lovely Bavarian countryside near Stuttgart. Selma's son, Charles, at the age of ten had accompanied his mother on a trip to visit his grandparents in 1935. Crossing Germany by train, mother and son had seen anti-Semitic slogans on buildings as they passed through cities and towns. Young Charles had endured anti-Semitic remarks made by a young German girl in his grandparents' village.[2]

Many Montgomery adults with access to a radio had tracked the gathering storm before the war's outbreak. Germany and Europe were far away, however, and two local events competed with the war for residents' attention in September. One was the beginning of the football season. The other was relocation (moving), for which the end of summer was the peak season.

In 1939, movers declared that there were more people departing for new domiciles, and more vans and trucks stuffed with furniture and other household items, than they had seen in years. Such activity indicated that the economy was rising, if slowly, from the doldrums. According to an analysis in the *Advertiser,* people were "turning to permanent residences and home ownership." Members of the incoming class of the Air Corps Tactical School (ACTS), the army's advanced school for air officers located at the area's army airfield, Maxwell Field, competed for rental property. The real estate situation augured the beginning of a housing shortage in Montgomery.[3]

Known locally as the Tac School, ACTS was part educational institution and part think tank for airpower theory, strategy, and tactics, a place of intellectual ferment unique among the world's air forces of the day. ACTS was to influence the army's waging of air warfare profoundly in the future. Most of the senior army air officers in the coming conflict were alumni of ACTS.[4]

Few Montgomerians knew precisely what went on at Maxwell, but the field's contribution to the Montgomery area's economy had been a rare bright spot in the decade-long depression. President Franklin D.

Roosevelt, popularly known as FDR, called in 1939 for an increase in spending on the military. Congress, in response, reluctantly authorized expenditures to invigorate the armed forces, which had been greatly neglected since the end of the Great War in 1918. The majority of funding went for airpower, which FDR viewed as decisive in future wars. By September 1939, Maxwell Field was beginning to enjoy some of the recent congressional largess. Work began on twenty-six barracks for enlisted men. The economic focus of Montgomery, however, was still overwhelmingly downtown, as it was in practically all cities and towns of the time.[5]

Residents who did not live within walking distance of downtown or who did not own a car—and most Montgomerians did not own one—used the relatively cheap public transportation system: the yellow-painted buses of the Montgomery City Lines, Inc., a private concern that operated with a municipal subsidy. Buses had replaced streetcars in 1936. In line with the hub-and-spoke principle, the buses on regular routes passed through downtown on their way to and from all outlying and suburban areas of the city. Each outward bound bus bore the name of its destination above the windshield—Cloverdale, Oak Park, Capitol Heights, Cleveland Avenue, Day Street, and so forth—changing its label when it headed back downtown.[6] In 1939 the one-way fare from Cloverdale to Day Street was five cents and included one transfer.[7]

By city ordinance blacks were required to take seats in the rear of the bus, while whites occupied seats in the front half. If a bus was nearly filled, with standing passengers clinging to the upper safety bars, a black person at a bus stop passed in his or her fare at the front and then hurried to the back entrance, where the doors were opened. A particularly mean-spirited driver might shut the doors prematurely and take off, leaving the black person behind to fume helplessly. Eventually the Montgomery city bus figured in the black reaction that gave rise to the national civil rights movement.[8]

In the daytime Montgomery's downtown streets were often clogged with passenger cars, trucks, and taxis (Yellow, Black-and-White, red-painted Dime, and various usually individually owned taxis that served the city's black residents). Statistics for the year 1939 show that the city had 16,000 cars in a population of 78,000. Buses, which did not require tracks to cross the city, enabled many whites to move to the suburbs and also transported black labor and servants to these suburbs as well as to menial jobs downtown. Buses allowed shoppers to visit stores downtown and return home, especially on Saturdays and holidays.[9]

Downtown Montgomery had several distinctive features that impressed passing strangers as well as natives. Dexter Avenue, one of two east-west boulevards that formed the main street, swept downward from the august white state capitol to the central plaza. This area, called Court Square, was graced by a fountain whose classical Greek figures, cast in dark metal, sprayed water into a basin surrounded by a metal fence. Traffic swirled constantly around the basin during busy hours, fed by Dexter and several other major streets such as Court Street, a thoroughfare that ran north-south. Pedestrians hurried across crossways when traffic lights afforded them the opportunity.[10]

Viewed from Court Square, the capitol gleamed in the sunlight like a Roman civic building. Nearby stood other state government buildings, also white. The state government was one of three chief employers in the city. The other two were the Works Progress Administration (WPA) and the municipal government. In 1939 Maxwell Field was not yet a major employer. The three other government bodies were consequently essential to the city's economy in the lingering depression.[11]

Montgomery, founded in the early nineteenth century, had been built, like Rome, amid seven hills near a river. Also like Rome, Montgomery—and indeed Alabama as a whole—had sanctioned slavery. Jefferson Davis had been sworn in as president of the Confederate States of America at Montgomery's capitol in 1861. The city of Montgomery had served as the Confederacy's first capital. Although the Confederacy, unlike Rome, had not triumphed militarily, state and capital retained a martial spirit.[12]

In the waning months of 1939, members of the four local chapters of the United Daughters of the Confederacy (UDC) opposed a move to place a bronze statue of Davis in front of the capitol on the broad knoll called Goat Hill. The Daughters argued that this particular statue by a Yankee sculptor looked too much like one he had made of Abraham Lincoln in Illinois. The women charged up Goat Hill in a last-ditch effort to sway Governor Frank Dixon and the legislature, but it was as futile as Pickett's charge. The statue was erected over their objections.[13]

The only nearby structure in direct spiritual conflict with Davis's statue was an unpretentious church constructed from red brick and timber that stood a block away on Dexter's south side. The Dexter Avenue Baptist Church had been founded by former slaves and other blacks in 1879. Its members were not involved in any controversy in 1939, however. Most whites were oblivious to them; only occasionally did a white person send a letter protesting their presence to the editor of the *Advertiser.* In time the church became the center of the black protest that gave rise to the national civil rights movement.[14]

Another noteworthy downtown feature was Union Station. This magnificent Romanesque structure, built in the 1890s, overlooked the Alabama River several blocks north of Montgomery Street, which formed the other stretch of the main street and, like Dexter, merged with Court Square. A long shed attached to Union Station's terminal building protected trains and people from the elements. Through the clouds of steam drifting back from idling engines one could gaze down from the shed at the muddy river and across to the wooded shore opposite. In the nineteenth century the river had played a key role in the city's commerce as steamboats carried cotton from Montgomery markets to Mobile.[15]

Montgomery's downtown area included the city's chief locus of black enterprise and entertainment. The district centered around Monroe Street, running parallel to and just north of Dexter, and Monroe's intersection with North Perry Street. Perry was one of several north-south thoroughfares that had been named after American naval heroes of the War of 1812 and that intersected Dexter consecutively from the capitol to within a block of Court Square.[16]

The district had originated before the Great War and included the Peking Theater, the only motion picture theater for blacks; pool halls;

a dance hall; the offices of most of the city's black medical doctors and dentists; the offices of black-run insurance agencies; Dean's, the largest black-owned drugstore; barbershops and beauty parlors patronized by blacks; and the only downtown hotel for blacks. In a society where people were segregated even after death, the district contained Ross-Clayton, one of the oldest black-owned funeral homes.[17]

Lonnie Coleman, a white Montgomerian, writing of a young black man in his 1944 novel *Escape the Thunder,* described the district's lure for blacks. Recently paroled from Kilby, the principal state prison, which was located at the northern reaches of the city, Coleman's hero "wandered about the streets he loved. . . . They were the streets of his people." He absorbed "the calm, lazy snip-snip of the scissors from the barbershops . . . , the sharp click of billiard cues against balls from the pool halls . . . , the laughter in the streets . . . , the earnest bargaining of the street peddlers."[18]

The black district was bounded by white commercial enterprises. These included fruit stands and secondhand clothing stores owned by immigrants or their second-generation relatives, stalls that stood close together and sometimes mingled with the enterprises of black citizens. Some of the newcomers had come from the Mediterranean area. Others were Jews from Europe and the Middle East who had left Europe to escape persecution. The two most prestigious restaurants downtown had been founded by immigrants with Mediterranean origins. Greek immigrant Pete Xides had founded the Elite (pronounced locally with the accent on the E) on Montgomery Street in 1910 and in 1939 still managed it. The Elite stayed open all night, serving guests at local balls or parties and concertgoers at the city auditorium. The Ridolphi family, with roots in Corsica, ran the Pickwick Café on Commerce Street, where police tolerated double parking by customers waiting for take-out food.[19]

A fruit stand shaded by a large umbrella on Dexter Avenue stood in marked contrast to the shops and stores in the last few blocks as the street leveled out before merging with the Square. Here too could be found the two most prestigious and oldest jewelers and some of the most upscale men's and women's clothing stores. Also here were the leading florist, rubbing shoulders with an immigrant-owned café named Cris's, famous for its gourmet hot dogs, and a cluster of five-and-dime stores—Woolworths', Silver's, and Kress's. Kress's impressive four-story facade had Corinthian columns.[20]

On the north corner where Dexter merged with the Square, a huge, round clock with four dials advertised Klein and Son, Jewelers. On the adjacent corner stood the Winter Building, where in 1861 a telegraph had been sent ordering troops to fire on Fort Sumter. In 1939 most Montgomerians were unaware of the building's historical significance.[21]

Emerging at a northwest angle from the Square was Commerce Street, running three long blocks to the railroad yards, and beyond the yards lay the former steamboat landing on the Alabama River. As the street's name implied, it was the city's most commercially important artery. Commerce was known as "furniture row." In the blocks nearest the railroad yards stood wholesale cotton and other warehouses and the largest hardware stores and office supply firms. Two eight-story hotels rose above all the street's other structures except the First National Bank Building, one of the city's two structures locally regarded as skyscrapers. The bank building soared twelve stories on a corner where Commerce merged with the Square. First National and two other banks on the street defined Montgomery's financial district.[22]

The second twelve-story "skyscraper," an office building known as the Bell Building, towered over Montgomery Street. With the three leading hotels, the Exchange, Whitley, and Jefferson Davis; the two leading motion picture theaters, the Paramount and the Empire; and the two radio stations—CBS affiliate WCOV in the Exchange Hotel at the corner of Montgomery and Commerce and NBC affiliate WSFA in the Jefferson Davis—Montgomery Street constituted the hotel and entertainment district. In 1938 a young "hillbilly" singer and guitar picker named Hank Williams had won an amateur hour contest at the Empire, launching his career. In 1940 WSFA sponsored a radio program featuring Hank and his band.[23]

The Whitley was the scene of excitement on the night of December 13, 1939. A rumor circulated that Clark Gable and his wife, the actress

Carole Lombard, had checked into the hotel, stopping over on their way to Atlanta for the premier of *Gone with the Wind*. Reporters hounded the hotel manager for interviews with the famous couple. The hotel had 256 rooms, and the manager refused to say which room they occupied. The couple escaped early the next morning, eluding the reporters waiting at the elevators and other exits. Attendants at the Montgomery municipal airport claimed that the two stars had left on a special flight to Atlanta.[24]

The Alabama premier of *Gone with the Wind* occurred a month later, in January 1940, in the Paramount Theater. The Paramount was not as grandiose as Birmingham's Alabama Theater, but it was dignified. The *Advertiser* reported that would-be viewers "formed a constant line that snaked at times from Court Square to Jesse French, Inc. in quest of tickets." The Jesse French Piano Company on Montgomery Street set up three ticket windows to handle the advance sales. The usual Paramount fares were $0.25 for adults and $0.10 for children under twelve years, but for the gala opening all seats were reserved, and all tickets, whether for children or adults, cost $0.76 for the matinee performance and $1.12 for the night showing. The depression notwithstanding, the house had been sold out in advance wherever the film played a six-day engagement.[25] Several months later, *Gone with the Wind* was shown for blacks at the Peking Theater. There were no long lines to purchase tickets.[26]

Away from entertainment and more consumer-oriented commercial activity, the city had an industrial park in 1939 that lay north of Madison Avenue, a thoroughfare one block north of Monroe and running from downtown eastward to the Atlanta highway. The industrial park had lumberyards, construction companies, coal companies (the gas space heater was just beginning to compete with the fireplace), moving companies, petroleum product headquarters and distributors, soft drink bottlers, and alcoholic beverage wholesalers.[27]

The local Coca-Cola bottler had opened its new plant in 1938 behind one of Montgomery's most historic churches, St. John's Episcopal on Madison Avenue. St. John's with its spire was best known as the church where Jefferson Davis had worshiped. Other historic churches downtown included the Reform synagogue Temple Beth Or, the First Presbyterian Church, and St. Peter's Catholic Church. Each dated to before the Civil War.[28]

Most black and white Montgomerians, however, did not belong to the Catholic, Jewish, Episcopalian, Lutheran, Seventh Day Adventist, Jehovah's Witnesses, Mormon, or other churches or sects considered peripheral in this center of the Bible Belt. Many were mainline Baptist, Methodist, Presbyterian, Christian Church, or African Methodist Episcopal. Others belonged to the Protestant Pentecostal or fundamentalist Church of Christ, the Church of God, Holiness, and various other faiths. No one questioned the propriety of starting the public school day with a prayer, and it was almost always a Christian prayer. High school and college football games at Cramton Bowl, out Madison Avenue, opened with a prayer, for which the unusually large "congregation" stood, with few, if any, exceptions. The prayer predictably ended with the phrase "in Christ's name, Amen."[29]

Perhaps oddly, Maxwell Field had no chapel in 1939. Military authorities expected the post's personnel and their families to catch a city bus at the main gate on Bell Street that would take them to a downtown church or, by means of a transfer, to a suburban place of worship of their choosing. No thought was given to black churches, for in 1939 no black troops were stationed at Maxwell.[30]

On all city streets, even downtown, until late 1941, enlisted men from Maxwell were hard to spot. When they were off duty, enlisted men generally chose to wear civilian clothes because of a postwar prejudice conveyed in the phrase "soldiers and dogs not allowed." While this prejudice was less common in Montgomery, middle- and upper-class females were taught to avoid enlisted men, who were poorly paid and could rarely afford the town's opportunities for entertainment and dining out.[31]

Enlisted men received a warmer welcome from the prostitutes of the city's only enduring large "redlight district," on Pollard Street near the railroad yards. Soldiers routinely received physical exams, however, and anyone found to have a venereal disease was punished sternly for having violated army regulations.[32]

Maxwell had its own hospital. The city's largest and best hospital, the Catholic-run St. Margaret's, a four-story gray structure, lay just east of the capitol. Though it served primarily whites, it allowed doctors to perform operations on a limited number of blacks. Black patients, however, were not permitted bed space in the main building and had to be wheeled on a stretcher to a small wooden building at the rear of the main building for recovery. This rule applied, regardless of the weather, even to patients just out of surgery.[33]

The best of the older medical facilities for blacks was Hale's Infirmary on Lake Street, which bordered Oak Park. A new hospital, part of the St. Jude's Catholic School and Church complex for blacks on West Fairview Avenue, had more up-to-date facilities.[34]

Blocks away from the capitol stood the massive city hall, a red brick structure with white columns. Located in the block bounded by North Court, Monroe, North Perry, and Madison, it held the city auditorium and the offices and forum of the three men who exercised the municipal executive authority.[35]

In 1939 the mayor and president of the city commission was William Adams Gunter, Jr. Gunter had served his first term from 1910 to 1915, and since 1919 he had ruled with a mix of compassion, tolerance, and firmness. In the depression Gunter put hundreds on the city payroll in a gesture that paralleled FDR's relief efforts. Gunter's compassion extended to blacks, but they received the more menial jobs. *Advertiser* editor Grover Hall, Sr., a friend of Gunter's, described the mayor's way of dealing with the many who sought his aid: "They waited in line outside his office. . . . A little job for a man or woman that could provide a little income for a family, a ton of coal that could keep another family warm in a freeze, a basket of food that could assuage hunger in another family. . . . He would greet each and every one. . . . 'Hi, partner! What can I do for you?'"[36]

"Partner" was Gunter's standard form of address. His organization, called the "Machine," was opposed by forces led by U.S. senator Lister Hill, a native of Montgomery. During a political race, Gunter could be "aggressive, fiery, bold, even ruthless." Many appreciated his lenient approach to public morality. He had refused to enforce prohibition laws and winked at gambling in such places as the Elks Club and the Veterans of Foreign Wars. He mounted no crusades against prostitution. He was unpopular with many of the lower middle class.[37]

Public Affairs Commissioner W. P. Screws, a veteran of the Spanish-American War and the former commander of the 167th Infantry Regiment (formerly the Fourth Alabama National Guard) in France, had a courtly air that women especially appreciated. Public Works Commissioner W. A. "Tacky" Gayle—whose nickname came from his boyhood habit of wearing mismatched socks—was smooth. But neither man equaled Gunter as a popular consummate politician.[38]

Screws presided over the fire and police departments. The police force, as in other southern cities, was expected first and foremost to enforce racial segregation, resorting on occasion to virtually unchecked brutality against hapless blacks. The Fifth Horseman of the Apocalypse for blacks, and often even poor whites, rode in the guise of local law enforcement officers. They were all white, like every exponent of the municipal and county criminal justice apparatus. A few poor persons were fortunate to have an influential white patron to protect them. But official documents do not record the beatings and consequent pleas, screams, and moans in the city jail and the county lockup. Federal authorities refused to allow their miscreants to be kept in Montgomery jails because of bad sanitary conditions and the legendary mistreatment of prisoners. Gunter named Ralph King as new police chief in 1940. A thirty-year veteran who had risen through the ranks, King was no reformer. A mild police effort to unionize was unsuccessful.[39]

In general, police brutality was moderated only for victims of stature. In October 1939, a police lieutenant struck a reporter from the *Advertiser* in the mouth in the belief that the reporter was interfering with the investigation of a crime. The Hall-Gunter alliance went into action. Although an apology was printed on the front page of the paper, the lieutenant was reduced to the rank of patrolman.[40]

The trial judges, whether at recorder's court in city hall or in the county and state courts, were all white males, for the most part reactionary and racist. The county courthouse, south of Dexter at the corner of Washington Avenue and South Lawrence, was the domain of state district judges Eugene Carter and Walter B. Jones.[41]

Jones, the star of all the courts—municipal, state, and federal—in Montgomery had in 1928 founded a local law school named for his father, a former governor and a Confederate general. Walter Jones seemed on occasion moderate. He was, for example, one of few jurists in the state to argue that women should serve on juries. But his deeper, enduring convictions were anything but moderate. In a column in the *Advertiser* titled "Off the Bench," he often romanticized the Old South and the Confederacy. He excused slavery with the statement, commonplace during the era, that blacks had been better off when they served benevolent white masters. In some of his columns Jones attacked the Nazis, stressing the disparity between Hitler's words and his deeds. Jones saw no inconsistency between his attacks on Nazism, with its extreme racism and its belief in a super race, and his own conviction that blacks were inferior to whites. Carter was not as extreme as Jones, but most whites sided with Jones.[42]

Idessa Taylor, born poor and black in Montgomery, grew up unafraid to assert her individuality in spite of the Fifth Horseman. She observed in local courts that the majority of judges, lawyers, prosecutors, clerks, and bailiffs demeaned blacks. She disliked Jones in particular. He appealed to more conservative blacks, showing them respect within patriarchal bounds.[43]

Tacky Gayle controlled the engineering and sanitary departments and the water works. The population of Montgomery had almost doubled in size since the Great War, from 40,000 to 78,000. Services were extended to the suburbs by a dynamic process. Garbage collection in 1939 was by open truck, with the black collectors gathering trash from the privately owned metal cans set out at the edge of the sidewalk. This service was popular because it was free. Street improvements, especially paving, were financed through assessments on the owners of affected property and funding from New Deal agencies such as the Works Progress Administration (WPA).[44]

The advent first of the automobile and then of the city bus hastened the paving of the thoroughfares that linked downtown with the mainly white suburbs of Capitol Heights on the east, Cloverdale on the south, and Oak Park more or less in between. Bell Street, which ran from east to west, connected downtown to Maxwell Field and then curved north to become the Birmingham highway. Posh Cloverdale, somewhat less posh Capitol Heights, and even less posh Oak Park, mainly twentieth-century developments, were substantially paved by 1939. Paving required affected property owners to hook up to sewer and water pipes. The extension of city-supplied water resources was funded partially by bonded indebtedness.[45]

The improvements made by 1939 for the most part excluded the principally black areas. The politicians, including Gunter, remembered blacks last when it came to improvements. Still, decisions had not been based entirely on race. When funding for improvements was sought, there was always the question of who could afford to pay part of the cost.[46]

The old textile mill community of West End, which sprawled about Bell Street from a railroad bridge west to Maxwell Field and beyond, had little pavement in 1939, save for a white housing project named Riverside Heights alongside Maxwell. Generations of white children had lived in rows or circles of mill-owned housing. Streets were dirt. Little if any grass grew in the yard. The houses had a kitchen, bedrooms, and a living room. The kitchen and living rooms doubled as bedrooms. A large potbellied stove in the kitchen served for cooking and heating. The family huddled around it in cold weather. An outside faucet provided water for washing and cooking. There was an outhouse for a toilet. The Alabama Power Company, a private utility, supplied a few houses with electricity. Some of the mill houses were still occupied, but the mills themselves had almost gone out of business.[47]

The same living conditions existed in areas of north Montgomery and parts of Chisholm. Conditions were worse in the vast black area of west Montgomery, which included Pollard Tract, Peacock Tract, and Washington Park from north to south, and in scattered other areas to the east and north that blacks had occupied since the Civil War. Streets and yards turned into muddy morasses or dusty stretches, depending on the weather. The majority of houses were dilapidated shanties and shacks of the shotgun or row type. A group of property owners and renters on Robinson Street, a blue-collar white enclave in Pollard Tract, petitioned the city commission in April 1940. The petition asked that property owners in the surrounding streets—where blacks lived—be compelled "to connect their properties with the sanitary sewers and do away with all surface toilets," because, the petitioners said, they could not "stand conditions as they had been in the past through another summer."[48]

Conditions remained deplorable at the end of 1940. After performing an inspection, the chief medical officer at Maxwell Field described the sanitary conditions in mostly black Pollard Tract and mainly white West End as intolerable and said that they threatened the health of post personnel.[49]

Mayor Gunter had taken advantage of New Deal legislation to give his city its first public housing in 1937, a black project located, ironically, just north of Cloverdale. The project was named Paterson Courts in honor of a white benefactor of black education. A white project, Riverside Heights, was completed in 1939 alongside Maxwell Field, with a steep embankment at its rear that ended in the Alabama River. Each of the projects had one- and two-story brick buildings. Most units rented for $8.50 a month, but a renter had to have an income of between $25.50 and $42.50 per month.[50]

A number of "grand" houses of varied architecture, new and old, existed in the white suburbs and on the connecting thoroughfares such as Madison, Court Street, and the naval hero streets of Hull, McDonough, Lawrence, and Perry. In the white suburbs the most common style was the bungalow. Cloverdale, the most prestigious suburb, was famous for its English-style parks and lovely gardens.[51]

As in all southern communities encompassing two or more races, and to some extent in much of the nation at the beginning of the Second World War, Montgomery had a caste system. The upper caste consisted entirely of whites and the lower entirely of blacks. Segregation of the castes was maintained by means of law, tradition, and too often coercion and even violence. The lower caste was not entirely untouchable. Black nannies, or mammies, cared for upper-class and many middle-class white infants and young children. Blacks had skins of different shades but not, as whites commonly supposed, because black males had been sexually aggressive to varying degrees. The rape of white females by black males was usually punished by death in the electric chair or by lynching. Though such executions were becoming less common, sometimes the mere accusation of wrongdoing was enough to ensure conviction. Rapes of white women by black men were relatively rare in Montgomery by 1939.[52]

Each caste had its own class divisions. Within each race there was an upper, a middle, and a lower economic group, with some blurring of distinctions at the boundaries. The white upper class was gentry. Many of its forebears had been planters or prosperous merchants. In many cases land and businesses had passed more or less intact through families. Except for a relatively small textile industry in 1939, Montgomery had no large factory-based enterprises comparable to Birmingham's steel industry and thus no powerful industrialists. All three city commissioners, like Judge Jones, had gentry origins. Most of the business leadership was gentry and included both Gentiles and Jews. This class was the elite.[53]

The white gentry was less homogeneous by 1939 than it had been before the Great War. The conflict had left the nation restless and had sent a wave of newcomers to many cities, including Montgomery. Montgomery's newcomers included William ("Bill") Lawrence, who had risen from a poor rural south Alabama background to become an army captain in World War I. His military achievements and his marriage to the daughter of one of the pioneers of the Jefferson County iron and steel industry gave him entrée into the ranks of Montgomery gentry.[54]

In the 1930s Bill Lawrence served a term as president of the Beauvoir Country Club on Narrow Lane Road in Cloverdale. Churches of the gentry and civic clubs included middle-class members. But the Beauvoir Club was almost exclusively the social center of the Gentile element of the white gentry. Narrow Lane Road was also the site of the Jewish social center the Standard Club, whose membership was largely gentry. Excluded from membership in the Beauvoir Club, the members of the Standard Club also ironically practiced ethnic exclusion. Membership was limited to Jews whose ancestry could be traced to Germany, Austria, or Western Europe and who were at least nominally members of the Reform synagogue, Temple Beth Or.[55]

The black upper class in 1939 was small and unrecognizable as such by the majority of whites. In the absence of a black country club, churches and the lodge halls of fraternal and sisterhood orders took on added importance as social centers. The black upper class was led by the few black physicians and dentists, the administrators of black Alabama State Normal College, and ministers and deacons of such leading black churches as Dexter Avenue Baptist. A few black businessmen reached the upper class. Robert D. Nesbitt, for example, was an insurance auditor and the deacon-clerk of Dexter Avenue Baptist. (He would, after the Second World War, play a leading role in bringing a young minister named Martin Luther King, Jr., to his church.)[56]

Both black and white upper-class families prized and usually sought a college education for their children. The black upper class lived in respectable neighborhoods in freshly painted white frame or brick veneer houses with well-tended grassy yards and flowers. But the average street on which they lived was unpaved or partially paved.[57]

The white middle class, much larger than the upper class, was a wide and diverse group occupationally. The white middle class consisted mainly of Anglo-Saxon Protestants, as did the upper class, and greatly outnumbered the Jewish middle class. The middle class tended to differ from the gentry in ancestral backgrounds and wealth. The most important difference, however, was social standing. Middle-class parents who themselves had often not gone beyond a high school education aspired to a college education for their children, but the majority of such parents could not afford to buy it.[58]

The white middle class had suffered in the depression. Many breadwinners had lost their jobs. Some deserted their families and disappeared. Others accepted more menial jobs at less pay. Some were chronically unemployed. A fair number of women were forced to seek employment as clerks in stores or as secretaries, and some became the family breadwinners. By 1939 the depression had eased somewhat. Readjustment had brought a degree of normalcy.[59]

The black middle class was considerably larger than the upper class but was proportionately much smaller and less diverse than its white equivalent. While whites often had jobs as salespersons of various kinds of goods, blacks rarely held such positions. The black middle class included locomotive firemen and switchmen, Pullman car porters, owners of small businesses, insurance salesmen and saleswomen, operators of funeral homes, postmen, practical nurses, beauticians, and clerks as well as butlers, maids, cooks, nursemaids, and chauffeurs for well-to-do whites. This group prized education and revered elementary and high school teachers such as Sadie Gardner Penn, a graduate of Alabama State and the daughter of a switchman on the L&N. A fair number of middle-class blacks had college training. The depression affected blacks much as it did whites.[60]

The white and black lower classes had certain common traits. Each was larger than the respective middle and upper classes combined, but poor blacks as a class were the most numerous of all. In both races the educational level was low, but that of poor blacks was the lowest of all. Poor whites battled the twin handicaps of class prejudice and poverty. Their poor grammar betrayed them even when their clothes did not. But poor blacks suffered the twin scourges of racial prejudice and dire poverty.[61]

Both poor whites and poor blacks were largely unemployed or underemployed. Blacks suffered proportionately more. Available jobs for poor whites were largely menial; they worked as skilled and unskilled laborers, waitresses, and seamstresses. At best they could aspire to be unordained preachers, police patrolmen, truck or bus drivers, beauticians, or practical nurses. Poor blacks were unskilled laborers, "yard boys," cooks in lowly cafés, garbage collectors, poorly paid domestics, and laundresses. Some raised vegetables and fruit on patches of land beside their homes and hawked the produce in the white suburbs. The crime rate was high for both lower classes, but that of poor blacks was the highest of all. In most cases crime was black on black.[62]

In 1939, society in Montgomery, like that in the nation as a whole, expected women to be homemakers for their husbands and children. The majority of girls were trained accordingly. Society prized physical attractiveness in women. Beauty shops and the cosmetic industry thrived as a result.[63]

Society expected women not to compete for occupations and civic duties traditionally reserved for males. The scarcity of jobs in the depression raised the barriers that kept women out of the workforce. Women were discouraged from entering certain key professions. A girl might reasonably aspire to be an elementary or high school teacher—or even a principal. A woman could also become a nurse, a beautician, a music or dancing instructor, a stenographer, or a secretary. But women were not welcome in the professions of law, medicine, and the ministry in 1939, and few could be found there. Sadie Frank and Alice Doyle were two female lawyers among eighty-odd male attorneys. One female medical doctor, Elise Stone, practiced alongside 100-odd male physicians. No church had a female minister. Neither of the two women lawyers had a full-time practice, and the doctor practiced with her husband.[64]

There were no women judges. No female served on the police force, as a sheriff's deputy, or on grand or petit juries. In a rare voice of protest, Hallie Farmer of Alabama College at Montevallo told the delegates of the Alabama chapter of the National Business and Professional Women's Clubs, which met in Montgomery in October 1939, that the denial of jury service threatened "the property rights and the very existence of women."[65]

In 1939, Montgomery women had carved out few places for themselves in the upper echelon of the business world. Esther Eisenberg had the rare distinction of serving an apprenticeship with the brokerage firm of Sterne, Agee, and Leach to be an investment banker. A few women were secretary-treasurers in family firms. A very few both owned and managed a significant business enterprise, usually as co-owner. Burt Morgan was partner and manager of the leading bookstore, the Little Book Shop, on South Perry downtown.[66]

Women often headed departments in large stores such as Montgomery Fair near the Square on North Court Street and ran shops specializing in women's and children's apparel. The Fair had an annual Women's Day, during which women employees ran the entire store after electing an all-female "management." In reality this device provided another way of having a sale. Women commonly clerked in department stores, drugstores, and especially in the five-and-dimes such as Kress. In the last-named stores, women clerks, paid comparatively low salaries, were particularly likely to suffer the depredations of males working in the nearby shops and other downtown businesses. In fact men might make passes at working women and professional women everywhere, or utter crude remarks or jokes, with little fear of retribution. Sexual harassment did not exist in the public consciousness. Nor did women necessarily treat each other well and fairly in the workplace. A clerk in the Lerner Shop on Dexter complained to her landlady that her "lady boss" had cheated the salesladies out of their commissions."[67]

In the last years of the depression, mothers with absent or unemployed husbands or mates continued to eke out a living for themselves and their children. They had a hard time competing with single women for available jobs. The New Deal's Farm Security Agency (FSA) and WPA had clerical, stenographic, and secretarial positions for white women with the requisite skills. Women also held a few of the WPA slots supervising women. Very few blacks, whether male or female, became supervisors and then only on work crews.

A few women had unusual occupations. Lois Yelverton was the city's only specialist in genealogical research in 1939. With most of the Confederate veterans now dead, many people with Confederate forebears were curious about the lives of their grandparents or parents. It was a form of ancestor worship that would grow in popularity. In a small number of occupations, a woman entered a field in which men had been competing with each other. A white woman, Winnie Westbrook, set up a furniture repair business on Mobile Road, competing with eight white males. Black businesses almost never competed with white ones.[68]

Segregation disadvantaged blacks nowhere more than in education, whether in the city or county. The traditional hovel-style black elementary school, with its lack of heat in the winter, cramped space, and outdoor privies, was gradually replaced by schools with modern features, thanks to the efforts of county superintendent of education Clarence M. Dannelly, Sr. Dannelly also initiated the city's first black public senior high schools. In 1937 he added a tenth grade to Booker T. Washington Junior High on Union Street south of the capitol and at the same time to Loveless School on West Jeff Davis Avenue. In the following two years grades eleven and twelve were added to both schools.[69]

Alabama State Normal College had a long-existing laboratory elementary school and junior and senior highs, but unlike the public schools, enrollment there was curbed by high tuition. Many of Montgomery's black middle class and gentry were alumni of the lab schools. A relatively small number of black students received a superior education under the tutelage of white nuns at St. Jude's, located on West Fairview Avenue near its Mobile highway juncture at the southern boundary of west Montgomery.[70]

Segregation meant that the white part of the local school system was necessarily far superior to the black visually, physically, and in its ability to open social doors. Among the white schools further disparities existed. Cloverdale Elementary, for example, had facilities that surpassed those of several other elementary schools such as West End.[71]

The jewel of the school system was the city's only white public senior high, Sidney Lanier, founded near downtown in 1910 but moved in 1929 to South Court Street a block from West Fairview Avenue. The architecture, with its collegiate Gothic style and central tower of Alabama limestone, was eye-catching. The faculty ranked among the finest in the South and had a national reputation. There were no social promotions at Lanier. The city had three fine white private schools— Starke military school, Barnes School, and Margaret Booth for girls— yet Lanier was preferred for most children of the gentry. In addition to academics, Lanier offered superior extracurricular activities. Its band had few rivals in the state. The athletic program, especially for football, equaled the best in the state. The Lanier Poets won the state football championship in 1939 with an undefeated season.[72]

Montgomery had two colleges, Huntingdon and Alabama State. Huntingdon, a small Methodist-connected liberal arts school for young white women, had a beautiful campus on East Fairview Avenue, with green grass, flowers, and dogwood, oak, and pine trees. Co-ed Alabama State for blacks sprawled just north of Cloverdale. Each of the two schools had had a vigorous young president. In 1939 Huntingdon's president was Herbert Searcy, thirty, who waged a successful campaign to reduce a debt that had brought probationary status from the regional accrediting agency. Alabama State's president that year was thirty-nine-year-old H. Councill Trenholm, who had taken over in 1925. In fourteen years he had made a two-year junior college into a four-year degree-granting institution. He had transformed a raw, open place with scattered buildings into a bustling campus, adding land, dormitories, a dining hall, more classrooms, and the first real library. Knowing the fanatical appeal of sports in Alabama, especially football, Trenholm boosted intercollegiate athletics.[73]

The Montgomery center for games was Cramton Bowl, off Madison Avenue just before it climbed to Capitol Heights. Lumber company magnate Fred Cramton had in 1922 leased the land free to the city in perpetuity. By 1939 the facility was well lighted and had concrete seats on one side and at one end. The other side and end had temporary stands for football that were removed for baseball season so that the infield and outfield could be completed for the city's Class B professional baseball team, a white city amateur baseball league, and touring teams of the Negro major leagues. The bowl seated 12,000 for football in 1939.[74]

From September until late in November, fans converged on the stadium every Friday night. The Lanier student body roared in the temporary stands as the band in Lanier blue and white marched smartly onto the white-striped green grass led by lanky, high-strutting Ed Bowman, a particular crowd favorite in 1939. Halting before the permanent west section, the band played the national anthem. As both teams stood by their benches, the captains, Lanier's in white helmets and blue pants and jerseys, waited as the zebra-shirted referee flipped the coin. At halftime the band played the school alma mater before the student-filled temporary east stands: "Dear Lanier, though fleeting time may bear us far away from thee . . ."[75]

Neither Booker T. Washington nor Loveless had an interscholastic football team before the end of the war. The Alabama State lab senior high had none. All of the high schools had basketball teams that competed against one another. The lab team won the black state basketball championship tournament in 1942.[76]

Cramton Bowl had been the site of one or more games each by the varsity football teams of the two flagship white universities, Alabama Polytechnic Institute (better known as Auburn, for its location) and the University of Alabama. (For obscure reasons the two had not played one another since 1907.) In the 1930s the Crimson Tide stopped scheduling varsity games at the bowl because of its small seating capacity. Because Montgomery was considered an "Auburn town," the Tigers still played one game a year but with a minor, nonconference opponent. Gunter launched a bowl expansion program in 1939 that was funded with federal money.[77]

In part the expansion program resulted from the inauguration of a college all-star football game in 1939, the Blue-Gray game. It was a symbolic reenactment of the Civil War by two all-white football teams, one in blue, the other in gray, in an appropriate setting, "The Cradle of the Confederacy." The Blue team was composed of senior college players from the Northeast and Midwest, the Gray, of seniors from the Southeast and Southwest. The Blue-Gray game was the inspiration of Alabama-born promoter Champ Pickens. He conceived the idea in 1938. Mayor Gunter persuaded him to hold the game in Cramton Bowl, with the proceeds going to welfare projects.[78]

The first game, played on January 2, 1939, brought a Blue victory. An Appomattox-like gloom extended over most of white Montgomery. Even without competition from a radio broadcast of this game, there were no profits. Gunter, however, persuaded Pickens to give

Montgomery another chance. A second game was played in 1939, on December 30, to avoid conflict with radio broadcasts of the traditional New Year's Day bowl games. While white Montgomerians were overjoyed with the Gray victory, the game remained a financial loser.[79]

A third game on December 28, 1940, brought a second Blue victory, disappointment in Montgomery, and still no profits. Mayor Gunter had died some three weeks before the contest. Pickens now felt free to denounce publicly the failure of the city commission to rally the business community behind the game. He also criticized Montgomerians in general for their failure to buy tickets. He noted that 65 percent of the ticket sales for the most recent game had been made to purchasers from outside the city. He threatened to take his game elsewhere, but Gunter's successor, Cyrus ("Cy") Brown, persuaded him to stay in Montgomery.[80]

The second game had been accompanied by several festivities. The morning before the game an elaborate parade stretched along the main street. It featured floats sponsored by cities and private white groups. The organizers at first emphasized the Old South and Confederate themes, but as the war progressed overseas, American patriotic themes became more prominent. The first Blue-Gray Ball was held in the city auditorium the night after the second game, highlighted by the crowning of the first Blue-Gray queen, Alice Martin, daughter of a local gentry family. Balls were popular.[81]

Blacks had their own annual sports extravaganza, staged each Thanksgiving. It featured the Alabama State Hornets and Tuskegee Tigers. On the morning of this game in 1939, reported the *Advertiser,* a "grand street parade" with bands and cheerleaders and cars filled with students began on Commerce, swung around Court Square, and proceeded up Dexter. The jukey, jazzy routines of both bands brought cheers from black spectators and laughter from whites. The 1939 Hornet-Tiger game drew more paid attendance than either of the Blue-Gray games that year.[82]

The masses appreciated Cramton Bowl activities more than other cultural highlights. The Montgomery Museum of Fine Arts, founded in 1930 near the downtown area, occupied a three-story building that had been a public school. Slowly it had accumulated artifacts from bygone eras with a particular focus on the Confederacy. At the museum on March 26, 1940, the *Advertiser* noted, "Montgomery's first grand symphony orchestra launched into its debut concert . . . last night, when Mrs. Fanny Marks Seibels, its diminutive organizer, director, and guiding spirit, raised her baton to silence a full house."[83]

The museum became a center for the arts. It sponsored art classes for white children. The chief instructor was Kelly Fitzpatrick, the doyen of Alabama painters. The children loved him, although he often had the strong smell of liquor on his breath. He was artistic director of the Dixie Art Colony, situated on Lake Jordan, an impounded body of water within easy travel of Montgomery. He was also the founder of the prestigious Alabama Art League. Fitzpatrick was a familiar figure in Alabama art circles. He was usually seen puffing on a curved pipe. His face was pitted from shrapnel wounds suffered in battle; he had been a machine gunner with the U.S. Army in France in the Great War and was the only survivor of his company. He rarely discussed his experience in the war.[84]

At about the same time, another artist worked from a seat on a wooden box alongside a fruit stand in Monroe Street's first block. "Uncle" Bill Traylor, then in his mid-eighties, had been born a slave on a plantation forty miles from Montgomery. As an artist he worked with a stick for a ruler, a pencil, and crayons. Few who passed by saw more than an old black man sitting on a box. After his death, he was hailed by art critics and painters as one of the great black folk artists and achieved the national recognition far beyond that accorded to Kelly Fitzpatrick. Both artists worked in a city soon to be profoundly affected by the new world war. In particular, the war would lay the foundations for a challenge to slavery's legacy of racial segregation.[85]

2

The Advent of Pearl Harbor

The 1941 Armistice Day parade down Dexter Avenue into Court Square and around the fountain to Montgomery Street. *Inset:* An aviation cadet from Maxwell Field and his fiancée wait to apply for a marriage license. *Courtesy of the estate of Horace Perry.*

The Nazis conquered much of Poland, and the Russians took over the rest. Then came the lull known as the Phony War between the French and British Allies and the Germans. The renewed German Blitzkrieg saw the conquest of Denmark, Norway, the Low Countries, and finally France. The last surviving remnants of the Allied forces were evacuated from the beach at Dunkirk in June 1940. The entrance of Fascist Italy into the war on the Nazi side in June was greeted with gloom in Montgomery.[1]

Viewers watched scenes from the battlefront in black, white, and gray at theaters. Paramount News at the Paramount and other newsreels showed the long lines of British and French troops on the beaches of Dunkirk, where they waited for the rescue armada, itself under attack by the diving and wailing Stuka dive-bombers of the Luftwaffe. Some of the ships sent up smoke and flame. On the other side of the Channel, hollow-eyed, unshaven men were cheered and embraced as they came off the gangplanks. The spectacle brought tears among Montgomery audiences.[2]

In July Royal Air Force (RAF) Spitfires and Hurricanes dove on incoming German formations bearing crooked black crosses. When tracers reached out and exploded a bomber or dive-bomber, the debris flew back as though leaping out of the screen. Moviegoers were as thrilled as if they had been watching a war film and not newsreel coverage of the ongoing Battle of Britain.[3]

The growing impact of airpower increasingly affected Maxwell Field. Colonel Walter R. Weaver had come to Maxwell in April 1939 to take command of the post and the Air Corps Tactical School. Weaver tightened discipline. In addition, he wanted to reestablish rapport with leaders among the white gentry. As Maxwell commander in 1927–1931, he had been responsible for inaugurating a close relationship between the post and the city. He had made a key contact in U.S. congressman Lister Hill, a Montgomerian. By the time Hill became a U.S. senator in 1939, Weaver was his protégé.[4]

The assignment of more troops to bases such as Maxwell after the outbreak of war in Europe led to increased construction. The post's expansion was closely watched by local governmental, civic, and business leaders, for it meant more jobs and more money spent in a city and county still laboring under a somewhat depressed economy. Renewing old contacts and making new friends, Weaver rejoined the Kiwanis Club, which met weekly at the Whitley Hotel, and the Beauvoir Country Club. He and his wife were a popular couple at parties and other functions of the elite.[5]

Dramatic developments in the war produced profound change at Maxwell in the summer of 1940. The Air Corps Tactical School was phased out. Maxwell became the headquarters for all Air Corps operational training east of the ninety-second meridian. Because of the weather, the training took place principally in the Southeast. When Weaver, soon to be promoted to brigadier general, was designated commander of the new headquarters, it was named Southeastern Air Corps Training Center (SEACTC). The RAF victory in the Battle of Britain in September brought renewed hope and emphasized the importance of airpower.[6]

In his official command diary, Weaver repeatedly noted conferences with Montgomery city officials and businessmen. He consulted with management of the Algernon Blair Construction Company, which became the leading Montgomery firm performing defense work at bases in Weaver's command. These conferences concerned such subjects as construction of 420 units in Bell Street's Riverside Heights housing project for Maxwell Field personnel with families. Washington was by this time restricting federal funds for construction to defense housing such as the Riverside project and buildings on Maxwell.[7]

Two schools to train flying cadets—a basic or second phase and an advanced or third phase school—were opened temporarily at Maxwell in the summer of 1940. Each graduated a class every ten weeks. As a result, congestion soon developed at the post and worsened as not only cadets but also support staff and other personnel swelled in numbers. The overcrowding soon affected housing, mess operations, sanitation, training, and practically every other aspect of base life. The Riverside housing addition, opened in early November 1940, allowed more military families to come to Montgomery, but it only slightly eased the congestion on the base. By fall, tent "cities" for enlisted men had cropped up on the post.[8]

The base situation also affected the surrounding community. Larger numbers of military personnel meant more money spent in the city and a growing amount of construction work for area companies and laborers as well as additional WPA crews. The need for civilian personnel increased. Maxwell's expansion marked the true beginning of the end of the depression in Montgomery. With it came problems such as a perpetual housing shortage and eventual worsening of the racial conflict.[9]

Plans were made to transfer the basic flight school to another field in the Montgomery area, but the new field did not yet exist. Construction of the new field was impeded by financial problems. On July 9 Weaver noted in his diary a telephone call that he had made to Commissioner Screws, in which he told Screws "that the War Department would not pay the $120,000 for the Municipal Airport and would go elsewhere unless the City made a decent offer." The Air Corps wanted to recast the municipal airport northeast of town as the site for the basic school. This airport, opened in 1929, had been Gunter's "baby." It now compared favorably with other fields at towns of Montgomery's size. It had lights and a paved runway, but it also had the only municipal golf course. By "decent offer" Weaver meant a lease for ninety-nine years for one dollar a year, which was becoming the standard arrangement throughout the country for the military's leasing municipal property for bases.[10]

After a trip to Washington, Weaver announced on June 22 that the government was ready to spend a million dollars converting the airport to a military field, with the unstated implication of what this would mean to a city not yet free of depression. The commissioners were eager to reap the economic benefits of another military airfield. There was the prospect of a substitute municipal airport in the near future. A Montgomery business clique, however, had persuaded the city fathers to seek to recoup some of the city's investment, estimated at $400,000, for the creation, development, and maintenance of the airport. This group had likely invested in the airport. The commissioners expressed reluctance to give up the golf course, "the principal recreation grounds for scores of working men and women" who did not include blacks. Military planners deemed certain acreage adjacent to the airport essential, but the owners asked more than the War Department felt was fair.[11]

There appeared to be an impasse between the parties from late June into early August 1940, but intense maneuvering went on behind the scenes. Weaver was a favorite with the city's elite, but he showed he could be a firm SEACTC commander. He used a press conference on July 28 as a bully pulpit, warning that the basic school would be opened in another city if the matter was not settled soon. The next day, at a second press conference, a reporter asked Weaver as to when an agreement might be reached. The colonel replied, "I've been trying to get in touch with someone who can tell me." The second press conference had been called to pressure the private landowners, who continued to seek their original demands. Weaver accused them of hitching their "evaluations to a golden star." After several weeks of further foot-dragging, the commissioners yielded and leased the airport to the War Department for the standard ninety-nine years at a fee of one dollar a year. The landowners held out a bit longer before a meeting of the minds occurred. Except to sign the lease agreement, Gunter, seriously ill with a heart condition, had been barely involved with the negotiations. Commissioner Screws was the main negotiator with Weaver.[12]

Part of the agreement between the city and the War Department had to do with Eastern Airlines, which had operated in and out of the municipal airport since 1938. There was soon no place for Eastern at the airport, as conversion began almost as soon as the lease had been signed. The War Department agreed to allow Eastern to have facilities at Maxwell until the city could take the necessary action to build a new airport.[13]

The city commissioners took the first steps in November 1940. Congress had recently passed a $44 million appropriation to develop municipal airports and similar projects deemed necessary for national defense. Montgomery's public airport facilities, now nonexistent, were considered by Washington "inadequate for national defense," and the commissioners resolved to "communicate with" the Civil Aeronautics Authority (CAA) to obtain funds for a new municipal airport. When the CAA authorities visited Montgomery in December, Brigadier General Walter Weaver assisted the city in briefing them. The CAA approved the funding. In March 1941, the commissioners voted to purchase property "seven and seven-tenths . . . miles from Montgomery" down the new Selma highway.[14]

Another federal action was much more significant for many young

Colonel Walter R. Weaver (center, in uniform), the senior commander at Maxwell Field and the creator of Gunter Field, in 1939 meets with Governor Frank Dixon (on Weaver's right), Mayor W. A. Gunter of Montgomery (on Weaver's left), and Grover C. Hall (at the far left in the front row). *Courtesy of the Office of History, Air University, Maxwell Air Force Base.*

men in Montgomery. FDR decided on a widespread military call-up. In the summer of 1940, the first units of federalized national guardsmen left for active duty. Montgomery units did not go until the late fall. When the federalized National Guard had departed, it was gradually replaced by a state guard recruited by the state adjutant general's office, as in many other states. In September 1940, Congress passed the Selective Service and Training Act. It was America's first military conscription in peacetime. All men between the ages of twenty-one and thirty-five had to register for a year's service. A lottery based on experience in the Great War determined which of the registrants would serve. Ultimately the lower limit was set at twenty. The law prohibited service outside the continental United States.[15]

In Alabama, registration took place on October 16. The machinery for the draft was established by October 29, the date when the first lottery drawing was to be held in Washington. Composed of locally prominent men, four draft boards for the city and one for the county stood ready to receive the numbers that would begin to emerge from a fishbowl in the nation's capital.[16]

The first number drawn was 158. The five men in the Montgomery area who had received this number when they registered with their boards became instant pioneers. Paul Kendall Roney, a white clerk with an insurance company, was photographed smiling at his desk in the Bell Building after a friend had called him with the news. Roney allegedly exclaimed, "You're kidding!" He told a reporter, "I pity my creditors. Tell them to be lenient." Reporters found Luther Larkins, a black lottery pioneer, at the local YMCA where he was janitor. "I don't care if I go and I don't care if I don't. 'Aire one of 'em will do. . . . But I'd sorta like to stay," Larkins told them. William Cotton, another black holder of number 158, was tracked to his house on Oak Street in Peacock Tract, where "all the neighbors had met in the dim kerosene lamp light" in the belief that he had won a different kind of lottery.[17]

For two consecutive days the *Advertiser* listed the numbers drawn in Washington. Then the novelty ceased. Setting the tone for private employers, the city commission passed a resolution protecting the jobs of city employees who enlisted in the armed forces or were drafted.

Enlisted men were given thirty days after discharge to reclaim their jobs.[18]

An *Advertiser* reporter was on hand when the "first troop train to leave Montgomery since 1918 pulled out of Union Station at 10:25 A.M." on December 5 bound for Fort Barrancas near Pensacola. On board were Montgomery County's quota of first draftees under the Selective Service Act, along with "men and boys" from other counties. None of those who had received number 158 were in the first group to be sent notices of conscription by their draft boards. All were white; the army would be segregated. Walter Lawrence, a veteran of the Spanish War and the chairman of local Board No. 1, presented all the men selected by his board with a Bible donated by his Sunday school class at the First Baptist Church on South Perry.[19]

December 11 saw the first group of black draftees from the Montgomery area depart from Union Station for Barrancas. Included in the group of five was Luther Larkins, characterized by the *Advertiser* as "YMCA's step-and-fetch-it janitor, the first Montgomery negro" called up.[20]

On December 14 an *Advertiser* reporter made telephone contact with Barrancas public relations. The first group of whites were "In the Army Now." An officer assured the Montgomery caller that the new soldiers "had been comfortably housed in properly heated barracks" and upon arrival had been given a "routine intelligence test and physical examination," had received "an explanation of government insurance and allotments," and had been "clothed in the U.S. uniform and assigned to a training company." They "received balanced meals [and in the] . . . evenings spent their time in the post theater and lounge in the Service Club."[21]

John C. Holley, a member of the pioneer group, wrote home: "Everything is fine here with plenty of food and I expect to get a lot out of it." Those waiting at home got a sanitized view of an experience that was often traumatic for the draftees—who eventually numbered in the millions—as a citizen army was molded. Holley went on to become the first commissioned officer of the pioneer white group of draftees from Montgomery.[22]

A reporter was on the scene in the late afternoon of December 12, when another group of Montgomery's early contribution to the armed forces "fell in on the sidewalk in front of a North Perry Street café." Here were fifty-seven enlisted men and officers from Company E, 106th Quartermaster Battalion, Thirty-first "Dixie" Division, Alabama National Guard, with orders to report to Camp Blanding, Florida. "A top sergeant bawled formal roll call and the men were marched into the café for mess." Later "Company captain, John P. Kohn, watched his men drift informally into Union Station. U.S. Army flannel and shoulder-slung belts" were everywhere in evidence. A twenty-minute delay in the train's departure allowed "time for smiles to wear off and real sentiment to show through. Oblivious to surroundings and even to flashing camera bulbs men kissed wives and sweethearts goodbye and mothers wept freely" before their sons. Trains were often late in leaving the station during wartime. The following day Company D of the 106th from Ramer in Montgomery County departed from Union Station.[23]

The following week another Montgomery-based unit of the "Dixie" Division assembled in Union Station. Known historically as the Montgomery Grays, it was officially Headquarters Company of the 167th Infantry Regiment, which had served with Pershing's "Punitive Expedition" in Mexico in 1916 and under the command of Colonel W. P. Screws, now city commissioner, in France in the Great War. In the gathering dusk men drifted to the edge of the tracks and looked down the high, steep embankment at the Alabama River and the wooded shore across the water. The station was crowded with 2,000 well-wishers and loved ones. One company officer was Second Lieutenant John T. Cherones, a married graduate of the University of Alabama, who had three Greek first cousins fighting the Italians and a fourth cousin who had recently been killed. The Montgomery Hellenic Society had established a Greek Relief Fund.[24]

Manfried Arie, formerly of Vienna, in a guest lecture at Temple Beth Or provided one of the earliest reliable accounts in Montgomery of the Holocaust. "Those Jews still in Germany," he stated, "are living an unending nightmare of brutality." Several foreign-born residents of the city later gave firsthand testimony regarding what later came to be known as crimes against humanity. *Advertiser* reporter Sara Crist interviewed several Jewish refugees who had endured concentration camps and other forms of Nazi persecution. A man "looked quietly out at the sunshine on Commerce Street as he talked of his three months at Dachau, the oldest but by no means the worst of these man-made hells. . . . He could still hear in the night, he said, the screams of men caught on the barbed wire trying to escape."[25]

Enlistments in the armed forces at the Montgomery federal court-house had remained relatively low after the beginning of the war. Men continued to volunteer for financial reasons. One example was Francis David Powell, who enlisted in the army at the age of fifteen and lied about his age. Enlistment picked up with the Nazi victories in the West and the narrow German defeat in the Battle of Britain, the first campaign in history mainly to pit airpower against airpower.[26]

But the economic incentives remained primary. Fred Burks, a young black man from Mount Meigs in eastern Montgomery County, entered Alabama State in the fall of 1940. He was from a landowning middle-class family and had attended the black county public high school. Burks enjoyed the fraternity dances and parties and football games but did well in his classes. He worked in the library to earn spending money. His parents were now both dead, and he needed a larger income to stay in school. But decent-paying jobs were scarce.[27]

Fred was in the Peking Theater in the summer of 1941 when he saw on the screen an army recruiting ad that mentioned "certain outfits" for blacks at Fort Benning, Georgia. The next day he went to the courthouse. The army recruiters, though white, were polite. After he signed the papers, he received train and meal tickets and was soon off on the great adventure. At Benning the pace of training would pick up with the nation's entry into the war. Burks received basic train-ing at the hands of white officers and black noncommissioned officers. He was assigned to a mainly black quartermaster company at the post. Because of his education, he soon became company clerk and was pro-moted to sergeant shortly thereafter.[28]

When draftees such as John Holley and enlistees such as Fred Burks came home on furlough, they had money in their pockets and were not burdens on their families. They introduced the folks at home to such army idioms as "chewing out" (scolding by an officer or non-commissioned officer).[29]

Montgomery in December 1940 suffered a crisis unrelated to the depression or the war. Since early that year, Mayor Gunter had suffered from a heart condition that prevented him from attending most city commission meetings and obliged him to run the city from his residence on South Perry Street. His condition worsened, and on December 2 he went into a coma. He died on December 4 at the age of sixty-eight. The demise of this long-reigning political boss who had shown himself capable of benevolence, compromise, and firmness sent a shock wave through the community but prompted some private rejoicing.[30]

During funeral services in St. John's Episcopal Church, the *Advertiser* noted, "negro citizens packed the balcony." Afterward Gunter was buried in Oakwood Cemetery. In an editorial entitled "So Long Partner!" supporter Grover Hall, Sr., called him "Father Christmas" whom "thousands of people came to interpret . . . as Santa Claus." "Unknowingly by their clamor, their piteous appeals," Hall added, "[Gunter's public] shortened the life of the eternally good Samaritan." Soon after his death, the local Chamber of Commerce petitioned Commissioners Screws and Gayle to approach the War Department to have the new army flying field named after Gunter. The commissioners appeared reluctant at first, probably because Gunter had taken little part in the negotiations that had brought about the new field. The chamber had to petition them again. The chamber based its rationale on Gunter's undeniable role as the father of commercial aviation in Montgomery, his support of Maxwell Field, and the fact that the municipal field had long been unofficially known as Gunter Field; the chamber did not claim that Gunter had led the way in gaining for his city a new army flying field. Unspoken was the fact that the person most responsible for obtaining a new field for the city was Walter

Weaver, and thus the field should have been named for him. That was impossible at the time, however, because he was still alive. The War Department named the field for Gunter.[31]

Two other deaths followed in December. Navy ensign and flight instructor Clarence M. Dannelly, Jr., son of the county superintendent of education, crashed with a student into Pensacola Bay on December 17. This was the first death of a Montgomerian in uniform attributed to military preparations for war. A fellow officer accompanied the casket from Pensacola to Montgomery. F. Scott Fitzgerald, a native of Minnesota, died of a heart attack in Hollywood on the December 22. Editor Hall eulogized the author of *The Great Gatsby,* whom few in Montgomery remembered. "He was the greatest prophet and interpreter of 'flaming youth,' that curious phenomenon of the post-war period. The flapper and the jelly bean were his meat. . . . He wrote beautifully and powerfully. . . . He was the husband of the charming and beautiful Zelda Sayre." Zelda, emotionally troubled and long separated from Scott, had returned to Montgomery to live with her mother.[32]

In January 1941 the crisis of leadership in Montgomery deepened. The *Advertiser* reported in a small article on the first page on January 7 that Grover Hall "was said . . . to have reacted favorably to a blood transfusion given several hours earlier when he was taken to the hospital suffering from a serious stomach ailment." A small number of Montgomerians knew that Hall was a heavy drinker and had a stomach ulcer. On January 9 he died after a serious of hemorrhages and six blood transfusions.[33]

The reaction to Hall's death was widespread, not only in the city, the state, and the South, but nationally. On January 10, as his paper pictured it, "a funeral possession more than a mile long climbed the slow ascent to Greenwood cemetery. . . . He was buried on a hillside overlooking the city, where with his unceasing campaigns against intolerance, his hearty, robust humor, he had become one of America's foremost personalities." That day his son, *Advertiser* columnist Grover C. Hall. Jr., received a telegram with condolences from Franklin D. Roosevelt. The *Advertiser* on January 15 printed a letter from George

Washington Carver of Tuskegee. It read: "I share in a real sense the universal grief occasioned by the passing from labor to reward of Grover C. Hall, our personal friend and lover of all right thinking humanity. 'Of a truth, a prince and a great man has fallen amongst us.'"[34]

Hall had lived to see a profound change in the newspaper scene in Montgomery. In November the publisher of the *Advertiser*, R. F. Hudson, Sr., announced that his paper had purchased the city's evening paper, the *Alabama Journal*, and that the *Advertiser* would move from its quarters on Dexter into the *Journal's* quarters on Washington Avenue. The papers would continue to be printed separately. Publisher Hudson, his son R.F., Jr., and other members of the staff prepared the editorials that Hall had once written.[35]

The political vacuum was soon filled, though not by Gunter's equal. The Machine that Gunter had built was in a sense self-perpetuating. The mayoral contest was not between the Hill faction and the Machine but rather between two candidates with Machine credentials. The runaway winner in a nasty contest was Cyrus ("Cy") Brown, formerly president of the county governing body, who swept the primary in January 1941 and then ran unopposed in the February general election. The most important triumph in this election was technological, not political. The February 18 ballot included a proposition for voting machines in future elections, which carried overwhelmingly. Technology had advanced in the city in other respects; in 1940 telephone operators had been replaced by dial phones.[36]

Veterans of the Great War, in which technology had played a devastating role, were mostly in their fifties and sixties at the start of the Second World War. Increasingly they suffered from the effects of their war experiences or the disabilities of advancing age. Many required hospitalization. The city was awarded a federal hospital for white veterans in 1938, with construction by the WPA and local concerns. By September 1940 the large four-story brick building was nearing completion on Perry Hill Road several miles beyond the eastern boundary of the city and close to the Atlanta highway. On November 1 the new hospital opened.[37]

On November 7, after the Tuscaloosa Veterans Hospital had been converted to a psychiatric facility, a train brought twenty-nine patients from Tuscaloosa, raising the census at the Montgomery hospital to seventy-five, a fourth of its capacity. The group on November 7 included a woman veteran, a former army nurse. Some of the twenty-nine patients to be admitted, according to the *Advertiser,* "were able to walk, some were very ill and many carried gunshot and bayonet wounds."[38]

A growing number of future veterans were not yet images on a silver screen or the subjects of blaring headlines and newspaper accounts. "Our boys" included draftees home on furlough and the increasingly acceptable local Air Corps personnel. Mayor Gunter had not lost his compassion on his deathbed. He sent a letter on November 28, 1940, to local civic and welfare organizations: "Ever since the opening of the national defense program and the arrival of soldiers in Montgomery in ever-increasing numbers, I have seen the need for a Soldiers' Club." It was to be "a place where these young men can gather together, read, relax, smoke, and talk . . . , a gathering place comfortably arranged where they meet for any clean enjoyment and fellowship." To be successful, he stated, "it must be a community endeavor. . . . For such a program will serve all groups and classes and creeds of our citizenship." He meant, perhaps without thinking, first class citizenship. The soldiers' club was intended for white servicemen only.[39]

In this case patriotism did not come swiftly or easily. Gunter's death on December 4 brought a temporary lull in the project. But by March 1941, the plan had picked up steam under the leadership of such stalwarts as sporting goods store owner Cliff Green, Coca Cola magnate Stanhope Elmore, and First World War veterans Colonel Millard Westcott—a Boy Scout official—Screws, and Gayle. For the Soldiers' Center, as it was officially named, the city had procured a two-story structure in the second block of Commerce that had been occupied by Sears before the store had moved to Dexter. Local funding for remodeling was restricted, and the center was available for limited use only from March until extensive remodeling became possible with federal funds obtained in August. These funds were available after August 1, when the center became part of an organization called the United Service Organizations (USO), established in February 1941 by an act of Congress. The YMCA was one member agency of the USO, and the local YMCA affiliate became the center's sponsor.[40]

A second USO club opened on October 25, 1941, on Lee Street a few blocks from Union Station, under the aegis of the local unit of the National Catholic Community Service, another member agency of the USO. Welcoming all white enlisted personnel and aviation cadets, as did the Commerce Street club, it was run by Catholics in the city. By early 1942 both clubs featured weekly dances, bridge, bingo, and group singing around the piano. The Commerce Street club also showed black-and-white and technicolor films of college football games.[41]

In March 1942, under the leadership of Virginia Laseter, a USO for women opened under the aegis of the local YWCA. Like its male counterpart, it restricted its membership to whites. The women's center eventually found a permanent clubhouse on Dexter. Until the creation of the women's auxiliaries of the armed forces, the center appealed principally to female relatives of servicemen, but local women could join to take advantage of its various programs, such as those discussing health. The USO for women in the beginning focused more on programs than on games and recreation. All the clubhouses were identified by the letters USO in neon lights. The USO became the downtown day-to-day operation most generally identified with the home front. There was no shortage of volunteers to help run the clubs and welcome and entertain service people.[42]

The local Red Cross chapter sponsored the knitting of warm clothing for war refugees abroad, a project with headquarters in a section of a department store on Dexter. Amelie Laslie, Senator Hill's sister, who had helped to found the chapter in the First World War, was in charge of Red Cross volunteer programs. Early in 1941 the chapter opened a surgical bandage unit at Maxwell Field and later a second unit downtown. The bandages were produced by military spouses organized by Elizabeth Weaver, the wife of the general, and civilian women volunteers. The bandages went to a collection point in Washington, D.C., which dispensed them, according to the *Advertiser,* to "any part of the country which has been the target of fifth columnists or saboteurs." The Montgomery volunteers, members of the gentry, were dressed, like their Maxwell counterparts, in white uniforms with blue veils, cuffs, and tabs. The Red Cross volunteer operations were by tacit understanding limited to whites early in the war.[43]

With the launching of flight training at Maxwell in September 1940 and at Gunter in November, the city saw a type of military trainee it had not known since the Great War—the army flying cadet. Part fledgling, part officer candidate, cadets of the army's air operations had trained in 1918 several miles to the east of Montgomery at a base called Taylor Field on Pike Road. No such flight training had taken place in the period between the wars at Maxwell Field, the base that had survived the Great War's end.[44]

The basic school moved from Maxwell to Gunter in November. Flight training continued at Gunter throughout the war. The advanced school at Maxwell turned out second lieutenants with wings of silver until it moved elsewhere in the summer of 1942. In the meantime, in the fall of 1941, a preflight training school for cadets was created at Maxwell. It was the largest such school in the army branch devoted to air operations. Cadet training had a system of discipline modeled on that of West Point. General Weaver saw to it that the preflight cadets were subjected to hazing by upperclassmen and to exhausting physical exercise, both of which he considered more important preparation for the rigors of combat than academic classes.[45]

During the limited hours of "open post," cadets could have visitors on the post or could go into town. They appeared at theaters, shops, and restaurants and at games at Cramton Bowl. In warm weather they wore khaki or "suntan" uniforms; in cold weather, olive drab uniforms. On their garrison hats, blouses, collars, and sleeves was the Air Corps insignia, a silver propeller sprouting bronze wings. The Army Air Corps and naval aviation competed for men. They were considered to be physically and mentally the most fit of the young white American males.[46]

As in the Great War, cadets helped spur Montgomery's economy. Dibby Carter, a feature writer for the *Advertiser,* wrote in December

1940: it had "come to pass, and all in such a short while, the Cadets' need of us, and our need of them. . . . This meeting of the minds, amalgamation of personalities, challenge to cooperation, stimulus to exchange of interest." She gave examples of what their $75 a month was spent on: "For instance, it was settled that 67 cadets of the upper class (only upper-classmen are allowed to have cars) will buy cars. At the end of the year thousands will have bought cars of our merchants." But, she pointed out, "that is not all. They (thousands) will buy new suits, wedding gifts, birthday gifts, holiday gifts, socks, lunches, dinners, radios, and every conceivable kind of luxury."[47]

At a 1940 Christmas season tea dance at the "ballroom" in the Jefferson Davis Hotel, an area set aside for cadets, the cadet officers of Advanced Class SE-41B introduced to their class the members of new class SE-41C. Many cadets had come from outside the South, such as 41C's Gordon H. Sterling, Jr., from Connecticut and Philip M. Rasmussen from Boston. Lacking at the time their own recreation hall, cadets also held dances in the Rainbow Room of the officers' club or in a hangar when Maxwell had open post. In the city, Carter pointed out, they were welcomed at synagogues and churches, such as the First United Methodist Church in Cloverdale, where a special Sunday school class was "well attended by young women of Huntingdon and cadets."[48]

Huntingdon was a natural preserve for all ranks at Maxwell and Gunter and particularly for cadets. Huntingdon students occasionally became romantically involved, and a number of marriages resulted over the course of the war. In the spring of 1941, for example, Huntingdon student Dorothy Ghent from Montgomery began to date advanced school cadet John T. Moore from South Carolina.[49]

Advertiser social columnist Go Peep zeroed in on officers. At the officers' club, "after the first course an entire dinner party had to dash from the terrace into the dining room. . . . the capable club hostess had planned for a sudden shower and the guests found a table decorated with flowers and places set for the correct number." Inside "the squab was served on schedule and from the laughter and active conversation a good time was had by all." The guests included navy lieutenant commander Henry Crommelin and his wife, Sally. Crommelin, who was stationed in Washington, D.C., was one of five brothers from the Wetumpka/Montgomery area who were Annapolis graduates. According to Go Peep, "Sally Crommelin chose a green frock for this party."[50]

Planes from Maxwell and Gunter flew over the city night and day. Some Montgomerians complained of the noise. Lee Allen, a Lanier student in the early part of the war, later commented, "Perhaps my most vivid recollection of wartime Montgomery was the incessant drone of airplanes." The periodic complaints about airplane noise during the war were always answered by letters to the *Advertiser* from indignant local residents, like the woman who wrote that she was "very much ashamed to be a part of a city that houses individuals who have nothing more to do than complain about the noise of peaceful bombers in this war-torn world."[51]

Fatal air accidents involving training planes from Maxwell and Gunter began in the fall of 1940. Maxwell Field had been named for an officer from Alabama who had died in an air accident in the Philippines in the early 1920s. The start of flight training at Maxwell seemed calculated to parallel the career of the field's namesake. On September 19 and again on September 20, a crash killed the instructor and cadet of each plane. Local papers were replete with grisly details of burning wrecks and charred corpses. Residents were both fascinated and horrified. Fatalities continued to occur periodically, on occasion in clusters, but new SEACTC regulations restricted the details that could be released to the media.[52]

One group of cadets in blue uniforms seemed statistically more prone to accidents than the others. These were Royal Air Force cadets, who learned to fly at Army Air Corps bases in the American South as part of the Lend Lease arrangement. U.S. officials accused these men of being too reckless in the sky.[53]

Under the British government's policy, all servicemen killed overseas had to be buried permanently in the land of their death. The site for all SEACTC bases was the Oakwood Cemetery Annex, where a steep hill leveled off. The British flyers were given a place of their own over which flew the Union Jack. Montgomery women, members of the Federated Garden Clubs, brought flowers and kept up the graves.[54]

When the blue-clad cadets came from Maxwell and Gunter into the city, they were favorites but only after it had been ascertained that they were British. They wore RAF blue overseas caps with white flashes. Their uniforms were khakis in the summer and blue wool in cold weather. Motherly women and Anglophiles loved to invite these cadets home for a meal. Some of them were young combat veterans who had flown as nonpilot crew in the RAF night bombing campaign against the Reich. All had spent time in the United Kingdom on an island under siege and had experienced the enemy bombing campaign known as the Blitz.[55]

The RAF cadets pursued the local young women, as did the Americans on British soil. A few relationships led to marriage. When Richard Ian Trotter of Newcastle-on-Tyne, England, received his commission as a pilot officer at the advanced single engine school at Craig Field in Selma in February 1942, he married Montgomerian Susan Wells in St. John's. The cadets in blue also seemed especially fond of the cinema. In the summer of 1941, they watched newsreels with images of the Nazi invasion of Russia in June 1941. They saw German panzers rolling across plains, columns of dusty infantrymen, and dive-bombers producing explosions on bridges and airfields and in villages. The audience responded with the same alarm that had greeted the conquest of France a year before.[56]

Montgomerians hardly noticed when FDR froze Japan's credits in the United States, effectively cutting off the Japanese from access to U.S. oil. This action in combination with the earlier U.S. embargo on scrap iron and steel to nations outside the Western Hemisphere meant that the Japanese had to seek some strategic materials elsewhere and perhaps resort to less than peaceful means of procuring them. Iron and steel were essential for continued Japanese expansion in Asia and for the creation of a strategic stockpile for an ultimate strike at the United States.[57]

The Montgomery City Commission took steps to ensure local preparedness. In May 1941, it decreed that city softball fields and tennis courts could no longer turn on their lights for night play.[58] Families of men drafted into the Army had hoped that at the end of their one-year hitch they would be home in time to enjoy Christmas 1941. Hopes were dashed in August when, by one vote in the House, Congress passed and FDR signed an eighteen-month extension of army service for the draftees.[59]

On November 11, 1941, the city held its "mightiest and most impressive Armistice Day parade," according to the *Advertiser*. It rolled down Dexter, through the Square, "and up Montgomery Street past a reviewing stand filled with civilians and military officers," including Governor Dixon, Mayor Brown, and General Weaver. The weather was sunny and cool. The 7,000 paraders included units from all branches of the American armed forces, including "a company of negroes" from a nearby camp for army ground forces. Veterans' groups—Veterans of Foreign Wars and the American Legion, wearing their distinctive overseas caps—passed the reviewing stand. Next came Red Cross women in red and white and the Gray Ladies; the Gold Star mothers of the Great War; and the Boy Scouts and the Girl Scouts. Also present were the blue-and-white uniformed Lanier band, the gold-and-black clad Alabama State band, and the Maxwell band in brown. The military core of the parade consisted of 3,000 U.S. Army Air Corps flying cadets and "several hundred" RAF cadets.[60]

The *Advertiser* commented that though thousands lined the parade route, they "viewed it with the curiously unemotional attitude characteristic of Montgomery audiences. Only a few spectators, and most of them negroes, bothered to uncover when the colors were carried past . . . , the British cadets alone waking applause from the onlookers and in no great volume."[61]

On December 5, 1941, a reporter for the *Advertiser* observed downtown Montgomery: "It was . . . splashed with light and color as Christmas windows, ornamental signs and streets lights were suddenly turned on." The colorful display ended a ban on Christmas lights for several nights to conserve power in the interest of national defense. The Alabama Power Company announced that residents could now have illuminated trees on their lawns as in the past.[62]

Royal Air Force aviation cadets and officer in the Armistice Day parade, 1941. *Courtesy of the Office of History, Air University, Maxwell Air Force Base.*

On Saturday, December 6, shoppers flocked to downtown stores filled with Christmas wares. People felt festive. The expansion of Maxwell Field and the construction of Gunter Field had added greatly to the local economy. The Great Depression's decade-long grip was slowly beginning to relax. The peacetime military draft meant that more uniformed servicemen were in the crowds than had been a year before. The temperature was in the forties, and the weather was partly cloudy.[63]

Decorations festooned the poles and beckoned in red and green cheer from shop windows. Advertisements for the Blue-Gray game decorated the Square. Sears on Dexter Avenue had on sale a Flying Eagle Steel Wagon for $2.39 and "Big Adorable 26-in. Babies" for $2.19. For the affluent, the Jesse French Piano Company featured an RCA "Magic Brain" needleless Victrola for $199.50. The new car dealerships had many models, such as the 1942 Studebaker Commander Land Cruiser for $1,243 at Byars Motors downtown.[64]

The main headline in the *Advertiser* on the morning of December 7 read "ROOSEVELT SENDS MESSAGE TO JAP EMPEROR," and the copy immediately below declared, "Personal Letter Is Final Effort to Insure Peace."[65] Even on Sunday some early-rising Montgomerians listened to the WCOV broadcast of CBS's "The World Today" at 7:00 or WSFA's network news at 7:45. Sunday school and church occupied perhaps a majority of people on Sunday morning until noon. Sunday dinner kept the family together until early afternoon.[66]

Theaters were crowded on Sunday afternoon. The Paramount had *Sergeant York* with Gary Cooper, the story of the World War I winner of the Medal of Honor from the hills of Tennessee. It had rained in the night, but the sun came out in the afternoon. A game of tackle football at Cloverdale Junior High School between teams representing the Commodore and Cavalier high school social fraternities got underway at 2:30. The field had already been churned up by the game between the Beta Gammas and the Night Owls. After a quarter of rugged play, two bruised, muddy Commodore players lay on the sidelines near a pickup truck that had hauled equipment. Listening to the truck radio, the adolescent driver suddenly poked his head out the window. "Hey," he said, "They bombed Pearl Harbor." The players looked up. One asked, "Where's Pearl Harbor?" The other raised himself on his elbows. "*Who* bombed?"[67]

That afternoon two coeds at the University of Alabama from Montgomery learned about the Japanese attack on Pearl Harbor in different ways. Jean Severence heard the news from a sorority sister while she studied German in the attic of the Chi Omega house. It was the sole topic of conversation at the sorority and fraternity houses that night. Algie Hill and a friend were at a drive-in movie near Birmingham with RAF cadet dates from the primary flight school at Tuscaloosa. They heard the news on the car radio. Hill's date said, "I am so awfully sorry." Hill, not yet realizing the import of the attack, replied, "Why?"[68]

At Mitchel Field, Long Island, Dorothy Ghent waited on the afternoon of the seventh at the flight line in her fiancé's Buick convertible, purchased in Montgomery when he was an aviation cadet. John T.

Moore was now a second lieutenant assigned to the New York–New England air defense zone. He was sent rushing to the flight line by a siren's wailing. After he took off in his Curtiss P-40 fighter plane for what might or might not be a practice patrol, Ghent turned on the car radio in time to hear an announcer comment that New York City might soon be bombed.[69]

When Moore returned, they drove back to the officers' club, where the siren had interrupted him and other flyers engaged in "pilot talk." He and Ghent decided to speed up wedding plans. A chaplain married them the following week in the post chapel.[70]

By nightfall of the seventh, Montgomerians with radios had learned where the attack had occurred, knew the nationality of the attackers, and had passed the information on to family and friends. But in the poorer sections of the city, electricity was for many people either unaffordable or unavailable. Aaron Harris, Jr., a student at Booker T. Washington High, would later remember that late on the afternoon of December 7 a truck with a loudspeaker drove through his neighborhood on North Decatur telling of the attack. It went on to other black neighborhoods. Harris never found out who had sponsored the truck.[71]

"JAPS KILL 350 AMERICANS IN SURPRISE PLANE ATTACK," screamed the *Advertiser* headlines on Monday, December 8. It was the largest headline in many years. The initial shock wave, which had abated after a night's sleep, gave way at first to feelings of anger and uncertainty. Sounding a positive call to action, the *Advertiser* editorialized, "America awakens this Monday morning, unified, alert, with a singleness of purpose as it looks back upon the long ago of Saturday." But the nation should only take a "glance at that closed chapter of complacency, of misgivings, of business-as-usual. . . . [Now is] a different America, an America that has been surprised, but one in which surprise has given way to determination."[72]

At 12:30 P.M. on the eighth, President Roosevelt addressed Congress. Much of the nation tuned in. At Lanier High, the student body listened over a loudspeaker system. In the lunchroom junior Wesley Newton looked around at the sober faces: senior Neal Howard, fellow juniors Billy Crane, Ralph Loeb, Bob Lawrence, Tommy Oliver, Bobby Young, James Donald Godwin, Billy Robinson, Neal's first cousin Mary Ellen Mathews, Betty Baldwin, Caroline ("Dootsie") Ball, Isabel Dunn, Betty Holloway, Mary Henrie Harris, Norma Jean Somerset, Virginia Waits. At the time the boys were exempt from the draft until age twenty.[73]

Montgomerian Margaret ("Peggy") Penton, a slender, dark-haired, and vivacious freshman, stood in a crowd of students on the Auburn campus around the front of Langdon Hall, next to the main administration building, Samford Hall. From a nearby loudspeaker on a truck, FDR's stentorian voice spoke of "a date which will live in infamy." Penton registered cold fear on a chilly day. With her was Marguerite Sherlock of Montgomery, her roommate, whose reaction was less anxious. On the night of the ninth, Roosevelt made a much more detailed White House address, also broadcast over the radio, "not designed to satisfy the curious, or to be a super news broadcast, or as a bit of bragging chest-thumping," according to the *Advertiser,* "[but] . . . a solemn address of a leader speaking to those to whom he is responsible. Its great value was in the vivid perspective of the forces locked in the death grip of survival and our role in the struggle," for "it was a reminder that the attacks upon us in the Pacific were but skirmishes in the larger battle-ground."[74]

Maxwell and Gunter Fields were on full alert. Guards walked the fences, including black soldiers of the recently activated Fourth Aviation Service Squadron at Maxwell. The gates were closed to all but those who had assignments or jobs or were dependents. Identification was demanded of each person. The only aircraft now allowed to fly over military and naval bases were warplanes or airliners.[75]

The *Advertiser* on December 11 tried to caution people that the danger came not only from the "Yellow Peril" but also from a "White Peril," the Germans and Italians having declared war on the United States. But the Japanese remained the most despised foe. The Office of Production Management (OPM) announced on December 10 that henceforth its press releases would carry the slogan "Remember Pearl Harbor." A fight occurred at a dance when a U.S. citizen of Spanish descent was mistaken for a Japanese. Police nabbed the first alien on Coosa Street downtown on the tenth, but he turned out to be a native of Russia, a country that became an automatic ally when Germany and Italy declared war on the United States the next day.[76]

When the city commission had its first meeting after Pearl Harbor, on December 9, a delegation from Japan Street in Capitol Heights petitioned to change the name of their street "because of the dastardly and unprovoked attack by Japan upon the United States." They asked that the street's former name be expunged "from all official records." The commissioners renamed it Glendale Avenue.[77]

The commissioners also ordered a twenty-four-hour guard to be placed over sensitive points in the city that might be the targets of saboteurs. Just which sites were the most sensitive had not been fully decided, and some confusion ensued. Realtor William Nicrosi, the chairman of the Montgomery County Civil Defense Council, called the council's first meeting on the ninth. It accomplished little, for the organization was only a skeleton force, and its military adviser had yet to be appointed.[78]

The reaction in the city, like the response elsewhere, was understandably visceral. A record number of fifty young men attempted on the eighth to enlist in the recruiting offices in the federal courthouse building on Church Street. The recruiters turned down most of the men, a few because they were beyond the upper age limit, the rest because they had dependents or physical defects. The stream of volunteers remained steady for most of December. Now and then friends enlisted as a group in one branch or the other during the weeks after Pearl Harbor. Verbon Sanders from Cottage Hill and several friends enlisted together in the marines on December 27 to avenge, they declared, the recent fall of Wake Island. Eager to go, Riley Jeffcoat carried a small bag with toilet articles and underwear. Sanders would have a rendezvous with fate in less than a year.[79]

A black postman named John Sawyer, at home on Cleveland Avenue, had heard on radio of the attack on Hawaii. He made his rounds the next day in Cottage Hill. In that original city suburb at the crest of Montgomery Street hill, still substantially white, women met him at their mailboxes, asking with anxious eyes and tones if he had brought them any communication from their relatives in the armed forces. The women wanted to be reassured that their loved ones were not now at Pearl Harbor. Telephone calls had not gone through. Sawyer felt compassion, but little from his mailbag brought comfort.[80]

Over the next few days, the local papers began to report some of the details of what had happened beginning at 7:55 A.M. Pacific time on Sunday, December 7. Montgomerians had been on board the battleships at anchor along Ford Island in the midst of Pearl Harbor. All of these men had survived. The only person from the Montgomery area to die in the Pearl Harbor attack was a navy man, Chief Petty Officer Walter Tisdale from the textile mill area of Boylston in north Montgomery. He disappeared in an attack on his fleet water tender and was never found. Americans killed in the attack included some 2,000 navy men, 200 in the army, and 80 civilians.[81]

A black sailor from the Montgomery area, Steward's Mate Robert Coley, age eighteen, was at his battle station on a submarine repair ship. He saw a fireball shatter the battleship *Arizona:* "It was horrible," he recalled fifty years later. "Debris was flying everywhere, guys were swimming in the water with oil all over them. I'll never forget it."[82]

Second Lieutenants Gordon Sterling and Philip Rasmussen, both from New England, had gotten most of their flight training at Maxwell Field. Receiving their wings of silver there in the spring of 1941, they had been posted to the Hawaiian air defense command. They were among the few army fighter pilots who managed to get into the air and engage the attackers. Flying obsolete P-36s, Sterling and Rasmussen each shot down an enemy plane, two of only twenty-nine losses suffered by the Japanese. Sterling became one of the first army pilots to die in combat when a Zero fighter, the best in the Pacific at the time, sent his P-36 spiraling into the sea.[83]

Montgomerian Catherine Thorington, in Honolulu with Katrina, her young daughter, was frightened for her husband, Lieutenant Commander Clark Thorington. Thorington was on one of the Pacific Fleet aircraft carriers that the Japanese had hoped to find on the seventh, but none was at Pearl Harbor that morning. Clark was at sea, and his

Montgomerians in the marines. Left to right, seated: "Rip" Carrie, Johnny Wilkerson, Reginald Wilkerson, Charles Highes, Riley Jeffcoat; standing: J. E. McElvaine, Dorsey Jordan, Rudolph Hamn (with black eye), recruiting sergeant R. M. Henry, Sergeant J. P. Waites, Bill Derickson, and Verbon Sanders. *Courtesy of the estate of Horace Perry.*

wife and daughter had been in more danger than he was. Unharmed, Catherine and Katrina Thorington soon flew back to the United States in a Pan American Airways clipper. The Texas-born wife of army infantry first lieutenant Charles W. Davis, a Montgomerian stationed at Schofield Barracks, gave birth to a son on December 8.[84]

Second Lieutenant James Tucker Fite of the army, whose parents lived on Allendale Road in Cloverdale, was a light bomb group pilot who had last communicated with his mother in a telegram from Honolulu early in November. He had left Hawaii before the Pearl Harbor attack and was in the Philippines on December 8. The *Advertiser*'s banner headline on December 9 read: "JAPS THREATEN WEST COAST AND LAND IN THE PHILIPPINES." On December 8 the Japanese had bombed Clark Field, the chief U.S. Army airfield in the Philippines, and invaded the islands. Fite's group had not received its aircraft. He, like the rest of the unit's personnel, would have to take up a rifle and fight as an infantryman. Private Douglas Kittrell, whose mother lived on

South McDonough, was on Corregidor with a coast artillery battery. Major James C. Knowles, whose mother and sister lived in Montgomery, was a staff officer on Corregidor. During the weeks ahead, each of these army men would become a Japanese prisoner; the three survived the Bataan "death march," but it was many months before their loved ones learned their fates.[85]

At home, Sidney Lanier High School principal J. C. McCants announced that most male students were engaged in defense activities such as the army's Reserve Officers' Training Corps (ROTC). Many boys who had avoided ROTC rushed to join or were pressured by peers into it. The *Advertiser* described how "out on the windy drill field . . . details of youngsters in their school clothes were taking their first lessons in 'squads right,' and 'about face' under the orders of 16- and 17-year old ROTC sergeants." After the excitement of the attack and the first flush of patriotism waned, many of the recruits went back to playing touch football during the physical education period.[86]

As Christmas neared, the city seemed in many respects its old holiday self but with new patriotic highlights. Before Pearl Harbor, the USO had sponsored a campaign encouraging Montgomerians to invite servicemen to their homes for a holiday meal on December 14. Although the fields' alert status kept most personnel on base, the spirit of the season and the times was manifested in the large number of citizens who asked for a serviceman.[87]

The USO holiday campaign involved only whites, and so black citizens came forward with their own appreciation for servicemen of their race. They held a party in the Alabama State gym on December 17 with lavish food and dancing. Men turned out in large numbers from the black aviation service squadrons at Maxwell and Gunter and from Tuskegee, where black aviation cadets were being trained to fly. These were the first blacks to receive flight training in the history of the American armed forces.[88]

The OPM announced that the city could have outdoor Christmas lights. On December 21, Christmas carols were sung in Court Square as in earlier years. By 9:00 P.M., with lights glowing and traffic barred from the Square, people had filled the area and adjacent sidewalks.

Rain was expected but did not fall, and the crowd was estimated at 4,000. Erle Danley, a music professor from Huntingdon, began leading the caroling. Loudspeakers sent the familiar songs of Christmas beyond the lights far into the dark. A choir from Alabama State sang spirituals. The crowd included a few blacks. A Maxwell Field soldier from New York took over the improvised podium and led the crowd in singing "Yankee Doodle." Immediately thereafter, members of the crowd responded with "Dixie." At the end of the evening, Danley led the gathering in "The Star Spangled Banner."[89]

With rigid security relaxed for two hours on the twenty-third, a number of townspeople joined personnel from Maxwell for a candlelight singing of carols in a hangar. British cadets were featured in such native carols as "God Rest Ye Merry, Gentlemen." On Christmas Eve, Aviation Recreation Unit No. 1, composed of women from gentry families, put on a party for white enlisted men at Gunter. The hosts included such notables as former governor Bibb Graves and his wife and the wife of Governor Frank Dixon. Vera Ruth ("Millie") Prentiss, the social director of the Commerce Street USO club, ushered in twenty-five young women to mix and dance with the soldiers. Guiding her charges like a moral first sergeant, she gave strict marching orders that kept them from accepting dates for later in the evening.[90]

Christmas Day seemed much as it had in the recent past. For children as a whole, it was better because of an improving economy. Many children received roller skates. The city blocked off some streets for young skaters. Even before dawn, the intermittent popping of firecrackers could be heard despite a ban on fireworks.[91]

Not many members of the armed forces would be able to come home to Montgomery for Christmas. Not many service people from the local airfields were released to come into the city, but the mess halls served bountiful meals on Christmas Day. RAF training in the United States had reached its peak, and blue-clad cadets accounted for a majority of the servicemen on the downtown streets. People sought them out. The *Advertiser* called it "an old world flavor . . . as Englishmen and Americans sat down to dinner together."[92]

The Blue-Gray game was played as usual. The draft made no crip-

pling inroads into the ranks of college athletics as long as eighteen-
and nineteen-year-olds were spared. On game day, December 27, a
dreary day, crowds lined the Blue-Gray parade route downtown. Patriotism was a favorite theme, as illustrated by a float from the city of
Selma. It had a silver plane, young women in flyers' uniforms, and the
slogan "Defense Bonds Will Keep 'Em Flying," symbolizing Craig
Field at Selma, where advanced flight training took place.[93]

The game itself, attended by 15,000 in cloudy but dry conditions,
was for the first time broadcast over a nationwide network, the Mutual. The Grays won 16-0, to the delight of most whites in Montgomery. The Blue-Gray Ball and other balls and the New Year's Eve parties proceeded on schedule. *Advertiser* social columnist Go Peep declared that while "there was a steady ripple of conversations about the
war . . . , there must be a normalcy here at home and a war against
nerves and hysteria." After all, "our forefathers left us the heritage of
all-high courage in the face of difficulties. It has made our country the
home of the brave and the land of the free."[94]

Some of the theaters advertised the usual special inducements for
New Year's Eve picture shows. The Paramount offered noisemakers,
party hats, and favors along with the film *Bahama Passage,* with the
blonde British beauty Madeleine Carroll and her much younger leading man, Sterling Hayden, later her husband and a strikingly hand-
some blond newcomer whose acting ability would only gradually develop. The Strand on Court Square featured the top-rated band of
1941, Glenn Miller and his orchestra, in *Sun Valley Serenade.* The theater offered "no favors, no noisemakers—but two hours of the grand-
est entertainment ever."[95]

Chief Ralph King reported that during the celebrations downtown
both on Christmas Eve and New Year's Eve in 1941, "People had a
good time, I think, but they seemed to be more reluctant to celebrate
and did not let themselves go as they have done at times in the past."
Cars circled the Square honking away on New Year's Eve, but no one
tried to scale the fence around the Court Square basin and take a swim
in the pool as in the past. Few auto accidents were reported and no
fatalities. King surmised that "the war and its effects probably placed

a damper on celebrations. . . . Citizens may already be girding for what seems sure to come."[96]

In January 1942 Judge Walter B. Jones attacked "blind, stupid vilification of the South" in a speech before the Junior Chamber of Commerce. Certain unnamed politicians, the "negro press, the radical white press, the Communist press and the Association for the Advancement of Colored People," he asserted, were vilifying "a great people," by which he meant white southerners, "whose loyalty has been the nation's bulwark through the centuries." Jones made no mention of the Civil War. The South "is sending its sons to the battlefields . . . and is doing its full part battling for the preservation of the American way of life."[97]

The vilifiers were seeking "to disrupt [the South's] civilization by forcing on it conditions which it will not tolerate." They were, he claimed, obstructing "the war effort and obeying the wishes of Hitler, Mussolini and the Fifth Columnists in our midst." Jones had succeeded, as far as white Montgomery was concerned, in identifying the Confederacy and the "civilization" that had followed, meaning segregation, with the "preservation of the American way of life." The judge, however, had more insight than most white Montgomerians into what a war avowedly fought for democracy might mean for southern "civilization."[98]

3

The Creation of Citizen Armed Forces

First Lieutenant Esther
Eisenberg, Womens
Army Corps. *Courtesy
of Martin Epsman,
Calera, Alabama.*

Montgomery-area draft boards were geared to the increasing demands of the armed forces in 1942. The Registrants' Advisory Board, whose function was to help potential draftees fill out a questionnaire after registration, met periodically with Judge Walter B. Jones at the county courthouse. The advisory board included a committee of blacks headed by John T. Alexander, the minority county demonstration agent, that assisted black registrants. Alexander commanded respect and was named co-chair with Judge Jones of the advisory board. While the setup may have been equal, it remained separate. On several occasions, however, Jones praised the patriotism of the black volunteers who worked at three centers where blacks registered for the draft.[1]

The five draft boards, composed of white males who were primarily members of the gentry, actually determined which of the registrants would be called up and which would be exempt. Two white women, Mary Crump, the wife of a prominent businessman, and Ella Pearl Oliver, the chief clerk of the state insurance board, served as registrars on draft boards. After delays caused by a nationwide mothers' lobby, Congress lowered the draft age from twenty to eighteen in November 1942, making the draft boards' tasks more difficult. The navy had been accepting volunteers at seventeen, and the army had taken eighteen-year-old volunteers, but rapidly expanding U.S. involvement in the war made a drop in the draft age inevitable. A short time later married men with children became subject to conscription.[2]

The number of draft evaders, or dodgers, in Montgomery and across the nation was not large, for this was a popular war, a "good war." Occasionally the papers published a list of draft delinquents from the local area. On May 17, 1942, the *Advertiser* listed twenty-four blacks and one white who were being sought by their draft boards. On June 28 the paper listed eight whites.[3]

The people subjected to the most widespread scorn were not those who evaded the draft illegally. Throughout the war, young men ranging in age from the late teens to early middle age could be seen in civilian clothes everywhere. The inevitable thought on the part of women, older men, and service people was, "Why isn't he in the service?" Often the person in question was greeted with a disapproving stare or a cutting remark. Those exempt at least for a time included married men with children, before the draft took them in; men who could not meet even the lowered physical standards; and teenagers who had not yet been called up. With the lowering of the age limit to eighteen, volunteering was sharply restricted to keep men from avoiding the least desirable branches, in particular the infantry. Workers in essential war industries were spared in parts of the nation but not in the Montgomery area, where there was virtually no such industry.[4]

Army corporal Emmett Poundstone, Jr., from Montgomery sent his mother a poem written by some of his buddies at Camp Wheeler, Georgia. Entitled "To All Draft Dodgers," it spoke to those "who cook up your pitiful story so the draft board will turn you down." A central theme of the poem was the same that enemy propagandists such as the radio broadcaster Axis Sally employed to undermine the morale of Allied servicemen: "You never think of the real men, who leave their home day by day. You just think of their girl friends, that you can get while they are away."[5]

In their senior year at Lanier in the fall of 1942, several male students decided after a Poet football game to visit the "red light district" on Pollard Street. While they debated whether to enter one of the houses with beckoning bright lights, recurrent shrills of laughter, and throbbing refrains from a jukebox, a group of soldiers passed nearby. The GIs loudly and contemptuously questioned both the patriotism and the manhood of the high school boys, who beat a hasty retreat from Pollard Street. Within a year all of these Lanier students were in the armed forces.[6]

The draftees' experience of being inducted or rejected was universal. At Fort McClellan, Anniston, where most Montgomery draftees were first sent, it took two days to go through the physical exam and the process of induction. During the night in between, most draftees slept for the first time in barracks. Some of the youngsters showed distress that first night. A lanky country youth knelt between bunks and chanted an obscene litany as he masturbated. For some it was a solitary journey; others, recounted the *Advertiser,* had encountered friends or had made new acquaintances from home while they "stood naked for three hours in room 12 on the Fort McClellan reservation awaiting their pre-induction physical examinations." One such group "organized themselves into 'The Room 12 Club.'" When they returned home, they set aside a night for "their first and last pre-induction dinner."[7]

When local army inductees departed for their reception center, usu-ally Fort McPherson in Atlanta for whites and sometimes Fort Benning for blacks, they routinely made the trip by chartered Greyhound bus. Trains were more often used for troop movements. A designated con-tingent of inductees met at the bus station on Lee Street as daylight was breaking. After the noncommissioned officer in charge had checked them in, they said their last goodbyes to loved ones and boarded the bus. The city was stirring outside the depot. Female high school grads sometimes rose early to come downtown and wave goodbye to men in their class. Dootsie Ball, Isabel Dunn, and Betty Baldwin of the Lanier class of '43 would, many years afterward, re-member the occasion. The bus left the terminal and went down to Madison Avenue and out to the Atlanta highway. Some of its occu-pants were homesick already as familiar blocks, houses, and trees spun past; others were excited. Many, having awakened too early, dozed off. Early rising would be a new fact of daily life.[8]

Grover Hall, Jr., formerly a columnist for the *Advertiser,* was drafted early in 1942 and summed up the reception experience: "The first days at Ft. McPherson, Ga. produced considerable emotional shock. All personality was completely submerged—every man a Zombie. No one knew which way to turn, or whether it was in order to take a drink of water between meals. The result was that the most independent and poised among us developed intense gregariousness."[9]

In retrospect, he wrote, "it appears ridiculous. But not then, for the merest private, had he sounded off in authoritative and martial voice, could have marched 1,000 citizen soldiers off a cliff into the sea be-low." Toward the end, "personality and individualism began to reas-sert [themselves], and [one] . . . was almost himself again. . . . The lions began slipping into the main post exchange for a prohibited beer, or into the theater. The lambs remained in their bunks and sighed at the daring of their fellows."[10]

Robert ("Bob") Lawrence wanted to become an aviation cadet. As a boy he had been well acquainted with Maxwell. His father, William, Sr., a civic leader, had often been invited to the base and sometimes took Bob along. Maxwell brass—dignitaries such as Walter Weaver—

had also come to the Lawrence home on social occasions. When cadets came into the city in droves from Maxwell and Gunter, Bob Lawrence "envied and despised" them, as did many other Montgomery youths who saw the cadets with some of the city's choicest girls. Lawrence yearned to wear the "sharp" cadet uniform and the insignia. He passed the exams and in May 1943 left his home, a lovely two-story red brick house with white columns in Cloverdale. He "walked down those same front steps, down the same brick walkway, holding a small suitcase in one hand and leading a tearful mother with the other."[11]

All the way to Union Station and then to Keesler Field, Mississippi, Lawrence "was about as excited and filled with anticipation as any time in my life." But basic training brought disillusionment. Instead of the planes in which he had dreamed of ultimately being a fighter pilot, there were infantry drill, KP, "policing the area," and lectures implying that women amounted to a vast army of whores with venereal disease. He also knew the void of separation. Not only was he parted from old friends, but he also saw new buddies shipped elsewhere. Only later did he perceive that his experience as a recruit was universal.[12]

Preflight training in California and classification as a bombardier cadet did little to improve his morale. Gone was the opportunity to be a hero pilot. And he still encountered "chicken shit" right and left. Two experiences provided some relief. He qualified for the wings of an aerial gunner, making him eligible to be a member of a combat air crew, and he was allowed to come home on furlough. Home felt strange at first without old friends. All of the males seemed to be away in the service, and all the females were off at college. But he enjoyed being with his parents. The ending of the furlough was for him, as for most service people, a low moment. But he looked forward to his military future—the silver wings of a bombardier and the gold bars of a second lieutenant. Then he would go off to fly in combat.[13]

The flight training of an aviation cadet did not always end happily; often it terminated in failure to win the silver wings or—increasingly likely—in accidental death. In October 1943, cadet Ed Bowman, cheered for his strutting as a Lanier drum major in 1939 and 1940, was killed in a plane crash in Kansas in his last week of basic flight training.[14]

At the less glamorous end of the spectrum was infantry basic (recruit) training in the army or boot training in the Marine Corps. The marines had access to stouter physical specimens and made boot camp more of a deliberate ordeal. The underlying purpose of all such training was to strip away the independence and "softness" of civilian habits and substitute a conditioned, automatic response to orders, whatever they might be and however exhausting and dangerous the actions they ordered.[15]

In training at Camp Croft, South Carolina, in August 1943, Private Neal Howard, Lanier class of '42, wrote home almost every weekend. Like most unmarried servicemen, Howard usually addressed the regular family letters to his mother, who lived with her husband and two daughters in Cloverdale. He told of seeing another Montgomerian, Private William ("Billy") Crane, Lanier class of '43, writing home at a nearby table in the post service club. Howard described his training in detail for his family. About learning to dig a foxhole he wrote: "We started digging in about 9:00 A.M. You've heard of the infantry digging in—It doesn't sound so bad, does it? Well, I didn't think it would take so much to dig a little foxhole—Did I get fooled! I finished mine about 2:00 after we had eaten our dinner of 'C' Ration (two cans in one—6 biscuits-candy-chocolate to mix in water—in the other some kind of hash or stew—They were pretty good)." But, he wrote, "we had to get along on one (1) canteen of water all day. That's about 1 qt. and it was plenty hot that day." As part of the day's exercise, a tank passed over his hole: "I'll admit I was a little worried when that thing roared down on *me*. I lived!"[16]

Army ground forces basic training involved various specialties other than infantry. Aaron Harris, Jr., the son of the black owner of a dry cleaner on North Decatur Street, was spared the infantry. A month after Pearl Harbor, he and George Matthews, a close friend, together volunteered for the army. After passing their physicals at Fort Benning, Harris was sent with other black recruits by train to Fort Dix in New

Jersey, while Matthews was sent elsewhere. Harris was to receive basic training in the Signal Corps. He had never been far from Montgomery and was fascinated by all he saw from the train window.[17]

In New Jersey he walked in deep snow and on patches of ice for the first time and "didn't mind it." In basic training the noncommissioned officers were black and the officers white. His first sergeant was "hell," but he detected no racism in the officers. Yet, he thought it strange that, although the men drilled with rifles and went to the firing range, no rifles were kept in the barrack. A white soldier told him it was standard operating procedure in white barracks to have rifles in rifle racks.[18]

Harris was too intrigued with his new surroundings to get homesick; besides, as he would recall many years later, "We had each other." He learned code. The slogan for trainees was "If you hear that sound, you have to call it." New York City was "crazy." He "couldn't understand it." He sampled the floor shows and dances of Harlem but did not want to live there. He met a young woman in Trenton, New Jersey. She had a car, and she drove him back and forth between the Fort Dix main gate and her apartment.[19]

Robert ("Bobby") Young graduated from Lanier, like Bob Lawrence and Billy Crane, in the class of '43, the first class whose males knew, barring physical reasons or some special deferment, that they were draft "bait." Drafted after graduation, Young was sent to Fort Riley, Kansas, for cavalry basic training, which was actually infantry basic, for the army no longer used horse cavalry units in combat. But to keep the cavalry tradition alive, the trainees had to learn to ride horses. While in basic, Young attended radio school, probably because he had been an Eagle Scout with demonstrated mechanical aptitude. He was excused from KP because he was acting leader of a trainee platoon. But the position did not get him excused from "stable police," and he shoveled his share of horse manure in part to keep cavalry tradition alive.[20]

After basic, he received advanced communications training at Riley, which involved such complex subjects as cryptography. Then suddenly in January 1944, as was customary in the army, he was transferred to

Fort Bragg, North Carolina, to join a heavy artillery battalion. Artillery units were in need of communications specialists.[21]

Injuries in basic training sometimes played a cruel trick of fate. While Private William S. ("Billy") Robinson, also Lanier class of '43, was in basic training as a combat engineer at Fort Leonard Wood, Missouri, he was selected to attend college under the Army Specialized Training Program (ASTP). Feeling homesick, he wrote his mother, who lived with her husband and three younger sons in an apartment in Riverside Heights: "If I have any choice I'm going to ask for Auburn." Both of his parents had attended Auburn. On a night exercise or "problem," Robinson fell off a truck and seriously injured a knee. By the time he was released from the hospital, his chance to attend any college under ASTP had vanished along with any opportunity to receive special training such as electrical. "It seems," he wrote his father, "I get the worst end of everything. That is everything works against me going to school." He soon found himself headed for overseas duty as a combat engineer replacement.[22]

Ralph Loeb, Jr., Lanier class of '43, went into the navy in the summer of 1943 following graduation from Lanier. He was an only son, with a sister who had married and left home. His father, Ralph, Sr., a food broker, and his mother, Rebecca Loeb, wept at Union Station when he departed for Bainbridge Naval Station. They returned sadly to their home on Ponce DeLeon Avenue in Cloverdale. In boot camp, as he later recalled, instructors told the trainees at the beginning of their ordeal that they were lower than "whale shit on the bottom of the ocean." Some rough youths from northern big cities gave him an occasional hard time. They seemed to pick on him more because he was a southerner than because he was Jewish. Loeb, in his senior year at Lanier, had qualified to study radar by passing the Eddy Test. During boot camp he scored very high on the basic IQ test and was accordingly permitted to attend a special navy school.[23]

Mail carrier John Sawyer was drafted into the navy in January 1944 when fathers were no longer exempt. It was hard to leave his wife, Mildred, and his small children, who pleaded, "Daddy, please don't

Seaman Ralph Loeb, Jr., U.S. Navy, 1943.
Courtesy of Ralph Loeb, Jr.

leave us." He was inducted into the navy in Columbus, Georgia, and was then appointed to lead a contingent of fellow black draftees by train to Great Lakes Naval Station for boot training. There all the officers and noncommissioned officers in charge of their training were white.[24]

Robert Sternenberg, a native New Yorker who had graduated from Auburn in landscape architecture, had married Erin Crum of Montgomery. Employed by TVA in Chattanooga, he enlisted in the Marine Corps in 1942 to avoid being drafted. After boot camp at Quantico, Virginia, he was selected for marine officer candidate school at Quantico and graduated as a second lieutenant of artillery. Boot camp and officer candidate school were equally rugged. Afterward Sternenberg went to New River, North Carolina, for extensive artillery training before an overseas assignment.[25]

Montgomerians went to various service schools, which were often held on civilian campuses. ASTP, offering sharply accelerated programs leading to a bachelor's degree in engineering, foreign languages, medicine, or dentistry, had three basic purposes—to keep men with high IQs from becoming cannon fodder, to give the army more specialists, and to provide civilian colleges with students in uniform to fill some of the space left by the drafting and enlistment of so many civilian males. ASTP was limited to whites. The navy had a similar degree program called V-12.[26]

The army sent Billy Crane to the Clemson ASTP engineering unit. Neal Howard, who had finished one year at Louisiana State University majoring in forestry before being drafted, likewise qualified for the ASTP engineering program. After basic training, he was sent to the University of Connecticut in Storrs in the late summer of 1943. He reacted like many other young men suddenly liberated from the hard grind of regular soldiering at some sweltering camp in places such as South Carolina or Texas: "This really is a nice place. . . . we eat like kings. All the buildings are new and beautiful. . . . We are living 6 men to a group of 3 rooms adjoining—in a former women's dormitory—What a life—I still can't believe it. What's more the [co-eds] . . . here outnumber us. How about that?"[27]

After boot camp, Ralph Loeb went to Texas A&M to master the revolutionary technology of radar. There was no social life for the navy trainees at A&M, so all-consuming were their studies, with one exception. They were guests of the college at A&M football games. Ralph saw how devoted the Aggie fans were, but as a Crimson Tide fan he was able to hold up his head, for the Tide had defeated the Aggies in the 1943 Cotton Bowl game. He failed the comprehensives late in 1943 and was sent to electricians' school at St. Louis, Missouri. It was a low point.[28]

At Great Lakes during his boot training, John Sawyer took a test that qualified him for both quartermaster (navigation) and signal training. These were "paired rates," for each had interchangeable duties on shipboard. Although he had encountered no black officers, Sawyer had experienced no overt discrimination. He was sent to Hampton Institute, a pioneer all-black college in Virginia, for quartermaster and signal training. The FDR administration had told the Navy Department that the trainees at Hampton Institute could not suddenly be diverted into traditional occupations for blacks in the navy such as mess steward. Looking back, Sawyer believes that this directive was an early harbinger of the integration of the armed forces.[29]

Sergeant Fred Burks at Fort Benning was selected after Pearl Harbor to attend quartermaster officer candidate school at Camp Lee, Virginia. Commissioned a second lieutenant in May 1942, he was then assigned to the newly formed Ninety-third Infantry Division at Fort Huachuca, Arizona, as a member of the division's quartermaster company—one of two mainly black infantry divisions in the army. The division's highest ranking officers were white.[30]

Trains took young Montgomery men to many distant places in their own country, exposing them to scenes and sights that many would otherwise never have had the opportunity to see—the Rockies (awesome to people who had never seen mountains), the deserts of the West (looking strangely luminous on a clear night to passengers gazing out the windows of a troop train), the beauty of autumn leaves in New England in such places as Storrs, Connecticut; and the teeming metropolises of Chicago, Boston, Miami, Dallas, Los Angeles, San Francisco, and New York City, all of which had skyscrapers that put those in Montgomery, Birmingham, Mobile, and even Atlanta to shame.[31]

Until May 1942, only a very few American women could share any of these experiences as members of the armed forces. Although women could serve in the British armed forces, the U.S. services and a majority of civilians did not favor military status for American women. Though the U.S. Army and the Navy Nurse Corps came into existence in the early part of the century, it took the crisis of a second world war for these women to receive full military rank as commissioned officers and equal pay. Gould Beech, a staff member at the *Advertiser* and one of a few locals to be openly liberal, wrote an editorial that seemed to endorse a military role for women. Publication of his editorial coincided with the attack on Pearl Harbor, which alone prevented him from being the target of a barrage of angry letters.[32]

Two forces brought change in the status of women. One was unrelenting pressure on the federal government from U.S. congresswoman

Edith Norse Rogers of Massachusetts, who had the support of a number of women's organizations. The other was changing conditions in the armed forces as the Second World War progressed. The global nature of American involvement in the war and the evolution of military technology had reduced the number of men actually in combat to one in eight. Among the noncombatants, only 34.1 had clearly military occupations. Of the nonmilitary specialties, 10 percent were administrative and clerical. Thus the door opened, and women were allowed to don uniforms to fill positions that males were not eager to have. From the outset the new military women were prohibited from direct involvement in battle. An idea emerged, partly propaganda, that military women would free up military men for combat. Twenty was the minimum age for all the women's branches. Certain restrictions were imposed on women volunteers who had children.[33]

A bill to establish the Women's Army Auxiliary Corps (WAAC) passed the house in March 1942. On May 13 an *Advertiser* headline read: "Female Army Approved by Congress." The accompanying article revealed that with senate passage of the WAAC bill, "a women's auxiliary army corps to permit 150,000 volunteers to serve in non-combat capacity" was on the verge of becoming reality. FDR immediately signed the bill into law. A similar proposal to establish in the navy the Women Appointed for Voluntary Emergency Service (WAVES) soon became law. In November 1942, a U.S. Coast Guard women's auxiliary called Semper Paratus Always Ready (SPAR) was established, and in February 1943 the Women's Reserve of the U.S. Marine Corps came into existence.[34]

The marines' branch for women had no catchy acronym. Male marines tended to call their female counterparts BAMs ("Big Ass Marines"). Such denigrating language showed how the men felt about the women's auxiliaries. An *Advertiser* article concerning the need for quarters at the WAAC's first training camp at Fort Des Moines, Iowa, carried the headline "More Space Needed for U.S. WAAC Girlies." The first Montgomerian to be accepted into the WAAC was Ramona Tripp. She was no girlie but the daughter of one of the city's most prominent ministers, and she had a degree from William Jewell College in Missouri. Tripp had been a service representative for Southern Bell for four years before she had applied for WAAC officer candidate school. In June 1942 she spent two days at Fort McClellan for a "mental alertness test" and a few days afterward went to Atlanta for a physical. Later in the summer, she reported for officer training at Des Moines.[35]

In September 1942, Go Peep highlighted the WAAC: "Strong arches, a sense of humor and the speed of a fire horse may not be listed as requirements for entrance into the Women's Army Auxiliary Corps, . . . but they are indispensable in Army life." All three attributes were required for WAAC officer candidate school for "a day that begins at 5:15 and proceeds from breakfast to drills to classes to calisthenics to dinner to study and to bed with less than ten minutes between events . . . plus plenty of energy." Ramona Tripp had what it took. She became a third officer, the WAAC equivalent of second lieutenant. Esther Eisenberg, who left a job as an apprentice investment banker, also had what it took. She trained at Fort Des Moines at about the same time.[36]

By early 1943 the WAACs and the WAVES had commissioned recruiters with offices in the federal courthouse. The recruiters brought an increase in the number of volunteers. Jean Tate from South Perry, a violinist who gave private lessons, was one of the first Montgomerians to join the WAVES. She later became a recruiter of women for the navy. Olivia Ann Turner of South Court, the first woman marine from the Montgomery area, had worked as a civilian at Maxwell. She took boot training at Camp Lejeune, North Carolina, then went to Cherry Point, North Carolina, for instruction in the technical aspects of aviation. A very small number of WAVES and women marines flew in flight crews, but none served as pilots. Private Turner was assigned to the technical library in the assembly and repair of airplanes at Cherry Point. The SPARs were late in recruiting women in Montgomery. Eleanor Manegold, secretary to Postmaster Roy Nolen, was one of the first.[37]

At first the military women came from a variety of primarily middle-class white and black backgrounds. Mae Belle Bryant from Alabama Street, a draftsman with the state Highway Department, enlisted in the WAAC, while her sister, Bobby Ruth Bryant, a civilian aircraft mechanic at Maxwell Field, joined the WAVES. Miriam Hayssem from LeBron Avenue, clerk in the finance office at Maxwell, became a woman marine. Jessie M. Cotton from Hall Street, the office manager for Dr. Wayman West, a black dentist, volunteered for the WAAC. Roosevelt Taylor, a black public school teacher, entered the WAAC. The navy resisted having black WAVES until 1944, and fewer than 100 served in the war. The Coast Guard had even fewer black women.[38]

In February 1943, Marylou Felder of the Stones Community in Montgomery County enlisted in the WAAC. A graduate of Lanier and formerly a student at Alabama College, she had left her job as chief clerk in the state Bureau of Vital Statistics to take basic training at Fort Des Moines. She was then assigned to Key Army Air Field in Mississippi. She was there on July 1, 1943, when FDR signed legislation that converted all the women's auxiliaries into regular divisions of their respective armed forces, changing the name of her rank from auxiliary to that of private and from WAAC to WAC. She was later promoted to technician (sergeant) third grade (T-3), the equivalent of her civilian grade as chief clerk.[39]

In March 1944, Marguerite Sherlock left her college studies in biology to come to Montgomery and join the WAVES. Her father, Cris, former state highway director and an unsuccessful candidate for governor in 1942, was at the time a major in the army. At her swearing-in ceremony in the WAVES recruiting office, she wore the casual coed garb of sweater, skirt, saddle oxfords, and bobby sox. After boot camp at Hunter College, New York, Sherlock qualified for specialist training as a laboratory technician. Posing for a photograph, she made a dignified appearance in a dress uniform as a pharmacist mate second class.[40]

One of the most unusual experiences of these various women was that of Corporal May Belle Bryant, a tower operator at a Texas army airfield. Hitching a ride in an AT-6 trainer after visiting her father in Alabama, she and the pilot were forced to parachute when the plane became lost in a nighttime storm and ran out of gas. As they prepared to jump, she told the officer over the plane's intercom, "Good night,

Lieutenant Hooten, I'll see you in the morning." Both landed safely, and Corporal Bryant was one of the first Alabama women to become a member of the "Caterpillar Club"—survivors of an emergency parachute descent.[41]

What motivated women to join the armed forces in World War II? Captain Esther Eisenberg, a Montgomerian who became executive officer of a WAC training regiment at Fort Oglethorp, Georgia, maintained that patriotism was the primary driving force. "They're patriotic deep down inside—so darn willing to do whatever they're asked to do. . . . They enlist, thinking of all the things they can do for the Army, and soon [they] find out that the Army has done more for them." The new type of recruit, however, initially resented being ordered about, probably more so than men, because women had little experience with military discipline. But the outlook changed after KP, drill, retreat formations, and parades. Eisenberg reflected: "You soon thrill to the quick when a military band starts playing."[42]

In addition, unemployed women and those with jobs that lacked security and/or dignity entered the military for the same reason that men had joined the Civilian Conservation Corps (CCC) in the 1930s: they saw a chance to be a part of an organization that provided discipline, the necessities of life, and dignified work with pay. Alice Oliver, a black seamstress, and Joyce Stripling, a white clerk at Silver's five-and-dime, were among those thus motivated to join the WAC.[43]

Montgomerians became increasingly familiar with servicewomen when the first company of WAACs arrived at Maxwell in April 1943 and one reached Gunter in June. Initial reaction on the two bases combined curiosity with suspicion, though covertly in the military scheme of things. The uniformed women began to appear more and more on downtown streets. They looked in shop windows, lined up to buy tickets to movie theaters, and ate in downtown restaurants such as the Elite. They even appeared in the bar in the Whitley Hotel but always in groups or with dates.[44]

By June, women in uniform had begun to gain acceptance and were rarely subjected to stares or snide remarks. Then a nationwide campaign of slander commenced that was specially aimed at the WAACs (soon to be WACs). Rumors spread of "loose" sexual behavior, including lesbianism. Servicewomen were accused of having a high venereal disease rate and numerous out-of-wedlock pregnancies, often terminated by abortions, which remained illegal in Alabama and in most other states. An unfounded rumor claimed that problems had led to a policy of issuing condoms to WACs so that they could be passed out to sexual partners.[45]

Defenders of servicewomen soon stepped forward. Secretary of War Henry Stimson condemned "sinister rumors aimed at destroying the reputation" of the women soldiers. The few women members of Congress blasted the allegations, and a delegation of prominent church leaders who visited Fort Des Moines attacked the rumors as unfounded. The base commanders at Maxwell and Gunter defended and praised their WAC personnel for doing well a "soldier's job." A WAC recruiting advertisement in November 1943 contained a statement by FDR praising the women.[46]

The rumors and stories persisted. On the local scene, military-civil cooperation began to turn the tide. Maxwell and Gunter Field air WACs and aviation cadets put on a musical review in the city auditorium in November. "An enthusiastic capacity house" heard Colonel Raymond L. Winn, the commander at Gunter Field, declare, "Our cry at Gunter Field is for more Air-WACs. They are working in airplane and radio maintenance, in the airdrome control tower, in administrative jobs and special service—but we do not have enough."[47]

An editorial in the *Advertiser* in February 1944 entitled "The WAC" called "the harm done by thoughtless people, people of good intentions who repeat malicious slanders," "beyond calculation." It denounced the rumors as well as the fad of joking about WACs as "reflecting on the fine young women who compose the Women's Army Corps." In the kind of ringing rhetoric that helped to beat back the slander, the writer stated: "When Joan Smith becomes a WAC, she is still the same Joan Smith who taught school or worked in Mr. Doe's office, and if she was a fine, intelligent girl she will be a fine, intelligent WAC." Individual Montgomery women came to the WAC's defense. Mrs. C. M. Hammonds of South McDonough wrote to the paper, "I saw in this morning's *Advertiser* where the WACs are trying to defend themselves and I think it is time as they are doing a grand job." She wished the WAC "good luck" and noted that she was a "mother with three sons in the service."[48]

In same period, however, Atticus Mullin, a columnist for the *Advertiser,* while not impugning the morals of WACs questioned the patriotism of American women who did not sign up. Mullin, who had a daughter commissioned as an ensign in the WAVES, charged in his column "The Passing Throng" of December 2, 1943, that "the failure of the young women of America to enlist in their branch of the Army has caused the War and Navy Departments to add to the quotas of men, fathers and all, to be called up in January."[49]

Several women reacted, accosting Mullin. He pronounced himself in agreement with a woman he admired and respected who had said: "I would like you to know that the women of this nation are as patriotic as the men." But he did not back down about the alleged failure of women to enlist in the WAC. Even when the numbers of volunteers soared following a news release in January 1944 that described the brutal treatment on the Bataan death march, Mullin was slow to retreat.[50]

In April the *Advertiser* featured white WAC private Mary Ann Robinson, who had returned on furlough. Robinson, formerly the office assistant of Dr. Paul Mertins, an optometrist who was himself in the service, was pictured by a reporter as a "symphony of brown—hair, eyes, uniform." She displayed a sense of humor as she described training at a WAC center at Daytona Beach. The sunrise there was "exquisite," she stated, and "the officers were so proud of it, they woke us up every morning at 6 o'clock to see it." She was glad to be home, she said, but was looking forward to going overseas soon. Her only regret was that she would have to leave her boyfriend, an enlisted military policeman who had only recently returned from duty in North Africa, where he had been wounded. She was sad that, once again, an ocean was to separate them. By spring, the campaign of negativisms against the WAC had largely faded in Montgomery and elsewhere.[51]

Most Montgomerians in military service did not go overseas following initial training. They were posted to naval or Coast Guard stations, marine bases, or army camps across the country. But wherever they were, most of them longed for home. To ease the homesickness, in 1943 radio station WSFA began publishing *Letter from Home* for local members of the armed forces. Most Montgomerians welcomed these newsy monthly bulletins wherever they were serving. The best remedy for service people, however, was a furlough, or leave to come home. Travel within the zone of the interior, meaning the continental United States, was usually by train when the distance to be crossed was significant. It was an ordeal. The packed day coaches often smelled like a sardine can and were overheated or chilly and gritty, with unreliable toilet and washroom facilities. Sleep was at a premium. Berths could be claimed only by those with high priority or "pull."[52]

When the train slid slowly alongside the river, viewed by passengers from the high bluff, a service person was instantaneously fresh and pumped up. The train jerked to a halt beneath the shed. If loved ones waited on a platform, the reunion was loudly happy and often tearful. Many of those who waited for the trains had witnessed similar celebrations on the same platform in other wars.[53]

Visiting Montgomery, service persons often hailed one of the taxis that lined the front of Union Station if they were not picked up in the family car or in the vehicle of a friend. Frequently, the service person asked to be driven to Court Square and around the basin, then up Dexter to Goat Hill.[54]

Letters to WSFA, in response to *Letter from Home,* reflected over and over the symbolic importance of this strip of downtown: "Hoping soon to return to Dexter Avenue and Court Square." A "picture of Court Square and Dexter Avenue is worth a million." "This South Sea island is not like Court Square or Dexter Avenue." "I have been around quite a bit since I left Montgomery but the place I would like to go around is Court Square." "A look at Dexter Avenue would do my heart a world of good." These sentiments were undoubtedly voiced by whites. No letters to WSFA mentioned the area of most importance to blacks—the strip of Monroe Street and the blocks just north and south of North Perry at the intersection with Monroe.[55]

The returnees were for the most part embraced by their friends and family networks. Church or school bulletins and newsletters commonly noted the homecomings. Some, probably all whites, were listed in *Letter from Home* or in a Sunday section of the *Advertiser* called *Alabama at the Front.*[56]

In May 1942, new Second Lieutenant Fred Burks, on his way from Virginia to join the Ninety-third Infantry Division at Fort Huachuca, Arizona, received a delay en route to come home for a week's visit at Mount Meigs. Friends and family were proud of the new gold bar that he wore on his collar. Despite his designation by Congress as an officer and a gentleman, however, Burks had to travel in the coaches for blacks only as he made his way to Montgomery.[57]

Civilian Montgomerians with loved ones stationed in the zone of the interior tried to visit them as often as possible and often tried to be with them until they went overseas. The relatives of members of the armed forces who traveled to be with their loved ones usually went by train. With the rarest of exceptions, such visits were limited to the zone of the interior, where travelers endured the miserable wartime conditions. In 1943, Peggy Penton accompanied Erin Crum Sternenberg, a married friend, to visit Robert Sternenberg, Erin's husband, a Marine Corps artillery officer stationed in North Carolina. Sternenberg brought William, her baby son, in his bassinet. Peggy Penton would later recall that "*nothing* had prepared two nineteen-year-old girls like us for this trip." They were fortunate to find seats in the crowded day coaches, including one on which to place the bassinet. The train windows had no screens, so "in order to get some ventilation we had to dodge the cinders which flew in through open windows." Eating was a problem, except for the baby, who had his formula. The Montgomery travelers found it impossible to find seats in the diner. They looked around for the vendors who ordinarily worked the trains, "but alas no Butch was aboard ..., [and] even when we had layover stops no food was available at the lunch counters." Night was welcome even if the heat was stifling, for in daylight the summer sun was fierce.[58]

To ease the tedium, Penton took a walk when darkness fell. She

First Lieutenant Robert
Sternenberg, U.S. Marine
Corps, with his wife, Erin,
and his son, William, 1943.
*Courtesy of Robert
Sternenberg, Sr.*

had to work her way through those on board who had no seats. In the swaying *clack-clack* of the train during the interminably long night, standing passengers sometimes dozed against one another. Others without seats hunched on suitcases or bags in the aisles. In the vestibules several men and women in the service, and sometimes a civilian or two, smoked and watched lights flash by in the dark. A serviceman and a woman, most often a civilian, would usually be intertwined vertically in a corner. Penton's thoughts drifted back to Montgomery, to Mac McMillan, the officer at Maxwell Field she had been dating.[59]

4

Montgomerians Head Overseas

Major Charles Willis "Gordo" Davis, U.S. Army, the only resident of Montgomery to be awarded the Medal of Honor in World War II. *Courtesy of Mrs. Charles W. (Joan) Davis.*

Two categories of service people eventually underwent the sometimes tedious, sometimes exciting process of readying to move overseas. One group consisted of members of an existing organization stationed somewhere in the zone of the interior or of the crew of a naval vessel assigned to a port in the zone of the interior—organization or vessel having received orders to ship out to some foreign destination. The chief virtue of this category was that at the lowest echelons, for example, in an infantry squad of twelve men, close bonding was possible between members. The higher echelons to which each service person also belonged—companies, battalions, and regiments—afforded progressively less opportunity for closeness with each increase in unit size. In the higher echelons, a single private or seaman was like one leaf in a forest.[1]

The second category was that of replacement. After undergoing recruit or boot training, an individual was assigned to a replacement pool, through the mysterious workings of the military bureaucratic process, and, like a spare part, was shipped from one replacement depot to another. There was little opportunity to bond with those on whom one's life might ultimately depend. Eventually a replacement joined the type of organization or ship for which he had been trained. It might be during a battle or campaign in which a ground or air unit or ship was currently engaged. A replacement was initially a stranger among those he joined. It was a lonely business, but such were the practical ways in which armies, air forces, and fleets faced the enemy and maintained troop strength.[2]

The end of the line for troops departing the zone of the interior was one of several ports of embarkation up and down the east and west coasts. The principal ports were San Francisco for war theaters in Alaska, the Pacific, and China-Burma-India and New York City for those in Europe, Africa, and the Middle East. Now and then, troops in full combat gear rode on ferries side by side with civilian passengers across a harbor to the docks.[3]

When soldiers or marines were herded through the cordoned-off sheds that abutted the docks where troop ships were anchored, several Red Cross field workers in red and white waited at the bottom of a gangplank. To each serviceman, bent under the weight of a weapon and a full field pack, and to each servicewoman, the Red Cross women handed out a cloth kit bag with playing cards, cigarettes, candy, envelopes, paper, pencil, and—for the men alone—razor blades. The kit also contained a soap that would lather in the saltwater-fed showers of a troop ship, a sewing pouch called a "housewife," and a pocketbook edition of detective, humorous, or western fiction or, in some bags, more highbrow literature. People in the service might, as they lay in bunks or hammocks, for the first time encounter Willa Cather's *O Pioneers* or F. Scott Fitzgerald's *The Great Gatsby*. They might not appreciate the reading matter, but the voyage was long, and a book was better than nothing when the crap games (in which women rarely indulged) or cards had died down.[4]

Troops en masse crossed the Atlantic and Pacific either in convoys of troop ships or on a single swift former luxury liner such as *Queen Elizabeth*. Tedium was common everywhere but especially in the slow-moving convoys and particularly in those bound for the far Pacific. Danger lurked in the unseen form of submarines. When there were unannounced drills, with sirens, whistles, and clipped loudspeaker commands, passengers did not know if these were practice or the real thing. Repetition took the edge off the drills. Service people in transit whiled away the time as best they might in their bunks or hammocks, writing letters to be mailed at their destinations, reading, or conversing (known among men as "shooting the shit") with those in nearby bunks or hammocks.[5]

A line stretched around the deck to the temporary kitchen and mess hall. Hunger had to be sharp before anyone would want to eat the often tasteless and limited meals that were slopped into the mess kits. Games of chance went on much of the day and part of the night. During the day you could go on deck from time to time for exercise and to gaze at vast, seemingly endless sea. If anyone fell overboard, there was no attempt at rescue, for the convoy would be endangered if a ship slowed and lost its position in the protective web.[6]

Stormy weather meant staying in quarters while the ship heaved and rolled. Seasickness was a common complaint, and the smell of vomit often lingered in the air. When the destination was sighted at last, everyone's spirits rose.[7]

Military Montgomerians felt like tourists in places such as Australia. Army sergeant Gus Knabe wrote his mother on South Hull that the "Australians have been mighty good to us and naturally are glad to have us here." He had never seen "such pasture land as they have over here and cows and milk are plentiful. In fact our food has been plentiful since we got off the boat." Such was not the case in northern

Australia, where the U.S. Army and Australian troops hastened to build an airfield in anticipation of a Japanese invasion. Living conditions were primitive. The troops had to subsist on three tins a day of Australian army rations. No matter what was in the tin each man opened at breakfast, lunch, or supper, he had to consume it or do without. Nelson Van Pelt, a lieutenant in the U.S. Army Air Forces (AAF), would later tell his postwar college roommate that one morning he opened his tin and dumped into his mess kit a small squid in oil. He was staring disconsolately at the squid and feeling the pit of his stomach rise, when an Aussie soldier sidled up and said, "Sy, Lefttenant, you wouldn't swop for me beans 'ere? I fancies them squid."[8]

John Donovan, a graduate of Lanier and the University of Southern California and a former navy aviator, wound up in Burma. He had resigned his commission in 1941 to become a flying mercenary with Claire Chennault's American Volunteer Group (AVG), a group that FDR had covertly approved a year before Pearl Harbor to fight for beleaguered China. The unit, composed of former army, navy, and marine flyers, was better known as the "Flying Tigers," from one of its insignia. Employing the almost obsolete Curtiss P-40 pursuit aircraft, the AVG operated from Burmese bases in the winter and spring of 1941–1942. Donovan faithfully wrote home to his mother, Mary Stella Donovan. He was not limited by censorship. He told her that they had only the bunkhouse and old "picture shows" in a native village for relaxation and recreation. He refrained from writing his mother about the bar and an available brothel. Mother and son were members of the Clayton Street Baptist Church near downtown. He was not modest about his achievements. He wrote, "Got another Jap plane and one more probable in [a] fight. We are still going strong but need more airplanes badly."[9]

On May 12, 1942, Donovan participated in an attack on a Japanese-held airfield at Hanoi. Another AVG pilot on the raid told of Donovan's fate: "I follow [Frank] Schiel down to 300 feet over the airfield. [Tom] Jones and [John] Donovan are scudding down the runway unloading their fifty-calibers and dropping weed cutters like they were going out of style. The field is erupting like it was the end of the world."

Suddenly "Donovan's hit! He goes straight into the runway and skids clear off the end in a big rolling ball of flame." Chennault cabled Donovan's mother that he was missing in action, and two weeks later a telegram arrived stating that he had been killed in action.[10]

Convoys took troops across the sub-infested Atlantic to England and Northern Ireland, where American forces were slowly being built up. Americans were impressed by the scenic beauty of the British Isles. One of the few Montgomerians to serve in the armed forces of the British Empire, D. Collier Houston, of a Canadian-Scottish kilted unit of the kind known as the "Ladies from Hades," wrote his parents in Oak Park, "It is a beautiful view. The grass stays green the year round. And there are plenty of rabbits and deer around our hut." From his base somewhere in southern England, near a duke's estate, he could see the castle.[11]

The first American offensive strikes were not launched from England or Ireland. After some preliminary U.S. carrier actions in the Pacific, in April 1942 AAF lieutenant colonel James ("Jimmy") Doolittle led an audacious raid of army B-25 medium bombers against the Japanese home islands. The planes launched from the carrier *Hornet* marked the beginning of the tide's turning against the Japanese. No Montgomerians flew with Doolittle, but he came to the city in July, after he had returned, had been awarded the Medal of Honor, and had been promoted to brigadier general. Following a brief inspection of Maxwell Field, Doolittle visited his old friend L. B. Whitfield, Jr., in Cloverdale.[12]

In the annals of naval engagements, the Battles of the Coral Sea and Midway in the Pacific were the first in which the chief damage and the biggest contribution to the outcome could be attributed to aircraft from the carriers of opposing forces. In May 1942, navy lieutenant (junior grade) Richard Crommelin took off in his stubby Grumman Wildcat fighter from the carrier *Yorktown* of a U.S. task force. He was soon in the swirling mix of dueling aircraft whose contrails streaked the sky over the Coral Sea. One of five Montgomery area naval officer brothers, Crommelin shot down two enemy planes before running out of gas and having to belly-land on the sea. A friendly ship took him from the water. He received the Navy Cross. Each side lost a carrier. Significantly, a Japanese convoy and the carrier escort turned back. Its troops had been intended to occupy Port Moresby on the southern coast of New Guinea, the planned jumping-off place for an invasion of Australia.[13]

Obsolete U.S. Navy torpedo planes flew from carrier decks on June 4 near Midway Island. Their target was four large enemy carriers, the core of a task force seeking the defeat of the outnumbered U.S. Pacific carriers that had been absent when Pearl Harbor was attacked. Sweeping just above the surface and into curtains of fire from enemy ships and diving Zero fighters, the torpedo planes launched their missiles. They failed to hit a single enemy ship, and their charge, while gallant, seemed more futile than that of the Light Brigade. Many pilots died, including ensigns Charles F. Brannon of Torpedo Squadron 8 and John Wiley Brock, Jr., of Torpedo Squadron 6, both from Oak Park, Montgomery. Both were awarded the Navy Cross posthumously.[14]

The sacrifice was not in vain. The torpedo plane assault drew down the Japanese Zero fighters flying cover over their carriers and enabled follow-up U.S. Navy and Marine dive-bombers in a matter of minutes to strike three of the four large enemy carriers fatally. U.S. dive-bombers sank the fourth later that day. Montgomerian lieutenant commander Clark Thorington survived the only sinking of a U.S. carrier, *Yorktown*. He was one of nineteen officers and men of its crew who were cited for bravery. Those decorated included fighter pilot Richard Crommelin, who received a second Navy Cross. Midway, one of the most decisive victories in naval history, marked the climax in the turning of the tide in the Pacific.[15]

After Midway the Japanese focused on an overland drive from the northeast coast of New Guinea southward to Port Moresby. To aid in the conquest of Australia, the Japanese began to occupy the Solomon Islands, which stretched southeast from New Guinea and were covered with tropical growth. The presence of an almost completed airstrip on Guadalcanal at the southern tip of the chain and a natural harbor on nearby smaller Tulagi represented a threat to the main supply line between Australia and the United States. The American reaction was an amphibious landing by the U.S. First Marine Division in August 1942. Tulagi fell quickly. Among the marines hitting the narrow beach east of the larger island's airstrip were four Montgomerians, including Private First Class (Lance Corporal) Verbon Sanders. The four had enlisted together three weeks after Pearl Harbor and were part of a group of seven enlisted men from Montgomery who had become close friends. The invaders seized the lightly defended airstrip easily.[16]

Marine captain William ("Bill") Hooper, an Auburn graduate, described the "steaming jungle" for his parents in the Montgomery County community of Snowdoun: "Recently on two successive nights it rained eight inches in about two hours and we thought we would be washed away." He and his fellow marines were careful "to tuck mosquito nets around the pad on a canvass cot . . . [and] to take quinine and atabrine as a malaria preventive." He watched "ants attack with success . . . lizards and battles between wasp-like things and large spiders ending by the former carrying the stunned spider . . . up a tree after removing its long legs."[17]

In the jungle men fought each other as viciously as the insects did. Marine private first class Charles Cox wrote his parents on Burton Avenue of his terror at being lost in the jungle. "I tried to make the best of it. The best was none too good. I had no bayonet with me and had asked someone to hold my rifle while I was stretcher bearing. I knew the Japs were in the woods around me and occasionally I heard the crack of their rifles." He was also endangered by "our mortar shells . . . whistling over my head and landing about 300 yards in front of me. I hoped one wouldn't drop short." Eventually, to his great good fortune, he found his fellow marines.[18]

Verbon Sanders waited in the dark when a large Japanese force launched an attack across a shallow river toward the airstrip. The citation accompanying the posthumous award of a Silver Star read: "Private First Class Sanders held his dangerously exposed position against a superior number of attacking Japanese. Even though severely wounded, he maintained stubborn resistance until he was killed by the onrushing enemy force. He gallantly gave up his life in the service of his country."[19]

The Japanese failed to take the airstrip despite reinforcements and banzai attacks. They punished the strip from the air with bombs. Bill Derickson, one of the seven closely bonded Montgomerians, miraculously escaped death when a bomb hit the radio shack on the field. The shack had been used to communicate with the field's small force of American planes. Derickson emerged from the wreckage traumatized but physically unhurt. The enemy punished the airstrip from the sea with shells. Chief Storekeeper George Andrew Morgan of the cruiser U.S.S. *Vincennes,* a veteran of twenty-four years' service, thought of his wife and five children in Montgomery as his ship lay in the passageway between the Solomons known as the "Slot." On the night of August 8–9, guns flashed and roared in the dark. During the worst American naval defeat of the war in open, equal battle, *Vincennes* went down. It was one of four Allied cruisers lost to a Japanese foray down the Slot. Morgan survived despite serious shrapnel wounds.[20]

Ultimately, the Americans learned how to compete in the dark as both navies fought a series of major engagements in the struggle for Guadalcanal. The approaches to Guadalcanal became known as "Iron Bottom Sound" from the number of ships sunk there. In mid-November the last chance for the Japanese to prevail faded in an air and naval clash called the Battle of Guadalcanal, in which a sizable number of Japanese reinforcements failed to get ashore when six troop-carrying transports joined other vessels on Iron Bottom. Some of the reinforcements scrambled ashore from their beached ships and ran into the jungle to escape the deadly aerial attack.[21]

By early 1943, an army general commanded the American forces. Two army infantry divisions and the marine Second Division, which had replaced the gallant but worn marine First Division, were advancing to dislodge the Japanese from Guadalcanal, which the latter now called the "Island of Death." The campaign stalled before a strong enemy position on four ridges whose shape gave them the name the "Galloping Horse." Unknown to the Americans, the Japanese had decided to remove their remaining troops, and Galloping Horse was meant to cover the evacuation. From there small arms and mortar rounds took their toll of the stalled Americans.[22]

An infantry battalion staff officer of the army's Twenty-fifth Division, Captain Charles W. Davis, once a football center at Sidney Lanier and a Crimson Tide moundsman, was sent to assess the situation on the line. A wild fury to end the resistance from the Galloping Horse caused Davis to organize a small party of enlisted men, which he led up a slope toward the enemy's strongest point. Two Japanese grenades fell nearby but failed to detonate. Davis and his men threw their own grenades into the enemy position. When the survivors fled, unhinging the defenses, follow-up American units drove the Japanese from the Galloping Horse.[23]

Davis was awarded the Medal of Honor. He was the first member of the army ground forces in the South Pacific to receive this highest U.S. decoration for valor in combat and the only Montgomerian to receive it in the war. The victory on Guadalcanal, the first significant triumph for American ground troops in the Pacific, was the denouement of the turning of the tide against the Japanese.[24]

The spring after the fighting had ended on Guadalcanal, Japanese graves, rusting equipment, temporary cemeteries with white crosses and stars of David, and the hulks of beached Japanese transports remained as visible reminders. AAF sergeant Herbert Anthony wrote his mother in Montgomery that he had attended Easter sunrise services. On "a beautiful day," they were held at the camp of a navy construction battalion, the "Seabees." "The altar was placed in an open field, with three crosses set up to the right of the altar. Services began with an organ prelude and even though it was played on a small field organ, it sounded beautiful." Then "as the sun rose and silhouetted the three crosses, the sound of two trumpets playing 'The Old Rugged Cross' rang out strong and clear. Next came 'Where Were You When They Crucified My Lord?,' sung by a negro quartet; then 'Christ Arose' played by the Marine band and sung by the Seabee chorus. . . ."[25]

"I truly wished you could have witnessed this gathering, for it was typical of our armed forces today. . . . A negro boy from Georgia sat next to me and shared the same hymn book with me, so you see it's a great Army we have and truly a democratic one."[26]

Montgomerians flew with the AAF over New Guinea in support of General Douglas MacArthur's efforts to check the Japanese drive on Port Moresby. Late in 1942 Captain Broughton McCord piloted a medium B-25 bomber of the AAF's Fifth Air Force from his Port Moresby base over the towering Owen Stanley Range to bomb Japanese-held Lae on the northern coast. Later, at home on College Street near Huntingdon, he remembered that "before I knew it I was watching a stream of bullets tear off our right engine." His crew managed to beat off the swarming Zeros, but the plane was too damaged to climb back over the mountain range and had to fly low along the coast in a roundabout journey to home base. Staff Sergeant Franklyn Timberlake, a Montgomerian, was not as fortunate on a mission to Lae. His B-25 crashed into Lae Harbor in March 1943. The following December, with a cold wind whipping the flags and banners at Maxwell Field, his parents received his Silver Star and Purple Heart. Then the aviation cadets passed in review.[27]

When the Allies moved into the Central Pacific by the fall of 1943, jungle warfare had been replaced by a different type of warfare—amphibious landings on atolls and on larger but primarily flat and open islands. Holland M. Smith, an Auburn graduate and a marine three-star general whose widowed mother lived in Montgomery, was the architect-in-chief of U.S. amphibious warfare in the Pacific. Known as "Howling Mad," he did not admire the U.S. Army's role in the island-hopping movement toward Japan and often quarrelled with his navy counterparts.[28]

The prototype of these landings began in the early hours of November 20, 1943, with a massive bombardment by surface vessels and dive-bombing by carrier planes of the designated landing and rear areas on Tarawa in the Gilberts. As the amphibious tractors (amptracs) and landing craft moved toward the shore, the receding tide hung some of the invaders on coral reefs. The Japanese opened fire from pillboxes that had withstood the shells and bombs. Those marines who reached the shore struggled under the fire and Japanese counterattacks to establish a narrow beachhead. Of the 5,000 assault marines, 1,500 were dead or wounded by nightfall. The bodies of marines littered the beach and bobbed in the incoming tide, their blood turning the water crimson. Foot by foot the reinforced assault troops moved inland, continuing to absorb heavy casualties from dug-in Japanese and from their banzai attacks. On the third day a navy cook, Chief Petty Officer Homer W. Harrison, a Montgomerian, brought supplies ashore from an assault transport to cook the marines a warm meal. He found the conflict still raging, with men falling from explosions and small arms fire. He was unable to light a fire and was forced to pass around cold K rations. Flame throwers and "satchel charge" explosives became weapons of choice as the enemy was slowly eliminated.[29]

Sergeant J. E. Maddox from Montgomery fought on Tarawa. He later likened John L. Lewis and his striking coal miners to the Japanese, as did many Americans. "Just last month we got the amount of about $7 for 72 hours of some of the bitterest fighting in the Pacific," he wrote his parents in Capitol Heights, referring to Tarawa. "I wonder what would have happened if we had stopped for more money or for a hot meal. . . . They should send us home to take charge of a few of the strikes." The miners could well have retorted by asking whether Tarawa was so strategic that it was worth the cost in blood.[30]

In the European, North African, and Middle Eastern theaters for much of 1942, the American and British allies' offensive efforts featured the air weapon. The AAF operated in the daylight, the RAF at night. In August 1942, Staff Sergeant Edward Breedlove of Montgomery, radio operator and gunner on a Boeing B-17 Flying Fortress, took part in the first American heavy bomber mission from England against the Continent. It was a small operation with little opposition against a French railroad yard. The American effort from England continued to be limited by a slow buildup.[31]

The British Eighth Army won a smashing victory at El Alamein in October 1942. The Americans followed up by invading North Africa in November to join the British. Coast Guard boatswain mate Peter Brown, a Lanier graduate, was a crew member of a landing craft infantry (LCI) that took GIs to a beach in French Morocco. He survived the fire from beach defenses and the bombing and strafing of German, Italian, and Vichy French planes.[32]

Army private Thomas Blake was not as fortunate. Early in 1943 a Western Union boy on a bicycle delivered a telegram to the widow Grace Blake on East Jeff Davis Avenue informing her that her son had died in a North African battle. Army corporal William Oates had temporary good luck. He made it to Montgomery late in 1943 from North Africa after discharge because of a wound, and his wife, small daughter, parents, brother, and sister rejoiced. Not long afterward, at the Alabama River bridge on the Birmingham highway early on a foggy morning, his motorcycle collided with an army truck. He was killed instantly.[33]

Captain Peyton Ward Williams, formerly a professor at the University of Chattanooga, wrote his parents in Ramer in Montgomery County of the low point and high point of U.S. Army ground operations in North Africa. He told of the disaster at Kasserine Pass in Tunisia in February 1943, where Field Marshal Erwin Rommel's Afrika Korps battered green U.S. troops: "I shall never forget the night we drove up to the front where the main portion of our troops in that area had withdrawn. For 20 miles it seemed that ours was the only convoy moving forward; everything was going back in seeming thousands through a moonlit haze of dust that made the whole vista appear like some dark and tortured corner of hell." But three months later, also in Tunisia, "the end to the campaign came quickly." Borrowing a term coined in the Great War, he wrote, "What we did to the Boche toward the last was at once magnificent and terrible.... They folded up completely and came marching out of the hills in orderly thousands to surrender."[34]

The different cultures in North Africa had an educational impact on Montgomerians but also produced ethnocentric reactions. Ed Meeker, a white army enlisted man and a former employee of the post office, wrote home that he and his buddies were "still doing our best at trading and bartering with these Arabs. The principal item that the native possesses, that is to say, that we dogfaces are interested in, is eggs. . . . If the Arabs don't seem to give in to us, we walk away, but are finally called back and our prices go into effect." Meeker said he was "so tired of looking at Arabs that I'd give my last dime to visit Monroe Street on some Saturday night."[35]

Flight officer Homer S. Gentry, Jr., whose parents lived on South Lawrence, trained in North Africa with his Consolidated Liberator B-24 group for the first AAF raid on the Ploesti oil fields in Rumania. A navigator, he flew in the low-level mission of August 1, 1943, against the target with its rings of antiaircraft artillery (called AAA) and squadrons of crack German fighter pilots. Through hell and flame the Liberators flew, inflicting great damage but suffering great losses in dead, wounded, and prisoners of war. Gentry survived this mission and received the Distinguished Flying Cross.[36]

On a July night in 1943, AAF first lieutenant Louis Haas flew as a navigator on a C-47 transport plane filled with paratroops over the Mediterranean bound for Sicily. He was fortunate to be able to write his parents on Norman Bridge Road about the experience. Below, in the dark on ships of the invasion fleet bearing Allied assault troops to Sicily, gunners mistook the transport planes with glider troops and paratroops for enemy and opened fire. Haas's plane went into the water. He was able to swim free and inflate a life raft. He spent eight hours floating on the open sea before he was rescued.[37]

When the invaders established a beachhead, German armor attacked and threatened to dislodge it. Private First Class Claude Hill of Montgomery was in the midst of paratroopers of the Eighty-second "All American" Airborne Division who helped to repulse the tanks. The Sicilian Campaign, an operation to take Sicily as a jumping-off place for the invasion of Italy, quickly became a contest of egos between the major American and British commanders, Lieutenant General George Patton and Field Marshal Sir Bernard Montgomery.[38]

When Patton slapped a GI in a field hospital, accusing him of cowardice because he claimed to be shell-shocked, the general suffered a loss of luster. He seemed likely to receive no future high commands. Montgomerians took sides in the controversy, as Americans did everywhere on the home front. Louise Tolbert of Oak Park, with a son serving as a B-17 gunner in England, wrote the *Advertiser:* "Mr. George Patton better stay in Europe, but as a general in the Army is unthinkable. . . . Sergeants, cadets, and others are busted often for minor things. Why not at least bust Patton back to private?" AAF sergeant James A. Darrock, stationed in Missouri, wrote his hometown paper: "General Patton is both a soldier and a good leader of men . . . . They are all under a great strain on mind and body. . . . Let's forget the General Patton affair for good and say a few more prayers for the boys over there."[39]

In August AAF first lieutenant Sherman W. White, Jr., of Montgomery, an alumnus of the University of Chicago, took off in his P-40 from the all-black Ninety-ninth Fighter Squadron's base in Sicily. A war correspondent sent back a report. In combat over water with technologically superior German FW-190 fighters, three of the pilots "from among us," including White, "did not have time to jump. . . . One day they were eating and playing games and talking about post-war plans back home—then they went on a mission—and never came back." On West Jeff Davis, public school teacher Sherman W. White, Sr., read the telegram to his wife saying that their son was missing in action. A second telegram later declared Sherman, Jr., killed in action.[40]

Early in September the Allies crossed over to Italy, coming ashore on the toe of the boot and in a few days landing up the west coast at Salerno in a flanking operation to reach Naples just to the north. The invasion played out against a backdrop of political intrigue that saw the fall of the Mussolini government, an armistice between the Allies and the Italian government, and the takeover of Rome and the war effort by the Germans. Private First Class Charles Trum, a Montgomerian, had volunteered for the draft midway in his senior year at Lanier. Less than a year later he was on the beach at Salerno, where he caught a shell fragment in the shoulder.[41]

After Salerno, the Allied push up the peninsula, slow and harsh, took on some of the mud-and-blood character of the Western Front in World War I. In January 1944, the Allies undertook a gamble to breech German defenses in Italy by landing at Anzio. The operation failed in a muddle of preparation and ill-advised command decisions.

Montgomery paratrooper Private James ("Buddy") Brasseale was serving with his mates as light infantry on the heavily shelled and bombed Anzio Beachhead: "We clinched our butts and went over the top again. Hadn't moved ten feet when there was a loud explosion. A Jerry 88 [shell] lit clear in the center of our squad. Two of us were dead and the rest of us were writhing around on the ground full of steel splinters." He gave his account a year later from a hospital in Rome, Georgia. He never fully recovered.[42]

A new AAF numbered strategic air force, the Fifteenth, began to operate from Italy in the winter of 1943 against oil refineries and other targets in the Reich and the Balkans. The Eighth Air Force had flown from England for over a year, gradually expanding its operations. In the summer of 1943, the Eighth had enough men and planes to increase its blows markedly. The expanded operations were part of a joint campaign called the Combined Bomber Offensive, in which the AAF hammered the Reich by day and the RAF by night around the clock. The effort was designed to increase steadily. The "bomber barons" in both forces hoped that the offensive would bring surrender without an invasion of the Continent.[43]

By the summer of 1943, a growing number of Montgomery-area airmen were joining the Eighth Air Force. Some of them, such as fighter pilot First Lieutenant Paul Saffold, had come through Maxwell Field's preflight school. He wrote his mother, Oneita Henderson, a secretary at Maxwell, that King George and Queen Mary had visited his base in East Anglia. "The queen was charming and she really stole the show. . . . She climbed up on the wing of a P-47 and I thought for a while she was going to get in the cockpit. We put on an aerial show for them, too." Censorship prevented Saffold from describing for his mother the role that his P-47 Thunderbolt fighter group was playing in the intensifying air campaign. At that time the Republic Corporation–built Thunderbolts, the top fighter plane of the Eighth, had the fuel capacity to escort bombers as far as the western edge of the Reich but no farther.[44]

AAF first lieutenants James ("Jimmy") Oakley from Oak Park and Silas ("Brook") Nettles from Cloverdale had gone through training together from Maxwell preflight to graduation as heavy bomber pilots. The two were then separated, but in the fall of 1943 both were B-17 pilots in England. Oakley had arrived in the summer and was finishing his twenty-five-mission tour just as Nettles was beginning his.[45]

The daylight air campaign picked up steam in September and the casualty rate rose proportionately. At Maxwell's Air Corps Tactical School, the prevailing maxim in the 1930s had been that the bombers in defensive clusters should always be able to fight their way to the target and back without the support of escorting fighters. This idea had translated into strategy and tactics, with the result that as late as the fall of 1943, the Eighth had no fighters with the range round-trip to escort the bombers to most of the major targets inside the Reich. These targets had to be attacked, in particular the aircraft industry supporting the Luftwaffe that controlled the skies all the way to the French Channel coast, where the Allies had projected an invasion to land.[46]

Although Oakley had avoided injury or capture, Brook Nettles became a victim of the theory that had originated in his own hometown. The Eighth intensified the campaign against the deep targets with mounting losses. The climax for both Nettles and the campaign came on the October 14 mission to Schweinfurt, where a factory complex producing most of Germany's ball bearings lay well beyond the range of the fighters. Nettles piloted his B-17 Bob Kat on only his second mission. The ugly and often accurate flak blossomed around the formation, causing the plane to vibrate, but it was a fighter that knocked out one Bob Kat engine as the plane neared the target. After the bombs were released, a gunner saw flame creeping along one wing. If it reached the wing tanks, the explosion would be spectacular. Nettles ordered the crew to abandon the aircraft. It was one of sixty AAF bombers lost on the mission.[47]

Nettles parachuted into a wheat field, fracturing his ankle. As he tried to hobble away, members of a local home guard unit spotted him. Shots brought him to a halt. A civilian woman with the unit said in English, "If you try to escape, we will kill you." Nettles was fortunate to have avoided outraged German civilians egged on by a Nazi fanatic.[48]

Most of the sixty bombers had been lost to the swarming fighters. It marked a defeat for the Eighth. The campaign was soon called off, supposedly because of the onset of winter weather. The *Montgomery Advertiser* of October 19 had a perceptive commentary: "Daylight expeditions, like the one of last Thursday against Schweinfurt . . . in which 60 Flying Fortresses were lost, suggest that we may be purchasing our success by means of pyrrhic victories as destructive to our own belligerent power as to our Nazi enemies."[49]

On the seas another costly operation was ongoing. The majority of supplies that sustained American forces on all the far-flung theaters traveled in U.S. merchant ships. The crews on these vessels were for the most part seamen in the U.S. Maritime Service (USMS), a wartime agency that oversaw all merchant marine operations. Montgomerians saw horrifying images on the silver screen: a Liberty Ship suddenly engulfed in a black eruption, the work of a torpedo fired by a U-boat; oil-soaked survivors clinging to debris; shock on the face of a rescued merchant marine seaman who knelt in a blanket on the deck of an enemy sub.[50]

White prisoner of war Wesley Newton from Montgomery met a black merchant marine seaman from Alabama in a German prison camp. The sailor had been picked up by a U-boat after his ship was torpedoed on the perilous run to Murmansk, Russia. Navy lieutenant (junior grade) Edward Wadsworth from Montgomery described duty on a destroyer escort in a convoy bound for Murmansk. In addition to U-boats stalking the vast array of ships, "the Germans at the time had land based planes that could shoot us up like ducks in the water"—water that contained ice. "We had general quarters for 18 hours a day and in the remaining six were in a foggy stupor. On one occasion I had no sleep for five days."[51]

Leslie Joyner had left his job as a foreman in the mailroom of the *Advertiser* in 1937 to join the maritime union. By 1942 he had served on three cargo ships that had been torpedoed. He wore on his chest three miniature silver torpedoes to commemorate the experiences. At one point he and other survivors lived for five days on a raft, fighting off sharks with rifles.[52]

All merchant seaman were volunteers, and most of the wartime merchant seamen were newcomers. Fletcher Holmes left his job in Montgomery as a meat cutter to sign up in 1942. Thomas ("Tommy") Oliver, Lanier class of '43, left Auburn in 1944 to join the navy but wound up in the merchant marine. John H. Stovall, a postal employee at Maxwell, signed up in 1944. After going through a special boot camp for USMS recruits, Holmes became a cook, Stovall a mess steward, and Oliver a member of the engine room complement. After passing an exam, Oliver received his license as third officer in the engine department.[53]

A thousand merchant seamen perished off the U.S. east coast in the first three months of 1942, when the German U-boat campaign reached its peak. On the far side of the Atlantic, Holmes, who survived several sinkings, was rescued by a tug of the Scottish sea rescue service as his ship foundered off the west coast of Scotland. In gratitude, he presented a USMS cookbook to Archie McGeachy, the cook of the tug. After the death of Holmes and McGeachy, Betty MacSporran, McGeachy's daughter, on December 16, 1995, returned the cookbook to Robert C. ("Chuck") Holmes, the son of the rescued Holmes, in Montgomery.[54]

The relatives who waited in Montgomery for men at sea had as much reason to be anxious as did families that sweated while a loved one fought in a battle zone. Bese Stovall wrote her husband during his voyage to New Guinea in July 1944: "I just wish it was so that I knew where you are. I worry myself to death not knowing. Still I know you will be all right, for I pray for you every nite & day."[55]

The U.S. merchant seamen endured criticism from media commentators such as Walter Winchell and in-your-face verbal abuse from members of the armed forces. The critics sometimes accused the seamen of resorting to sabotage. Servicemen felt that the men in the merchant marine were overpaid draft dodgers who had it "soft." Merchant seamen who returned to Montgomery frequently wore civilian clothes and went unrecognized in public.[56]

Returning members of the armed forces were usually greeted in a friendly way. A few were acclaimed. The *Advertiser* on October 21, 1943, carried a front page story: "Lieut.-Col. Charles Willis Davis, the hero of Galloping Horse, stepped from an Eastern Airlines plane at Dannelly Field [the recently opened new municipal airport] yesterday afternoon and was immediately imprisoned in the arms of his mother, who had not seen him for two years." The "tall, rather rangy possessor of the Congressional Medal of Honor," nicknamed Gordo because of his Alabama birthplace, was repeatedly honored during the next forty-eight hours. He sat on the Lanier bench at Cramton Bowl— where he had once played center for the Poets—at a Friday night game, which Lanier, the underdog, won over visiting Dothan. Earlier he had addressed the student body and staff at his high school alma mater. He had told them, "To be honored by my fellow students means more to me than I can express to you, but it is something I will carry with me with pride for the rest of my life." At Maxwell Field he saluted the "eyes right" from a training wing of aviation cadets, which passed in review in his honor.[57]

Five days later Lieutenant (Senior Grade) Richard Crommelin addressed an assembly of notables at the Whitley Hotel for the Navy Day luncheon. He wore the ribbon of the Navy Cross and the gold emblem of a second award for his feats as a fighter pilot on the carrier *Yorktown* in the Battles of the Coral Sea and Midway. He singled out the Coral Sea as the battle that "saved Australia from Japanese conquest."[58]

More nearly representative of the average person on leave was Private First Class Thornton S. Cody, a white male who came back to little acclaim. He had the good fortune to have returned healthy from a distant combat zone. In January 1944, Cody wrote WSFA from Camp Carson, Colorado, "at the foot of Pike's Peak just outside Colorado Springs." He had arrived there in December 1943 with the Eighty-seventh Mountain Infantry Regiment from the Aleutians, where in August he had been "the 2nd machine gunner ashore" on the island of Kiska. The "visibility on ridges was limited to perhaps 12 to 15 feet. . . . The wind, rain and general disagreeableness of it all made it very

difficult. We called those hurricane winds 'Williwaws,' and I can testify that it was hard to even crawl in some of them much less stand
up.[59]

"Actually we went through battle without its terrible horrors," for
"two days after we landed . . . it was definitely established that no Japs
were there." After reaching Camp Carson, "I did get to Montgomery
for 6 days to spend with my Mother and Grandmother. . . . It certainly
gave me a rejuvenated feeling to be back."[60]

5

The Emergence of the Home Front

Caroline Ball holds a coffee cup at the opening of the canteen operated by the
Red Cross and the Junior Chamber of Commerce near Union Station, October
1943. *Courtesy of Albert Krause Studio/Tommy Giles Photographic Services.*

Without a well-organized and well-functioning home front,
successful war fronts would have been impossible. Montgomery was
not an industrial city before the war, and no significant war industry
as such was established there during the war. The surrounding county
had agriculture, essential to a war effort; but apart from warm bodies,
what did the city itself contribute of significance to the armed forces?[1]

Maxwell, in the constantly expanding air war, was the headquarters for the training of many of the bomber crews and fighter pilots

for the AAF and, for a time, of a significant number of bomber and fighter pilots for the RAF. Gunter Field added the flight training of basic-phase aviation cadets throughout the war. The Montgomery area supplied most of the civilians who worked or labored at both Maxwell and Gunter. Maxwell and Montgomery had long nurtured each other. In May 1943, Major-General Walter Weaver, by then commanding the vast AAF Technical Training Command, wrote Lister Hill, "Certainly I will never forget Maxwell or Montgomery, the many friends I have there, or the many kindnesses bestowed on me." To varying degrees most service people who served any length of time at the two bases felt the same way.[2]

Civil defense seemed vital at first and received much attention. The images of the Blitz in England and of Pearl Harbor invigorated it. Civil defense efforts in the Montgomery area began shortly after Pearl Harbor when several Montgomery civic groups sponsored the installation of air raid warning posts in the county. In January 1942 the Office of Civil Defense (OCD) in Washington, D.C., came into being, with Mayor Fiorello La Guardia of New York City as its first director. The OCD worked through the nationwide state and local committees to prepare them for aerial bombing and sabotage and even for possible enemy invasion.[3]

The threat of aerial bombing became stronger once the United States had directly entered the war. Aerial assault on the Montgomery side of the continent seemed unlikely, but the federal government informed governors such as Alabama's Frank Dixon that the Germans were planning to build an ocean-spanning bomber. Sabotage in the form of explosives or arson was a stronger possibility. At the county-municipal level in the Montgomery area, the CD committee was staffed by prominent people, overwhelmingly white, who supervised many different activities. Initially, the leading task was the formation and training of local organizations that operated on a grid principle, particularly in the city. These units were air raid wardens and auxiliary police and fire personnel. The system dragged until the committee created a Citizens Defense Corps and on February 14, 1942, appointed Commissioner W. P. Screws to be its director. During a first exercise, a night "bombing attack" on West End Grammar School, volunteer CD personnel rushing to the scene were hampered by traffic. Afterward the city passed an ordinance that gave Screws complete authority to carry out blackout and air raid exercises in any part of the city and to clear public streets, sidewalks, and buildings in advance.[4]

One of the chief functions of the defense corps was to coordinate with the local air raid warning system, whose core was a filter center where army personnel supervised local white female volunteers. These women were trained to react to alert signals of a pending air attack by enemy planes flying in from the Gulf. The signals were telephoned in from the regional air raid warning headquarters in Mobile. The women also practiced reacting when volunteers manning observation posts in the county sent warnings that they had spotted enemy planes. Home from Auburn, Peggy Penton later described her work as a volunteer: "We went to our assigned tasks at night" at the center, located in the Bell Building, with "windows heavily draped as a precaution against attack."[5]

The filter center volunteers were shown films of the heroic RAF women's auxiliary members as they operated, often under air attack, the "Chain Home" air defense radar system that was vital to victory in the Battle of Britain. Although the Montgomery women lacked radar, they learned, with telephone headsets and mouthpieces, to move chesslike pieces representing aircraft on a plotting map. "We were given wings at the completion of our training and of a certain period of time served," Penton recalled. Even so, the army personnel and local community leaders issued plea after plea for volunteers to work the daytime shifts, because most available women had regular daytime employment. Peggy Penton, for example, worked for the Office of Price Administration (OPA).[6]

The army furnished everything for the Montgomery volunteers at the center. But a special unit of the auxiliary police, the Auxiliary Police Motorcycle Squad, furnished its own equipment. It was the first auxiliary unit to win approbation. One of its duties was to assist in moving military convoys, munitions, and war equipment through the city, which had no bypass highway. On average it had taken a convoy seven hours to pass through, but once the unit had formed, its thirty motorcycles led by police captain R. P. Dees "roared to their posts in 11 minutes," according to an *Advertiser* reporter who had trailed it by car, "and a huge olive drab cavalcade of men and machinery was shuttled through the city in less than two hours."[7]

The combined CD committee made more than token efforts to involve the black community in the majority of CD activities, but the local papers gave the blacks who were involved far less publicity than the whites. It was rare when the *Advertiser* printed in its semiweekly *Civil Defense Bulletin* such announcements as one on July 31, 1942, stating that "All Colored Wardens" in Zone Three, covering much of west Montgomery, were to report to George Washington Carver School for first aid training. The air raid wardens were predominantly black and white males, with a few white female wardens. Some black males were enrolled as auxiliary firemen, but as a matter of deliberate policy, only white males could become auxiliary police.[8]

Directed by the area army Fourth Service Corps headquarters in Atlanta, a blackout began the test of Montgomery area CD. Evidence of widespread interest and some anxiety surfaced before this first periodic air defense exercise in a series. A white grammar school student representing his class asked a teacher the zone of each class member, who was the warden for each student's particular block, and whether the students would be able to hear the air raid sirens. Commented the *Advertiser:* "Such intelligent interest . . . is a challenge to the rest of us to make this thing work." Before the blackout, scheduled for March 17, a white housewife wrote the paper that her black cook believed it meant a real air raid.[9]

On the seventeenth the regional headquarters at Mobile sent a "yellow" signal at 8:02 P.M. alerting key city and county CD personnel to take their posts. At 8:26 the "blue" signal came that the "enemy" was on the way. Since the large air raid sirens ordered by the defense corps had yet to arrive, the sirens of police cars posted at strategic areas of the city had to serve in their stead. Lieutenant Robert Register circling above the city in a Maxwell plane observed what took place when the sirens wailed. "In one minute, it was 85 per cent black, in two minutes it was 95 per cent black, and in three minutes it was at least 99 per cent black." Below, residents, in an interior room curtained off from the rest of the darkened dwelling, clutched their flashlights and huddled around a radio tuned to the CD-designated station.[10]

Register gave the scene below a poetic but unintentionally ominous touch: "The Old City seemed to disappear right before your eyes." After forty-five minutes, the "All Clear" sounded.[11]

The tests soon combined air raid alerts, blackouts, and mock air attacks that were scheduled to occur on a certain date. Such an attack on August 18 featured louder sirens, searchlights, and mock bomb explosions that supposedly caused heavy casualties and damage in Court Square. The exercise included the deployment, in the aftermath, of local units of the Alabama state guard, the replacement for the federalized National Guard, to protect several state buildings including the capitol. The tests made the town seem somewhat as it might have in a war zone during an air raid. On one occasion CD officials set off large firecrackers in the darkened downtown but without thundering AAA guns and orange flashes in the night, flaming buildings, or smoking rubble. For more of a martial flavor, one had to be on Maxwell or Gunter. There antiaircraft and machine guns protected hangar roofs, and guards had rifles, bayonets, gas masks, and steel helmets.[12]

Assessments of the populace's reaction were more positive than negative, but public response to tests conducted without advance notice was much poorer even as late as the summer of 1943. In August in a surprise exercise, twenty minutes elapsed after the "Yellow Alert" before all lights were off. Umpires for the Fourth Service Command concluded that the "attack" had "plastered" Montgomery with bombs and "buildings were demolished, citizens killed and maimed, and all the horrors of an air raid were visited on the city."[13]

Although only 66 percent of air raid wardens had reached their posts during this exercise, many, perhaps most, took their job seriously. East Fifth Street in Oak Park and several surrounding blocks were the domain of warden August Caton. He was intensely serious in his performance. Daughter Mary Louise Caton would later attribute his intensity to his "heavy time" in the trenches in France in the Great

War. But as daughter Pat Caton recalled, at the time his children were occasionally "tickled" by his irritation when regulations were not observed to the letter. A light in a house that was supposed to be totally darkened aroused his anger and prompted him to knock at the offending door and demand compliance.[14]

Inevitably, horseplay competed with serious intent. Go Peep reported that various male guests at a hotel had received after-midnight phone calls in their rooms from a voice that purred, "I'm lonesome." When each man "repaired with unaccustomed haste to the whispered number of a hotel room," he was greeted by a "charming Alabama girl," whose "husband stood smiling in the background. 'We are testing out a new air raid system,' she explained sweetly." Go Peep concluded that "a siren with a feminine whisper is more effective than the alley-cat-tenor type."[15]

Eventually Americans nationwide realized that aerial bombing by the enemy was unlikely to inflict damage on the continental United States. The filter center closed early in 1944, and the blackouts, alerts, and practice raids came to an end. The recruitment of air raid wardens and auxiliary fire and police volunteers was no longer extensive.[16]

On October 13, 1942, the Montgomery CD committee established a Citizens Service Corps to direct its several community service committees. The Service Corps coordinated the activities of various special interest groups with the war effort. It promoted the work of schoolchildren in drives to collect, for example, scrap metal and fostered summer youth recreational programs. The *Advertiser* termed an early program "Day Care Centers for Working Mothers" in Boylston and West End, where poor white women worked in textile factories.[17]

One of the most far-reaching initiatives of the Citizens Service Corps was the block leader system. The corps appointed a housewife in each city block to organize the other homemakers for campaigns such as preparing for a blackout, promoting war loan and scarcity drives, and combating "black market" operations. These women joined the wardens, police and fire auxiliaries, and volunteers who assisted the draft boards in forming the backbone of the home front. Like other aspects of the home front, the block plan reached the black districts last.[18]

Volunteers of the Citizens Service Corps in Montgomery, date unknown. *Courtesy of the Alabama Department of Archives and History, Montgomery, Alabama.*

Shortly after Pearl Harbor, the FDR administration decided to ration certain consumer goods because an increase in hoarding conflicted with the needs of the rapidly growing armed forces. The administration sought to curb the threat of dangerous inflation in a war-stimulated economy by a combination of rationing with higher taxes and price, wage, and rent controls. The Office of Price Administration under Leon Henderson was created to plan and direct these programs. It issued its first order, on December 27, 1941, to provide for the rationing of tires and tubes beginning in January 1942.[19]

On January 3, Federal Marshal Walter Bragg Smith swore in the first Montgomery tire rationing board. It was composed of prominent white men. For January, in all Alabama, the OPA-mandated quota was 2,906 tires and 2,432 tubes for passenger cars, motorcycles, and light trucks and 3,680 tires and 3,076 tubes for heavy trucks and buses.

These figures were cut in half in February. Curtailment on a month-by-month basis reduced the number of motor vehicles on the streets.[20]

On January 1, the Office of Production and Management announced that the production of new passenger cars for civilian sales would shortly be almost completely halted, with existing stock made available according to strict priorities. New trucks would soon join the vanishing category. If civilians had trouble imagining a world in which only steadily aging used cars moved about the streets and on the highways, a world in which these cars were, with the rationing of tires, restricted in their mileage seemed almost inconceivable.[21]

Several such government acts, along with the rapid call-up of young men, intensified public awareness of the war and its effect on lifestyles. There were instant protests when the highest priorities for tires and tubes were granted to construction companies, clergymen, physicians, dentists, and veterinarians "principally" for work and professionally related activities. Those engaged in farmwork using vehicles with authorized rubber could use them for pleasure as well. Eventually excessive violations of "principally" led OPA to decree that all vehicles with high priority for tires and tubes must be used "exclusively" for business purposes.[22]

Thefts of tires mounted over the first few months of rationing. On Goat Hill several black state prison trustees on work details stole tires from vehicles parked nearby and, through fences, sold them on the black market. Before long these men had gone back to their cells with additional time. Black and white thieves stole tires from car rental companies such as Dixie Drive Yourself until the ring was smashed through the combined efforts of the police and the FBI. In the neighborhoods an increasing number of owners found one or more tires missing from cars parked on the street after dark.[23]

Tire thieves joined draft dodgers and black marketeers as the chief villains on the home front. A full-page notice in the *Advertiser* depicted a sinister-looking man bathed in shadow making off with a tire. The ad proclaimed: "Tire theft . . . is not just petty larceny anymore. It is a direct stab-in-the-back [to] . . . vital American production." The notice, sponsored by the Pure Oil Company of Chicago, denounced the villain with patriotic rhetoric: "For want of a tire, the car was lost . . . , the man was lost . . . , the job was lost . . . , the bomber was lost; for want of a bomber the battle was lost." Thieves were "as obnoxious as a fifth columnist, as despicable as Benedict Arnold." Sometimes a tire dealer was found violating the law. The OPA suspended the right to sell new tires for two weeks when the Firestone Store on South Court downtown was caught selling new tires without the required trade-in.[24]

FDR delayed gas rationing to prevent a backlash with political ramifications, but over time, shortages created hardship. Urgent need hit Alabama late in 1942. Categories of eligibility, marked by stickers on windshields, were A for basic allotments; B for the general range of occupational needs; C for "preferred" driving such as that of physicians and dentists, governmental officials, defense workers, schoolteachers and officials, and essential farmworkers; D for motorcycles; and T for taxis. The fixed amounts varied from region to region and changed from time to time. In line with tire and gas rationing, the maximum speed limit was lowered to forty miles an hour, but the new limit was frequently not observed.[25]

High school students with access to cars raced up and down Fairview Avenue just before the advent of gas rationing as if they were thumbing their noses at this latest blow to their freedom. All too many adults, while denouncing the black market, tried to wheedle extra gallons from their favorite gas station without the requisite stamps but met with little success. Owners had to account to the OPA for gallons sold and coupons collected. People turned to carpooling and bicycles for transportation, but bicycles too were soon rationed. The city bus line quickly became overburdened.[26]

One of the few groups in the population to benefit from the situation comprised some 100 women between eighteen and twenty-five who, under the auspices of the Office of Defense Transportation (ODT), were trained as auto mechanics, parts clerks, lubrication experts, metalworkers, and welders for local employment. Chevrolet dealer Thomas McGough directed the program. None were employed permanently except as parts clerks.[27]

Sugar rationing began in May 1942. "Roses are red, violets are blue, sugar is short and getting shorter, thanks to Hitler, Hirohito, and their hordes," remarked the *Advertiser* on the morning of registration. Montgomerians registered at elementary schools throughout the county for War Rationing Book No. 1. It was a system "long in effect in most European countries." Petroleum rationing later had a separate book.[28]

The OPA warned that any hoarding of sugar would be subject to a $10,000 fine or ten years in prison. Hoarding was defined as accumulating for a single person or in a family more than two pounds per person. No evidence survives that any Montgomerians were thus penalized.[29]

Book No. 1 contained pages for tires and coffee. Meats and fats, canned fruits and vegetables, and other processed foods appeared in Book No. 2, which became available in February 1943.[30]

The registration for Book No. 1 was delayed because the process was new. Registration for Book No. 2 went much more smoothly. County Superintendent Clarence Dannelly complimented elementary school personnel, parents in the parent-teacher association (PTA), and members of the Citizens Service Corps who assisted in the registrations. He singled out the white Chisholm Elementary School, whose pupils were mainly from the families of blue-collar textile workers, for its efficiency in registering 3,363 people in the allotted time.[31]

War Ration Books No. 2 and No. 3, issued in July 1943, both reflected the addition of shoes—three pairs a year—to the rationing list. Book No. 4, issued in October 1943, reflected the addition of whiskey and wines. Many heavy drinkers soon resorted to the black market.[32]

Rationing was complicated by nature. The combined Rationing Board of Montgomery County, whose members were men and women (its executive secretary was Clara Cahn), was located on Washington Avenue downtown and had some discretion in establishing quotas. The *Advertiser* helped simplify matters by periodically publishing explanatory tables and charts and question-and-answer articles. When a housewife, the key consumer coping with rationing, opened her Sunday *Advertiser,* she turned to a "handy rationing guide" that indicated which stamps or coupons in which books were current. Entitled "Home Front Orders," the guide named such items as "SUGAR—War Ration Stamp No. 10 good for three pounds until Jan. 31, 1943" (Book No. 1); "MEATS AND FATS: Red stamps lettered L become valid for this today, June 6, [1943]" (Book No. 2); "CANNED FRUITS AND VEGETABLES: Blue stamps lettered K, L, and M are valid for these foods through July 7, [1943]" (Book No. 2); "SHOES: Stamp #18 good for pair of shoes through October 31, [1943]" (Book No. 3)."[33]

Meats, canned fruits and vegetables, and other processed foods were distributed under a point system. Newspapers printed several pages listing the types of food items and the number of points and the maximum price for each. The *Advertiser* explained the rationale for the point system: "The reason for adopting this system is that there are a great number of different items of processed foods. If the supply of each item were evenly divided, there would not be enough to go around." The system took into account "personal preference." If one person wanted canned peaches and another canned pears, each surrendered stamps worth points that the particular item at a given weight called for. If only pears were available, it would be first come, first served. The point system for meats, butter (which soon disappeared), margarine, lard, and cooking oils reflected more or less the same principle.[34]

To augment the food supply, people were encouraged to have "Victory" gardens. Victory gardens, borrowed from the Great War first by the embattled British, became part of the lore of World War II. An editor for the *Advertiser* summed up the feelings of the many successful gardeners: "One of the pleasures of Victory Gardening . . . is to sit down to a meal, preferably with appreciative guests, and to announce as nonchalantly as possible that the beans, corn, tomatoes, beets, and onions are all the products of our small patch."[35]

Price ceilings worked hand in glove with rationing. After Congress in January 1942 authorized the OPA to set controls for maximum prices, the agency at first tried selective controls. This approach did not work, and protests resulted. In April the OPA froze all retail prices at the highest level reached during the previous month. On May 17 the Sunday *Advertiser* announced that controls on all retail items were to become effective the next day. On the eighteenth the paper reported that ceilings had already forced down the prices of some items, including steak, which had dropped as much as five cents, according to local grocers. Rent controls for houses, apartments, and roominghouses and controls for hotel charges soon took effect.[36]

In October, at the president's urging, Congress passed a more detailed price control law and added wage controls as well. While discontent remained, especially among merchants and landlords, and the black market did not vanish, these devices helped keep inflation within reasonable bounds.[37]

Another tool to combat inflation was taxes. At the urging of the administration, Congress reluctantly passed the Revenue Act of October 1942, which imposed a flat 5 percent gross income tax on all incomes over $624 per year. Though the act also imposed some increases that affected the middle and upper classes, it hit those who were less well off the hardest. For the first time industrial workers—old-timers and new war workers—paid an income tax. The Montgomerians who grumbled the loudest were those who had recently acquired war-related jobs at Maxwell, Gunter, and a new military depot.[38]

Over the course of the war, an indeterminate number of people and enterprises evaded the various controls. In April 1943, in a crackdown on overcharging or false declarations of the amount of ration points of stocks on hand, OPA proceeded against six city restaurants. Two of these were popular places—the old, established Elite and a new, partly open-air restaurant, the Candlelight, between Montgomery and Clay Streets up the hill near Cottage Hill. The usual penalty in such cases was a slap on the wrist—suspension of the offender's ration books for several days. In May 1943, Judge Walter B. Jones, at the behest of the OPA, enjoined four Montgomery grocers from charging higher prices than allowed. The OPA threatened to seek criminal sanctions if further violations occurred.[39]

In June 1943, a taxi of the Blue Cab Company was caught speeding and had to forfeit fourteen of its T cards, worth five gallons of gas apiece. The OPA occasionally caught a landlord or landlady violating rent regulations. In May 1944, Juliette Sumers Boud was enjoined in federal court from exceeding the legal limit for rents being charged in her roominghouse on Catoma Street near downtown.[40]

After the war, army veteran Wesley Newton asked his mother, housewife Florence Newton, whether she had cheated in any way where rationing was concerned. She replied, "I was sorely tempted, but I decided that if I did it, it would be breaking faith with my three boys in service." Bobby, Newton's youngest son, had been an enlisted man in the army infantry, and her oldest son, Bill, a petty officer in the navy.[41]

In Montgomery the OPA, the object of much criticism, was headquartered in the old Post Office Building on Dexter and employed a number of people from the area. Peggy Penton took a job in the public relations office of the OPA after she decided not to return to Auburn. There were too many exciting things going on in Montgomery after Pearl Harbor. Mary Henrie Harris went to work for the OPA after graduating from Lanier in May 1943. Both later agreed that the work at OPA was not exciting, but the pay was good.[42]

In May 1943, the *Advertiser* had an editorial entitled "Salute to the OPA": "There's a whole lot of beefing at this whole business of rationing, price controls, and government management of business." The government's "quick-changing decisions" had too often proved "maddening to local volunteer workers in the control program and to business folks who comply at a loss with shifting regulations." But "most disheartening of anything has been the rush buying and planned hoarding by many citizens financially able to display their poor sportsmanship." These people were "not willing to join the great group determined to suffer as full members of the democracy."[43]

In spite of the negative aspects of the OPA, the paper praised it. The agency "is doing a swell job within the field that comes closest to us all." It had curbed the trend "toward sky-circling prices," a trend produced by "the appalling cost of modern war equipment, of tools for our own first truly mechanized conflict." One factor and "one only, we repeat, saves our homes from prices which could mean real ruination." This "complex machine may creak and groan as she lumbers along and may expose a lot of lost motion in her efforts at regulating the affairs of 135,000,000 extremely independent citizens, still she is a marvelous instrument. Our grocery bills establish this fact."[44]

Several campaigns on the home front relied upon voluntary public participation and willingness rather than compulsion. Crucial were the drives to collect scarce and salvageable materials that were essential to the war effort. Montgomery's first scarcity drive began in January 1942, when the Salvation Army used its trucks to collect paper from citizens who called in to the army's North Lawrence headquarters. Paper was soon eclipsed by metals, rubber, and fats but would become the most needed item near the end of the war.[45]

In February the state's manufacturers' association launched a drive for the collection of scrap steel and iron, but not until Governor Frank Dixon appointed a state scrap salvage committee in March did the salvage of scarce materials become a concerted effort. In Montgomery the salvage committee of the Citizens Service Corps became active in April.[46]

Public reaction to the earliest campaigns was initially enthusiastic as various civic, governmental, and business groups pitched in. A crusading spirit existed that included children's crusades. The rallying cry was, "*You* are doing something to help our boys overseas."[47]

Scrap metal was the first target of the Montgomery salvage committee. It listed the kinds of war implements that scrap could be turned into: "One stove (250 pounds) could supply iron for one 500-pound aerial bomb. . . . one hot water boiler could supply steel for one 37 m-m gun. . . . one bed spring (60 pounds) could supply steel for two four-inch 105 m-m shells."[48]

In the midst of this scrap drive in May 1942, the War Production Board (WPB) sent an emergency communication to the state CD council that scrap rubber was desperately needed. The state council passed the word down to the county-city salvage volunteers. The *Advertiser* pointed out that "with 92 per cent of our supply cut off by Japan, with vastly increased consumption made imperative by the requirements of our army and navy and the needs of our allies, and with the national stock-pile containing hardly enough for one year's military needs, the rubber situation has become acute."[49]

Filling stations were the collection points for rubber. Individuals turned in their contributions. Each received a fee of one cent a pound, the cost underwritten by the oil company whose products a particular filling station handled. The stations, according to Alabama Petroleum Industries Committee, depended upon "the public [to bring] in their mites of discarded rubber articles" from "attics, basements, garages and barns"—such items as "old tires, tubes, garden hose, hot water bottles, tennis shoes." At the end of the drive in July, Montgomery's total of almost 200,000 tons placed it among the state's leaders.[50]

As part of a nationwide campaign promoted by WPB, Montgomery-area housewives were to collect waste fats from bacon grease, frying fats, and meat drippings. This was to be an ongoing campaign. The *Advertiser* underscored the necessity: "The war in the Pacific had greatly curtailed imports of oils and fats—sources of war vital glycerine, the base for explosives." Housewives took waste fats in jars to their local grocers, who paid them four cents a pound. Florence Newton, among thousands of other area housewives, took her waste fats to the A & P Grocery on Cloverdale Road. The result, reported Go Peep, was "2,000 pounds of waste kitchen fats for the war effort."[51]

The most vigorous scrap metal drive of the war in the Montgomery area, for both city and county, took place in October 1942. At its core was a children's crusade. Children accounted directly for close to 100,000 of the total of 6,200,000-odd pounds of metal. "It was notable," editorialized the *Advertiser*, "because of the interest shown by the children." Maxwell and Gunter commanders lent a hand with trucks and personnel to assist in moving the scrap from collection points to boxcars in the marshaling yards. The Block Plan leaders organized the blocks for collection, and auxiliary firemen and police collected in their respective zones. Montgomery County finished fourth in the state in per capita collection.[52]

Salvage drives and rationing required volunteers from many backgrounds to do administrative work, with participation by many young and old in the drives. Rationing affected the vast majority. The Red Cross's voluntary work absorbed the time and energies of a more select group in Montgomery. Most of its members were white women, and its services were more specialized. In the towns and cities across the land, three ongoing volunteer services were, at the time of Pearl Harbor, the most closely related to the war effort—surgical bandage wrapping, sewing/knitting, and Gray Ladies.[53]

Bandage wrapping was at first the activity of women of the gentry. When the number of those who volunteered to prepare the dressings rose in response to appeals after Pearl Harbor, the group became more diverse. The cause continued to attract the gentry, but middle-class women and some from the lower class also turned out. The understanding was that volunteers must be white. Rebecca Loeb, the wife of a middle-class food broker, had begun to wrap bandages when the city division's work was on the second floor of a Dexter clothing store, and she continued when it was transferred to the Elk's Club on Madison. Her persistence stemmed partly from the fact that her only son, Ralph, Jr., had been drafted into the navy in 1943. Such personal ties were the motivation for many women. In the summer and during holidays, teenage girls came forward, both Girl Scouts and Junior Service members of the Civilian Service Corps. The latter included members of gentry families such as Barbara Vaden, a junior at Lanier, and members of middle-class families such as Pat Caton, a sophomore at Lanier.[54]

The military services anticipated that 90 percent of their bandages would come from Red Cross volunteers. No other volunteer activity in the city was as accurate a barometer of the level of overconfidence or enthusiasm for the war effort.[55]

An even more pressing need of the services was medical doctors. Early in 1942, an army general officer called a meeting of Montgomery area physicians and informed the gathering that this area would have to furnish a minimum of 100 doctors in the next few months. A physician stood and said, "Are you crazy? I'm not giving up my $30,000 a year practice." The general turned to his aide and said audibly, "Get that man's name. He'll be the first called." In July, however, the War

Top: Red Cross volunteers from Montgomery and Maxwell Field prepare surgical bandages for the armed forces, 1942. *Bottom:* Elizabeth Weaver, wife of Maxwell commander Walter R. Weaver, stands third from the left. *Courtesy of Laurens W. Pierce, Montgomery, Alabama.*

Manpower Commission ordered the medical recruiters out of the state, bowing to claims by the Alabama Defense Council that Alabama had furnished a disproportionate share of doctors.[56]

A willingness to give something more precious than money characterized the Montgomery Gray Ladies unit, which formed in 1941 several months before Pearl Harbor under the leadership of Gypsie Oliver. The women initially visited sick GIs in the Maxwell Hospital, where they talked with the patients, brought flowers and small gifts, wrote letters for those too ill to manage a pen, and bought small items such as books. After Pearl Harbor the services were extended to the Veterans Hospital. At the outset the Gray Ladies organization was almost exclusively the province of the gentry. It was their way of involving themselves directly in a cause, following a tradition that dated at least to the Civil War. A few cynics suggested that these ladies could afford so much time and energy along with some expense because they had servants to do their housework and care for their children.[57]

The Red Cross established offices at Maxwell and Gunter to coordinate various activities in a category called home services—the most active being as liaison between service people and their families in times of crisis at home and verification of the need for an emergency furlough. Red Cross funding enabled many a Montgomery serviceman and servicewoman to come home from bases in the zone of the interior to be with a family member who was sick or dying.[58]

The local Red Cross chapter furnished Montgomerians who had loved ones in prisoner-of-war camps with information about the International Red Cross's efforts to improve conditions for prisoners. It was through the Red Cross that the Fite family received a first communication from James Tucker Fite, who was being held by the Japanese. Touching many more people was the expansion of the Red Cross peacetime blood donor program. Plasma was now the form for overseas use.[59]

The Red Cross continued other work under way before Pearl Harbor. Sewing and knitting produced sweaters, gloves, and scarfs. Skills with sewing machines and knitting needles crossed class lines as middle-class and even some lower-class women held their own and may after Pearl Harbor even have outnumbered the gentry. Before Pearl Harbor most of the production went overseas to the Allies and war refugees. Afterward, most of the items produced—often in olive drab, navy blue, or hospital maroon—went to the U.S. armed forces. Commanders were especially grateful for surgical caps and gowns, hospital pajamas, and kit bags.[60]

As the war unfolded, the Red Cross offered other services. A Red Cross Motor Corps, formed shortly after Pearl Harbor, consisted of women of the gentry. It served as a free taxi service for Red Cross volunteers and staff and, more important, took patients from the Veterans and Maxwell hospitals for rides and picnics.[61]

In an effort to compensate for the dwindling number of registered nurses, the Red Cross developed the Nurses' Aide Program. It offered no financial compensation for either training or service and was strictly voluntary. Participants needed dedication to carry bedpans and assist crotchety ill folk without recompense. Florence Lobman, the director of the program and the wife of the president of the eminent old drygoods firm Steiner-Lobman, compared her troops with those in military service: "Nurses' aides are auxiliary forces for the professional nursing service, in the same manner in which ground crews help the aviators."[62]

The first nurse's aide class to graduate was middle class in social background. Its members were not likely to be found at the country clubs or in the columns written by Go Peep. In January 1943, Go Peep did comment upon the powder blue nurse's aide uniforms, but by this time women of the gentry had enrolled in the nurse's aide classes. "The Nurses' Aide Uniform is one you can be proud to don. The wearer is making things easier for the doctors and nurses in the hospitals and the insignia she wears on her blouse is the symbol of gallant courage."[63]

The Red Cross chapter was responsible for initiating a popular food service for members of the armed forces. In January 1942, Caroline Ball, wife of the prominent lawyer Fred Ball, Jr., organized the Red Cross Canteen Corps to serve food to military personnel passing in and out of Montgomery. The canteen corps of volunteers ranged from high schoolers such as Ball's daughter Caroline, a student at Lanier known as Dootsie, and her friends Isabel Dunn and Betty Baldwin, to middle-aged matrons. After taking courses in nutrition and food preparation and handling, the corps was ready to serve food by summer 1942.[64]

The women, with food and drink donated from restaurants, private sources, and the USO, at first set up shop at the Lee and Commerce Street USOs, using the kitchen of the Women's USO on Dexter to prepare the food. They served refreshments on such occasions as Christmas parties and fed soldiers from posts outside the area who came to the city to march in parades. The canteen corps furnished sandwiches, doughnuts, soup, tea, milk, and coffee at the USOs on Sunday afternoons. Ball commented early in 1943 that the "'feed' has become a legend. We often have new boys telling us that other boys send them."[65]

She planned from the beginning to have a canteen near Union Station to serve troop trains and transient service people passing through Union Station and the bus station on Lee Street, taking "up now where the Red Cross left off in the other World War," a reference to the Red Cross canteen that had been located near Union Station in 1918. The project was spurred by a letter from Major General Ralph Royce, the senior commander at Maxwell, who had written her in April 1943, "From my observation of the number of enlisted men and their families traveling in and out of Montgomery today . . . , there is a very great need for a canteen at the Montgomery railroad station. . . . A canteen staffed by the Red Cross or other civic agencies, in my opinion, would serve to make the enlisted men's stay in Montgomery, or departure from here, a much more pleasant occasion."[66]

Under the sponsorship of the Junior Chamber of Commerce, a canteen project developed. The old Windsor Hotel at the intersection of Commerce and Water Streets across from the railroad station, once the haunt of prostitutes, was purchased and torn down. On the site rose a one-story building that when finished resembled a short order café. When the canteen was ready to open, the sign on the building read: "JUNIOR CHAMBER OF COMMERCE FREE CANTEEN operated by RED CROSS CANTEEN CORPS."[67]

On October 30, 1943, there was an opening day ceremony in which civic, military, and Red Cross dignitaries took part. Local marine Hugh Stuart was the first to be served. The Hut, as it soon became known, was then ready for business. The first customers, recorded the *Advertiser,* "were three Marines and one sailor," sent there by "benevolent M.P.s" in the terminal. One of them exclaimed, "Gee, this is sure swell. What town is this, anyway?" Over the course of the first day, the canteen staff served 200 customers. They were all white, but ultimately black servicemen and servicewomen came to the canteen and were served on an unsegregated basis.[68]

The canteen corps soon reached 225 members working in shifts around the clock. Food and drink were supplied only to those troop trains whose commanders requested it. Dootsie Ball later recalled, "I was a 17-year-old waitress, but it was an exciting experience especially the time we got up in the middle of the night to make 100s of sandwiches for a troop train." The grimy and tired servicemen on the trains responded with an enthusiasm described by a witness who "watched them give a whoop of jumping joy when their troop train pulls into the shed and the Red Cross girls appear with food and drink. The girls carry magazines, gallons of cold drinks, cigarettes, and baskets of sacked cookies and sandwiches. They also wear smiles. . . . Typical comment when the boys meet the girls is: 'The manpower shortage must have brought these female Santa Clauses.'"[69] Montgomerians traveling on troop trains across the land often received the same hospitality and were just as grateful.[70]

The Red Cross encouraged local chapters to conduct two types of fund drives during the war. The Roll Call Drive, a holdover from peacetime, started each November with a fixed quota. Shortly after Pearl Harbor the War Relief Fund Drive began in Montgomery, chaired by stockyard owner W. C. Bowman. It also had a fixed quota. As with most such drives in Montgomery, the initial tide of contributions soon became a trickle. Follow-up statements from prominent persons appealed to the better angels. Ads and editorials in the local papers stressed the humanitarian nature of the Red Cross, especially its assistance to service people. Gradually business picked up and quotas were reached.[71]

The community did not find Red Cross drives as compelling as war loan drives. In 1941 before Pearl Harbor, Secretary of the Treasury Henry Morgenthau, Jr., began the task of selling Americans on the idea of purchasing large amounts of special government bonds to help finance the defense effort. After Pearl Harbor the bonds were to finance the war effort. Everyone, Morgenthau said, can contribute to the "defense of democracy."[72]

In March 1942 a Montgomery County Defense Bonds Savings Staff was formed. By April the term "war" had replaced "defense" for bonds and stamps. Montgomery housewives known as the Minute Maids canvassed homemakers in their own neighborhoods, took orders, and arranged later delivery for bonds and stamps. Caroline Strassberger of the Montgomery County defense bond staff headed the Minute Maids. "Occasionally," she told a reporter, "we hear some woman complain that she just doesn't have time to give to this essential work. I always think of one of our Minute Maids who has four small children and does all her housework but still has time to devote to the delivery of stamps to her neighbors." Auxiliary policemen became "Minute Men."[73]

The Montgomery area was well above the national average in filling the monthly quotas. In June 1942 the state placed second in the country in the percentage of sales above the quota. In July patriotic fever soared as a series of "War Hero" and "War Aid" events took place. The theme was "start shelling out your dough so the boys at the front can shell hell out of the Axis."[74]

On Friday night, July 10, such an event took place in the lobby of the First National Bank on Commerce, during which the Maxwell Field dance band, the Rhythmaires, played. Bank tellers were on duty to take pledges by phone, while two sales teams called the Stars and the Stripes circulated among people gathering in the lobby. WSFA and WCOV broadcast the name of each purchaser.[75]

Also broadcast from the lobby was an address by John Wiley Brock, Sr., of Plum Street in Oak Park, whose son, a naval officer, was missing after participation the month before in the Battle of Midway as a torpedo plane pilot. "My boy, John, always said that the American way of living was the only way," he told the hushed crowd. "Will you deny them the planes, tanks, guns they need? After all, they give what they can never get back—all we're doing here is lending some money to our country." It was the most effective appeal possible. The crowd and callers quickly shelled out $20,525.30. Brock's son was later declared dead.[76]

On December 1, 1942, the Treasury Department kicked off the first

of the war loan campaigns. It raised $9 billion and lasted through the
month of December. This venture and the second war loan campaign
of April 1943 were relatively low key. The purposes of each of the
campaigns throughout the war were twofold: first, to help finance the
war for a given short period and, second, to absorb current surplus
cash to keep inflation down.[77]

Circuit Judge Eugene Carter became head of the county group. The
first two campaigns were for the most part handled by state and county
war bond groups and at first involved little propaganda. When the
second drive seemed in trouble, however, newspaper ads began to appeal to the emotions: "Today on battle fronts around the world native
sons of Alabama are descendants of those who marched with Lee. . . .
Many more are sons of those who wrote another glorious chapter in
history for Alabama in World War I." Increasingly these ads were
designed to fan hatred of the enemy, something Treasurer Henry
Morgenthau had hoped to avoid. Full-page ads, sponsored by local
businesses, showed such scenes as Japanese soldiers committing atroci-
ties against American prisoners.[78]

War loan drives became more elaborate and aggressive, seeking
increased revenue as war expenses mounted. Montgomery County's
quota had been $4 million in the second drive but more than double
that for the third. To ring in the latter on September 9, 1943, bells
pealed, horns blew, and sirens wailed. The Minute Maids canvassed
the blocks. Subsequent war loan drives in general, with one exception, ran the same course. Beginning briskly, they soon lagged, received
fresh injections of individual energy and organizational striving, lagged
again, were revived by applications of show biz as celebrities such as
Bob Hope made appearances at Cramton Bowl to entreat purchases,
and finished respectably ahead of the quota. The appeal at first was
fairly moderate, but when money only trickled in, the appeal sought
to evoke gut patriotism.[79]

The offerings on a regular basis and during a drive consisted of
savings bonds, treasury bonds or savings notes, and treasury certificates
of indebtedness. The one category of offerings that had the hardest
time meeting its quota by the deadline was War Savings Bond Series

E. Its owners could be an individual, two individuals, or one individual upon whose death the bond was payable to another individual. Other offerings had similar provisions for individuals but also permitted corporations or other groups to be owners. Some imposed no restrictions on ownership.[80]

Series E bonds ranged in denomination from $25 to $1,000 and were thus more for individuals of average income who had relatively little to invest. The fact that Series E trailed in all but one of the drives and required an extension of time to fill its quota probably reflected, in part at least, the lingering effects of the depression.[81]

During the third drive, the Paramount divided its 1,252 seating capacity in sections and made the seats available through the purchase of a war bond. The higher the denomination, the better the seat. The war bond motion picture *So Proudly We Hail,* about heroic army nurses who performed their duties under fire on Corregidor until they were evacuated to Australia, sold out.[82]

Sybil Winn, wife of Gunter's commander, was a tireless leader representing the military community. The most persevering of all the spouses of the airfields' senior commanders, from whom much was expected, she conducted a dawn-to-dusk campaign in the third drive that brought out wallets, opened purses, and produced signatures on pledges. Her contingent of men and women in uniform worked the downtown area, moving out from Court Square, while she and other service people labored all day covering the drive in broadcasts from WSFA. The city and county later honored her for her work. Women were the shock troops of the drives.[83]

A constant problem for the coordinators of the multiple drives during the war was their competition for citizens' dollars and/or time. Go Peep summed up it with a lead: "THE TIME IS NEVER RIGHT": The "Third War Loan drive was launched in the midst of income tax troubles. On the heels of it comes the Welfare-Warfare Chest Appeal. There is a desperate need for scrap to keep our steel mills going. . . . The time is never 'right.' It is either on the heels of the predecessor or in the midst of another."[84]

She cited the task of John Rushin, manager of the Jefferson Davis

Hotel, who "accepted chairmanship of 'This is the Army' as a benefit for the Army Emergency Relief." The show enjoyed great popularity on Broadway and as a motion picture featuring composer Irving Berlin and young actor Ronald Reagan. Berlin sang his immortal World War I song with the lyrics "Some day I'm going to murder the bugler. . . . I'll amputate his Reveille and step upon it heavily and spend the rest of my life in bed." The roadshow version, brought to the Paramount, was slow to sell out, coming in the midst of the third war loan drive, but it had succeeded by opening day.[85]

On October 6, 1943, the day of the opening, one of the most colorful local wartime parades publicized the show. Overhead flew B-24 heavy bombers from a pilot transition school at Maxwell. Led by civilian and military dignitaries in convertibles, the parade showed off unit after unit: Maxwell Field marching band; company after company of aviation cadets, mostly AAF but with a contingent of Free French cadets who were flight trainees at Gunter Field; the WAC companies from Maxwell and Gunter; the blue-clad band and brown-uniformed ROTC cadets from Lanier; and cadets in military academy gray from Starke School. The weather was still warm, and the aviation cadets and WACs wore khaki uniforms. All parade participants were white. The crowds who lined Dexter, the Square, and Montgomery Street were mostly white. They made little noise at first, in the old Montgomery style, then warmed to the cadence and began to cheer each passing unit.[86]

6

The Black Community in Montgomery and Abroad

Full-page advertisement purchased by black citizens in Montgomery for the fourth war loan drive in 1943, showing First Lieutenant Sherman White, Jr., of Montgomery in the cockpit. *Courtesy of the Alabama Department of Archives and History, Montgomery, Alabama.*

The mistreatment in general of black citizens of the United States during "the Good War," besides being fueled by bigotry, continued to reflect legal segregation of the races in the former Confederate South. Elsewhere segregation was more de facto than de jure. Detroit, however, witnessed one of the war's largest race riots. The segregation of public facilities, transportation, and education had been sanctioned by the U.S. Supreme Court as "separate but equal." The majority of whites did not question the legal or moral correctness of segregation, nor did they assert that most segregation was separate and unequal.[1]

Black service people were quick to see the disparity between racial segregation in the armed forces and the call to defend democracy against tyranny abroad. They began to register protests, sometimes violent, against ill treatment in various places across the nation. The reactions, official and otherwise, particularly in the South, were repressive. Violence was often met with even more extreme violence.[2]

In Montgomery, seven months after Pearl Harbor, two policemen responded to a call from a city bus driver. Available records do not reveal what two black airmen from Gunter Field had done to provoke the call. Perhaps they had violated the segregation ordinance by taking forward seats on the bus or by doing something perceived to be disrespectful. Whatever the cause, the two policemen responded with a sudden violent assault. One of the officers fired his pistol, slightly wounding Private Joyner. At the driver's request the police arrested Joyner and took him to the city jail. They did not arrest the other airman.[3]

The next day, July 13, 1942, Colonel William Welsh, acting commanding officer of the Southeastern Army Air Forces Training Center headquartered at Maxwell, requested a morning meeting with police commissioner and retired army brigadier general W. P. Screws. The commissioner, perhaps a bit anxious, hurried to Welsh's office in Austin Hall, the headquarters building. Screws informed Welsh that the policemen's account made it appear that they were justified in their actions. The officers had been mistaken, however, in waiting to make the arrest until the bus driver asked them to do so and in arresting Private Joyner alone. Because of that error, Joyner had been released and some form of disciplinary step was being considered against the two policemen.[4]

In his official diary Welsh wrote: "General Screws . . . informed me action had been taken to instruct all police in the handling of military personnel, and that mutual agreement could be worked out between the city of Montgomery and the commanding officers of Gunter and Maxwell Fields." Welsh told Screws that he did not believe "a reprimand of the police concerned would be satisfactory to the military personnel and at the very least what should be done was to discharge the policemen guilty of this unwarranted attack, and that actually criminal action should be taken against them."[5]

The retort shook Screws. Welsh, who had been stationed at Maxwell since 1938, was a favorite with the city's leadership. Screws told him that he would get back to him that afternoon. At 3:30 P.M. Screws returned with a copy of the police officers' testimony. He was, he told Welsh, seriously contemplating suspending the officers for "a period." The colonel replied bluntly that this action would be unsatisfactory. He informed Screws that Colonel Aubrey Hornsby, the commanding officer of Gunter and a native white Alabamian, had asked that criminal charges be filed against the policemen. Then Welsh was conciliatory. He told Screws he "sincerely hoped that we could obtain full cooperation of the city of Montgomery in order to avoid repetition of these instances and to prevent undue publicity or necessitate action by higher authority." Screws promised to cooperate "fully" with whatever course of action military authorities felt was warranted.[6]

In a huddle the same day with Welsh and his staff, Hornsby, as Welsh noted in his diary, "stated in his opinion the action on the part of the police was unprovoked and a brutal assault on the colored soldiers and he felt criminal action should be taken against the police officers concerned." On July 14, Welsh and Hornsby traveled in their olive-drab-colored staff cars, from Maxwell and Gunter, respectively, to city hall.[7]

Screws told the officers that he had suspended the two policemen and that they would be dismissed if further action warranted suspension. Hornsby informed Screws that he intended to inform Joyner of his right to bring criminal action. Welsh presented Screws with the draft of an agreement for close cooperation between authorities at the two bases and Montgomery police in the handling and treatment of military personnel in the city. Screws indicated that he liked the draft but that Mayor Cy Brown would have to approve it also.[8]

The commissioner poured more oil on troubled waters. He promised "immediate action to instruct civil police in the arresting and con-

trol of military personnel, with particular reference to colored soldiers."
Policemen would be "required" to attend night classes. Screws promised "full cooperation to avoid any repetition of abuse of colored soldiers."[9]

Not only had no mention of this episode appeared in the *Advertiser*
or the *Journal* but no mention ever appeared. Apparently no record of
any agreement between municipal and base authorities concerning
the handling of military personnel was placed in Maxwell, Gunter, or
municipal archives, and no reference to classes for police on the handling and treatment of military personnel survives in extant records
of the Montgomery police force. The only known record of the episode appears in Colonel Welsh's command diary. The November 7,
1940, issue of the *Advertiser* indicates, however, that an agreement was
implemented. The paper noted that an FBI agent was conducting a
series of lectures for members of the Montgomery Police Department
on the "technical wiles of crime detection," including the interviewing of witnesses and the procedure for making arrests. Police Chief
King was pleased with the "experiment."[10]

No evidence of more black-white/military-civilian violent episodes
surfaced until March 1943. Then the *Advertiser* reported an incident
in which Corporal Rubin Pleasant, a black GI home on furlough, took
a front seat on a city bus eastbound up Adams Avenue from downtown. Ordered to the rear by driver Lamis Farmer, the soldier demanded a refund, in the driver's account, before he would move.
Farmer stopped the bus and threw Pleasant off. The driver told police
that Pleasant had drawn a knife, and the driver added, "I pulled my
gun and let him have a slug in the leg." Police took the soldier to nearby
St. Margaret's Hospital. He was then turned over to Maxwell authorities, apparently in line with an unwritten agreement between the city
and the base. His punishment, if any, was not recorded in Maxwell
records.[11]

The all-too-prevalent attitude of many bus drivers was illustrated
by an editorial in the *Advertiser* of August 10, 1943. The writer, unnamed but one of an editorial committee of moderates who filled the
gap after the death of Grover Hall, Sr., told of witnessing a scene on a

wrestling trunks and suitcases in the baggage room at Union Station. He had, he stated, "wanted one of those jobs on the Pullman car ever since I got down there and saw those porters standing up side the train with those white coats on, sharp and everything." Then "the man in charge of Pullman Company operation [at Montgomery] said to me, 'You know I'm going to need three porters. If you'd like to try out I'll be glad to give you a chance.'"[18]

By World War II Nixon had been around the country and had met celebrities and politicians. He kept his base in Montgomery, however, where he and his wife had a house in Peacock Tract. Feeling the injustice of the USO situation, he "decided to go out lonehanded for a USO club." He wrote a letter to Eleanor Roosevelt. Soon two well-known black men looked him up at home. One was Jessie Owens, the great Olympic runner and a native of Alabama. The other was James W. Jeetle, an employee of the federal recreation program. The latter, showing Nixon a telegram, said that in all his years in that program, "this is the first time Mrs. Roosevelt sent me out in the mud to see what a Negro's crying about."[19]

On June 21, 1942, under the sponsorship of the national YMCA, there being no local branch of the YMCA for blacks, a USO club for black service people opened at 215 Monroe Street in the heart of the black entrepreneurial district. Made aware of the high-level interest and the availability of funding, Cliff Green, a white businessman on the local USO executive committee, helped create the black club. With Nixon in the background, Dr. H. C. Trenholm of Alabama State presided at the club's opening. A glee club in summer khakis from the black Fourth Aviation Service Squadron at Maxwell Field and another in civies from Alabama State provided the music. A white major from Maxwell gave the main address.[20]

Segregation was the rule when Montgomery catered to the appetites, thirst, and civilian entertainment of service people, but there was a noteworthy exception. Soon after the Red Cross/Junior Chamber of Commerce canteen near Union Station opened in October 1943, it served blacks alongside whites—soldiers, sailors, marines, Coast Guard. This policy represented a departure from the "whites only"

Dance at the Monroe Street USO. *Courtesy of the Alabama Department of Archives and History, Montgomery, Alabama.*

policy of a Red Cross canteen that had operated near Union Station in the Great War. Apparently no discord accompanied what was, in essence, integration at the World War II canteen.[21]

The letters in the *Advertiser* on March 18, 1945, included a series of communications from servicemen expressing appreciation for the canteen. "Bankrupt" AAF private Parker L. Enright said he "certainly did welcome the sight of the breakfast of bacon and eggs." Two AAF aviation cadets wrote "to thank you for the sandwiches, coffee, and donuts. . . . You were really swell to us." Sergeant Paul F. Giroir, a medic stationed at the Fort Benning hospital, declared, "If every State treated the service men and women the way you do this would be a much better world." These letter writers were white.[22]

At the end of the column came a letter from a soldier stationed at Fort McPherson in Atlanta. Addressed to "My dear Mrs. Ball and co-workers," it extended "my appreciation for your splendid service not only to me but to all . . . service men no matter what his color is. May all your days and good work toward mankind continue to . . . brighten always." It was signed "S-Sergt. Jesse Taylor (colored)."[23]

In October 1942, the USO Travelers Aide Service Unit established a "whites only" lounge in Union Station for service personnel. Having learned from the USO club experience, Travelers Aide soon opened a separate lounge for black service personnel. The multicolored flow of uniforms that passed in and out of the station day and night saw skin colors separated not only at the lounges but at ticket counters, water fountains, and toilets and on the trains, whether civilian or troop. This scene—the USOs, the two airfields, and city buses—stood in sharp contrast to the situation at the Red Cross/Junior Chamber canteen.[24]

White USO clubs had guest choral groups of aviation cadets from Maxwell and Gunter. The Maxwell-based black Fourth Aviation Squadron's Jubilee Singers were sometimes featured at the clubs, and on occasion their singing was broadcast on WCOV. The white USOs also presented the Maxwell marching band, whose concerts were often carried on WSFA. This radio station also broadcast an occasional concert of the Fourth Aviation Squadron's drum and bugle corps. The highly regarded group substituted at parades at Maxwell when the all-white marching band was off promoting war loan drives in the South or was in the city giving concerts for war loan and Red Cross fund drives.[25]

The Red Cross chapter's relationship with blacks was checkered. Blacks were not invited to join Red Cross sewing, knitting, or surgical bandage activities until late in the war. There were no black Gray Ladies. The chapter organized at least one black nurse's aide class and encouraged black first aid training. A chapter news release in April 1942 reported that "approximately 3,000 white persons" and "approximately 2,500 [blacks]" had enrolled in Red Cross first aid classes since Pearl Harbor.[26]

Blacks were included in the scarcity drives. Particularly in the first year after Pearl Harbor, the need for fats and scrap rubber and metals was urgent. The black community, with leaders such as G. T. Alexander and O. C. Crow, responded energetically. In a rare acknowledgment, the *Advertiser* noted that blacks participated "with enthusiasm running high," although west Montgomery and other black districts had far fewer of the scarce items than white areas did. During a

Black army enlisted men hold Cokes and coffee alongside the free canteen operated by the Red Cross and the Junior Chamber of Commerce. *Courtesy of the Albert Krause Studio/Tommy Giles Photographic Services.*

children's crusade mounted to foster Montgomery's effort in a 1942 scrap metal drive, the *Advertiser* praised the Alabama State laboratory high school for its unusual contribution of a large box of keys marked "Our Compliments to the Japs and Nazis."[27]

The local papers covered blacks' part in the war loan drives more than other involvement by blacks in activities on the home front. Following the first war loan drive, which ended in early 1943, the *Advertiser* had an editorial entitled "BOND SALES AMONG NEGROES." The writer commented that the "war was brought home to them as never before and they were made to feel that they were part of it in a very impressive way." The editorial described the high point of black participation. It "closed with a big parade, headed by the Tuskegee airport band, and a rally at the city auditorium, where Gov. Sparks made an inspirational address." The "Tuskegee airport band" was a black military band from Tuskegee Army Air Field, where a pioneer experiment in training black army fighter pilots was in progress. The paper credited J. E. Pierce and R. L. Battle, officers of the Negro Civic and Improvement League, with the main leadership of the effort.[28]

Not until a year later, however, did black Montgomery's role in a war loan drive again receive special attention in a local paper. On February 3, 1944, the *Advertiser* carried a full-page advertisement that boosted the ongoing fourth war loan drive. This type of ad appeared frequently, sponsored by local businesses during the various drives. Such ads were expensive and required many sponsors.[29]

What made the February 3 ad distinctive was its particular sponsorship and content. Its headline proclaimed: "MONTGOMERY COUNTY NEGROES are behind the FOURTH WAR BOND DRIVE," and its sponsors were primarily black businesses. The list of sponsors revealed much about black enterprises almost halfway into the twentieth century. The list had no department stores, wholesale cotton or grocery warehouses, or banks, for blacks had been denied the opportunity to accumulate the requisite capital. Still, it was impressive, with the enterprises ranging from shoe shine parlors to insurance agencies. It included the Atlanta Insurance Company, the Caffey Realty Company, Dean's Drug Store, the Peking Theater, Hines Dry Cleaning Company, Matthew's Tavern on Day Street, Ross-Clayton Undertakers, The Goldstucker Burial Association, Darget and Darget's Grocery and Market, Hiawatha's Shoe Factory, J. L. Oliver's Auto Repairing & OK Service Station, and John A. Williams, the Plumber. The list also contained the City Federation of Colored Women Clubs—social outlets that because of segregation were more vital to black women than to white— and the two black public senior high schools in 1943, Booker T. Washington and Loveless. Black educators were anxious to demonstrate that black students and teachers were as patriotic as their white counterparts. War bonds could be purchased at white banks and the post office and also at the Atlanta Life Insurance Company, several other black insurance agencies, and the Goldstucker Burial Association.[30]

The ad contained a brief historical account of blacks' participation in the nation's wars. It excluded any reference to the role played by black soldiers and sailors in the Union army and navy or to the two black regular army cavalry and two infantry regiments created after the Civil War (called the "Buffalo Soldiers" by the Indians against whom they fought in the Indian Wars), perhaps in deference to prevailing white sentiment.[31] Two months after the ad's appearance, in April 1944, Technical Sergeant Robert Coprich from Mount Meigs in Montgomery County, a platoon sergeant in the U.S. Army's mainly black Twenty-fifth Infantry Regiment, was killed in action on Bougainville in the Solomons. As usual, the local papers carried no notice of his death.[32]

The ad singled out three other black Montgomery servicemen in the ongoing war. One was First Lieutenant Sherman White, Jr., of the all-black Ninety-ninth Pursuit Squadron, "the first casualty of that outfit." Another was Captain William Graham, a graduate of Alabama State, "the highest ranking officer of his battery," an AAA battery in the South Pacific that had "brought down several Japanese planes." The third was "James Scott, a Montgomery Negro [who] jumped from his ship to save one of his mates in South Pacific waters." Scott was probably the James Scott identified by the *Globe and Independent,* a black Nashville newspaper, as the Montgomerian who with two other members of a black engineering unit of the U.S. Army stationed in Australia rescued a white pilot when his plane accidentally crashed in "alligator infested waters" and began to burn. General Douglas MacArthur had pinned the Soldier's Medal, the award for bravery in a noncombat situation, on all three men.[33]

The ad called upon "THE NEGROES OF MONTGOMERY" to "SUPPORT THESE MEN. . . . We must not fail them now. LET'S SHOW HITLER AND TOJO we are united in our effort for a complete victory." Those purchasing bonds could serve the government and society in general and increase their own future yields. "NO ONE IS TOO POOR TO BUY A BOND," the ad asserted. It added, "Negroes have pledged to buy $100,000" worth of bonds out of a total quota of $8 million for Montgomery County.[34]

On February 12, 1944, a bond rally was held at the Square and up

Dexter. The ad of February 3 had called on blacks to take part by assembling at the Dexter Avenue Baptist Church. In a particularly effective appeal, Nellie White, mother of Sherman White, Jr., urged the assembly to purchase bonds so that her son would not have died in vain. The *Advertiser* reported that "patriotic negroes held a rousing bond rally yesterday at the Dexter Avenue Church and after it was over, J. E. Pierce announced that the total [black] sales for the Fourth War Loan amounted to $135,000." The rally had produced $22,000.[35]

Other black leaders made appeals through radio stations. President Trenholm of Alabama State was the most prominent. Neil Hudner, a visiting concert singer who had appeared in the celebrated all-black motion picture *Green Pastures*, sang over WSFA. The fourth drive, he declared, was for blacks in the armed forces from Montgomery and around the nation who were fighting and dying. A specific clue to the effectiveness of these appeals was a bulletin issued by the fourth drive leadership. It praised "negro cooks and other domestic help" for taking part in the weekly purchase of war stamps.[36]

The deaths of First Lieutenant Sherman White and Technical Sergeant Robert Coprich, both killed in action, had not been reported in the local papers. The deaths of many white service people were noted. White's death made the *Advertiser* only in the ad of February 3, 1944. The local newspapers never carried notices that blacks had been wounded in action, were missing in action or captured, or had been killed in a training accident or in action. This failure to inform may have been because black loved ones, after receiving the pertinent telegram from the War or Navy Departments, simply failed to notify the papers. The omission may also have reflected the fact that a majority of blacks could not afford to subscribe. But the general absence of news about black service people in the local papers did not encourage loved ones to submit news of any kind. It was almost as though the war were being waged by whites alone.[37]

Shortly before Pearl Harbor the *Advertiser* began to devote part of a page in the Sunday edition to news about service people, primarily those from Montgomery and other counties in the paper's coverage area. As the war expanded and more people entered the armed forces, the coverage became a whole page and sometimes a page and a half. The feature was called "Alabama at the Front," although the news was more often about training and other noncombat duties and routines. Again, what was included depended on the information that loved ones or friends sent to the *Advertiser*.[38]

Throughout the war less than half a dozen news items about black service people appeared in "Alabama at the Front." These were incidental to news about whites involved in the same set of circumstances as the blacks. Before the death of Grover Hall, Sr., the news and editorial sections of the paper had been separated. "Alabama at the Front" fell in the domain of news and features, which was under Managing Editor William J. Mahoney, Sr. The news portion of the paper detailed black crime and covered blacks' sports with less frequency. Montgomery blacks in the armed forces were seldom mentioned. The *Journal* followed the same practices—practices that generally accorded with the policy of the press owned by whites in the former Confederate South and even in many papers outside the South. Publisher R. F. Hudson, Sr., was the final authority on his papers' policies. The policies reflected majority white prejudice.[39]

Now and then the editorial staff of the *Advertiser* let its readers know that local blacks were fighting in the war and that their loved ones were as anxious as whites. In May 1943, Edna L. Sisselberger, a white Montgomerian, sent to the "Tell it to Grandma" column a letter that she had received from Mary A. Johnson, a black Montgomerian. The letter responded to one by Edna Sisselberger that the *Advertiser* had published under the heading "The Mothers of Soldiers." The *Advertiser* published Mary Johnson's letter on May 29.[40]

Johnson expressed "deep appreciation" to Sisselberger for "remembering the mothers of my race." Her son, Staff Sergeant Jenkins L. Johnson, was "somewhere in the southwest Pacific. I find that one of the hardest things for a mother to overcome, in trying to adjust herself to the circumstances that exist in this war, is—not knowing where your boy is. If it were not for prayer. . . , I do not know what would become of me." She then voiced one of the rare published criticisms of segregation in the 1940s to come from a local black person: "I have faith to believe that if all the mothers of soldiers of this land, for a while, could forget prejudice, inferior and superior positions in life, and go to God with the determination to begin in our own lives to carry out His peace . . . of which we have made such a mess. . . . He would hastily answer in a more glorious way than we are now able to comprehend."[41]

One black mother indirectly protested the lack of news about black service people. She avoided "Alabama at the Front" and sent a letter that the editorial staff published on March 28, 1945. From Selma she wrote, "I have been taking the *Advertiser* a long time and I read a good many letters written by white service men. I have just received a letter from my son, colored, and I would like to read it in the Tell It to Grandma." She signed her name "G. R. Pickens" and enclosed her son's letter. His letter was included under hers in the "Tell it to Grandma" column. From somewhere in Europe, combat veteran Sergeant Roy Pickens had written his mother that "men are testing each other's strength and skill; tearing down a mighty nation that an even mightier nation may live and enjoy peace and its birthright and the pursuit of happiness in its own way."[42]

Periodically the *Advertiser* ran a column entitled "Montgomery County News" under the byline of white correspondent Mildred Smith. Besides the usual descriptions of county life, the column carried news of county service people, mostly white, with occasional mentions of blacks. Mildred sent Christmas boxes to county service people whom she knew. She told of "finally hearing from Pvt. Joe Louis Watkins, colored boy from Dublin [Montgomery County], who is with a company of engineers in India." He wrote her "a letter of thanks" in which he said, "We have been very busy and still have a long ways to go and lots to do before this war is over and we'll be coming home."[43]

WSFA's *Letter from Home* was overwhelmingly about the white world. They described familiar scenes, often with photographs; told of municipal and private special events and entertainments; gave accounts of sports in Cramton Bowl; underscored the area's participation in war loan and other drives; and listed the names of Montgomery area servicemen and servicewomen on leave at the time a particular issue was compiled. Service people who received *Letter from Home* provided a major source of raw material for the history of the area in the "Good War."[44]

The letters written in response came overwhelmingly from white service people, as evidenced by the nature of their units and/or their loved ones' addresses listed in the Montgomery City Directory. In some cases, however, the writer's identity was uncertain. Black service people did receive *Letter from Home.* Captain Francis Thigpen wrote WSFA from somewhere in the European theater of war that while he was "riding in a convoy last week, moving with a hospital, the colored driver of my truck turned out to be from Montgomery. He was Corporal Horace Lowe, and he proudly showed me his latest LFH." Like information supplied to those who put together *Alabama at the Front,* the compilers of *Letter from Home* depended on addresses and changes of address received from men and women in the service and from their loved ones. The requests for *Letter from Home,* accompanied by addresses of service people, with few exceptions came from whites, although in some cases a request came from an ambiguous source.[45] The lack of evidence about the Montgomery area black military experience in World War II made black military Montgomerians the lost battalions.

During the war the black community challenged whites' denial of blacks' right to vote. Within his own community, E. D. Nixon had been advocating that blacks register. Even earlier Johnnie Carr had listened to NAACP representatives, speaking from the pulpit of the Hall Street Baptist Church, as they urged the members to register.[46]

None of these situations entailed leading a sizable group of blacks to the county courthouse in an effort to get them registered. Now and then, a daring white with status would bring to the courthouse an individual black with a fine education and status in the black community in hopes of getting him registered. The move occasionally succeeded but always with difficulty. White Methodist minister Dan C. Whitsett, who had questioned the necessity of the poll tax in a letter to the *Advertiser,* accompanied the director of the black USO on Monroe Street to the courthouse late in 1942. The director had done work toward a Ph.D. at the University of Chicago and was a minister and a former college professor. The chairman of the board of registration told Whitsett, "I'll approve him, but don't ever bring this class of person here again."[47]

Arthur Madison, the first black to practice law in Montgomery, eventually led a large group of blacks to the county courthouse to register to vote in the fall of 1943. Madison was a member of the Montgomery County family that in the late nineteenth century had established the small all-black community of Madison Park, located not far from Gunter Field on the highway to Wetumpka. Madison had practiced law in New York.[48]

When all the voter applications were rejected, Madison quickly filed an appeal for sixteen of the rejectees in circuit court. Members of the white political leadership, caught off guard, pointed fingers at one another. Senator Lister Hill suspected a plot by his opponent, arch conservative Birmingham lawyer James Simpson, in the pending senatorial election of 1944.[49]

In February 1944, six of the plaintiffs appeared before Judge Walter Jones and stated that they had not authorized Arthur Madison to file in their behalf. Two other plaintiffs asked that their names be dropped from the suit. The dissenters included Sarah Pearl Madison, Arthur Madison's niece. The applicants were mainly public school teachers, and threats to their jobs had apparently led them to back down. Jones, who would have opposed any black lawyer and who regarded Arthur Madison as an "agitator," granted their requests. He assured these black Montgomerians that "the court will undertake to see that every right you have under the law of the land, and according to the constitution, is enforced and respected."[50]

Arthur Madison was arrested on April 8 by Sheriff Addie Mosley on five counts of illegally representing people in court. Madison was tried in Judge Lomax Crum's Court of Common Pleas, which found him guilty as charged and imposed as a penalty a fine of $2,500 and disbarment from the practice of law in the state. At Lister Hill's request, Attorney Richard T. Rives of Hill, Hill, Whiting, and Rives assisted gruff, longtime County Solicitor Temple Seibels at the trial.

Senator Hill wanted to squelch the black voter registration drive in order to answer Simpson's charges that he was liberal on race issues. After the conviction Seibels told reporters that "the ends of justice and the preservation of harmonious relations between the white and black races have been well served by the conviction of Arthur Madison."[51]

Madison had represented himself in the Court of Common Pleas. When his appeal of the conviction was heard in circuit judge Eugene Carter's court, he was represented by black Birmingham lawyer Arthur Shores, a pioneer in NAACP legal cases in the state. Madison had waived his right to a jury trial, in spite of a rumor that the jury venire included both whites and blacks. He mistrusted the blacks he might get on a jury; it was virtually unheard of for blacks to serve on juries in Alabama. Perhaps Madison believed that he would have the best chance with the trial judge, Eugene Carter, who was known for his relative fairness. Rives again assisted the prosecution, arguing that Mildred Hardy, the plaintiff in the case being tried, had clearly not asked Madison to file a voting denial appeal for her. Shores argued that the state had not shown "criminal intent." Judge Carter denied Madison's appeal, which was then carried to the next level. In the end, however, Madison lost all the way through the Alabama Supreme Court, paid his fine, and accepted disbarment. He went back to New York and did not return alive to the Montgomery area. After the war, his body was sent for burial at Madison Park.[52]

At the grassroots level, some few individual black citizens refused to knuckle under completely to the system. Idessa Taylor worked as a machine operator in the white-owned Reliance Manufacturing Company, which produced shirts for the navy in its small west Montgomery plant. Attesting to her good work, she was placed in charge of her floor on the night shift. One night she was called into the white manager's officer. He told her that the women on her shift would do better work if they would quit going to a nearby nightclub for blacks, and he suggested that she speak to them. She responded by saying that she would not interfere in the private affairs of these women and noted that the manager did not discuss with her the private affairs of white

Idessa Redden stands in front of the building in west Montgomery where as a young woman she helped to make shirts for the U.S. Navy. *Courtesy of Idessa Redden; collection of Wesley Newton.*

women who worked in the office. Slavery, she told him, no longer existed. The manager commented that with her attitude she needed to go north, but he did not fire her.[53]

Black culture began to be displayed in connection with black pride during the war. In 1944, Alabama State hosted an exhibition of African sculpture, curios, paintings, and literature that was on loan from Howard University. The showing was open to the public at large, in contrast to an exhibit of paintings on loan from the Dutch government in exile to the Museum of Fine Arts in 1943. The Dutch paintings, including selections by the Impressionist Vincent Van Gogh, could be viewed only by appointment.[54]

The difference in the amount of attention that local newspapers paid to the lives of blacks and whites was stark in May 1944. Although interest in the city focused on the looming invasion of France by Allied forces preparing to cross the English Channel, Gunter Field celebrated Mother's Day by honoring local women who had sons and/or daughters in the service overseas, were Gold Star mothers, or had sons who were prisoners of war. The *Advertiser* printed a list of mothers, all white, who had signed up to attend the ceremony and a dinner following at the field. At the end of the article appeared a small paragraph: "Eight colored Gold Star mothers will be guests of the . . . [black] 22d Aviation Squadron for the day. They will also play hosts to the 17 colored mothers who have sons overseas." It gave no names of these black mothers.[55]

7

Life and Death at Home

Grand march at the Commerce Street USO. *Courtesy of the Alabama Department of Archives and History, Montgomery, Alabama.*

In the United States the two most popular transmitters of entertainment were generally the radio and the cinema, or the picture show, as the latter was known in Montgomery. War did not change this fact. In the recent gloomy past both media had offered relatively cheap diversion from the depression blues. Cinema-generated war propaganda was effective partly because of the medium's grip on the public and partly because of the federal government's unprecedented control over this means of mass communication.[1]

"War movies" increasingly appeared in theaters. Hollywood and Washington combined to give the public a sanitized version of the violence of war and also to disseminate war propaganda. Hollywood had yielded to pressure from Washington so that the cinema industry would not be considered nonessential, status that would have brought with it serious economic consequences. The briefer newsreels were permitted to depict the war somewhat more fully than motion pictures. Some pictures stressed combat in its various forms; others, the home front, espionage, and the underground movements in enemy-controlled territory. Musicals incorporated war themes in technicolor. The enemies' inhumanity to captive peoples, prisoners of war, and even their own peoples was a major theme. In portraying combat and training, most war-related movies were unrealistic and overly simplistic. Some had realism and were above average. A few, such as *The Story of G.I. Joe,* based on coverage of the Italian campaign by the great war correspondent Ernie Pyle, were outstanding. During the peak year 1943, war movies accounted for 33 percent of total films made. Thereafter, the populace gradually began to tire of the war in general.[2]

In February 1943, before the peak had been reached, Montgomery's Paramount booked a war movie entitled *Casablanca* for Thursday, the nineteenth, through Saturday, the twenty-first. This was the time of the week reserved for the least-ballyhooed pictures, those not likely to attract the largest attendance. After a trial run in a few major cities in the fall of 1942, in which the reaction was mixed, *Casablanca* had been released to theaters nationwide in January 1943. It contained no battle scenes, and one of the few things that gave it special attention was the meeting in December 1942 and January 1943 of Allied heads of state Roosevelt and Churchill with their military chiefs in Casablanca to plan future strategy.[3]

Few Montgomerians were aware of this indirect connection. *Casablanca*'s lead players, "tough guy" Humphrey Bogart and the young Swedish beauty Ingrid Bergman, were the big attractions. What the audience unexpectedly saw on the screen captured their emotions and lingered in their memories: the ambience of intrigue and entertainment at Rick's Café Américain, owned by the character played by Bogart; the ill-fated romance of the lead characters (begun in Paris in an intriguing flashback); the suave and opportunistic Vichy official, played by Claude Rains ("Round up the usual suspects"); Rick's black handyman, played by actor Dooley Wilson, who sang "As Time Goes By"; the heroine's husband, a charismatic leader of the Resistance, with whom she reluctantly departed for safety at Rick's urging; and the memorable last line uttered by Rick to the Vichy official after they had combined to thwart the Nazis and left to join a nearby Free French garrison: "Looie, I think this is the beginning of a beautiful friendship."[4]

At moments *Casablanca* was as transparent a piece of war propaganda as most other films of the genre, but it was not consigned to the permanent obscurity that awaited most such films in cinema history. It captured three Oscars, including Best Picture, in 1943. Yet not until well after the war did *Casablanca* become, like *Gone with the Wind,* one of the most celebrated motion pictures of all time.[5]

Montgomery area government, business activity (including the cinema), and society in general retained some of their old features while also changing profoundly. City hall faced a crisis a few months after Pearl Harbor. W. A. ("Tacky") Gayle, a major in the army reserve, was called to the colors. The other commissioners, Brown and Screws, decided that they could split his duties and carry on in his absence.[6]

The war made the government of a city of Montgomery's size easier in several respects. The expansion of Maxwell and the creation of Gunter brought about the eventual end of the long, harsh depression. The construction in 1942 of the Holding and Reconsignment (H&R) Point a mile or so to the southwest of Maxwell was another economic blessing. Though many incorrectly regarded this as a war plant, the H&R Point was a regional army supply depot. Local firms, particularly the Algernon Blair Construction Company, were the principal recipients of contracts to build the six large warehouses. Hundreds of locals worked at the H&R Point, congesting traffic on the access roads when a shift changed.[7]

By 1944, women filled about 2,000 of the 5,000 jobs available for civilians at the bases and the depot. Most jobs held by women were civil service employment traditionally regarded as appropriate for women, that is, the jobs of secretary, typist, file clerk, stock clerk, librarian, and salesperson (in the commissaries). These jobs paid better than equivalent work with city businesses or in state, county, and municipal government. Most civilian mess personnel were not civil service and were primarily black men and women, but these jobs had not existed before the war. Some black women began to find jobs that paid well in the handful of small defense-related enterprises in Montgomery. Idessa Taylor found employment in a workshop that produced uniforms for the navy, but after she married she accompanied her husband to Tennessee, where he had obtained a defense job. A small number of white women residing in Montgomery could identify with Rosie the Riveter, the figure who represented women defense workers. In the summer of 1942, Mary Lett, a recent graduate of Verbena High School, saw in Montgomery's main post office a federal civil service announcement encouraging women to apply for training at Maxwell as mechanics in one of three specialties—engines and other aircraft systems, aircraft frames, and sheet metal. Lett qualified and joined a class that included women who were both single and married. The war had greatly increased job opportunities for married women. Upon graduation Lett was assigned to Gunter as an airframe mechanic. She took her first paycheck, ninety dollars for two weeks' work, to Cris's Café on Dexter for all the hot dogs she could eat.[8]

The increasing shortage of men opened to women a certain number of jobs that had previously been unavailable. By 1944, as an *Advertiser* headline put it, "WOMEN 'MAN' SCHOOL BUSES IN THIS COUNTY." American women in the paid wartime labor force grew by 6.5 million, and Mary Lett was one. When she married an aviation cadet at Gunter, she became one of the 2.3 million women who left their jobs during the war.[9]

Prewar businesses and financial institutions flourished in the good times created by the war. In 1942 each of the city's three banks reported the most successful year in its history. The war accelerated an effort begun in the late 1930s to lower the city's bonded indebtedness.

In 1942 the first city bonds since 1929 were retired. By the end of fiscal 1943, the city had its first credit balance since before the depression and boosted the pay of city police and firemen for the first time since 1929. Federal grants enabled the city to expand the waterworks to keep up with Maxwell's and Gunter's growth and a sudden population increase.[10]

The war economy also had its downside. In addition to the problems associated with rationing, price and wage ceilings, and taxes, the war severely limited construction and paving supplies. After Pearl Harbor there were no new appropriations in the city budget for paving streets because materials were lacking. One example was asphalt, in great demand for defense work. New construction of houses and apartments fell off drastically and was authorized only if dwellings were directly for defense plants and military projects or housed essential war workers who were emigrants ("in-migrant workers") to the plant site.[11]

Montgomery gained a new municipal airport in the summer of 1943 with the opening of an airport seven miles up the Selma highway. Named Dannelly Field for a dead U.S. Navy aviator from Montgomery, the field should have been named for the dead mayor W. A. Gunter, the father of commercial aviation in Montgomery. Instead, Gunter's name was attached to the army basic phase flying field northeast of the city. At the War Department's request, the city leased Dannelly to the AAF as an auxiliary field for training planes from Gunter in touch-and-go landings. Shortly before the ceremony opening the airport, city officials learned that work on an extension of Maxwell's runways meant the suspension of Eastern's service in and out of that field, cutting off the city from airline service. Mayor Cy Brown and a delegation from the Chamber of Commerce called on the senior commander at Maxwell, Brigadier General W. W. Welsh. They asked that Eastern be allowed to share the airport with Gunter. Welsh agreed to share the operations building with Eastern. Airline service for civilians without a government priority had been reduced to a minimum, but city officials knew that such service would grow when the war wound down.[12]

On July 1, notables assembled at Dannelly, named for Clarence Dannelly, Jr., a navy pilot who had died in a training accident in 1940. During the dedication ceremony, the Maxwell Field band played "Anchors Aweigh" and then "The Star Spangled Banner" as Mary Dannelly, the mother of Clarence, Jr., christened the field. A southbound Eastern DC-3 mail plane then landed.[13]

The housing shortage that had existed in Montgomery since 1939 became desperate after Pearl Harbor. Want ads in the local papers reflected the problem. At one time an ad might have read: "Couple with four year-old daughter desires immediate possession of modern furnished apartment, Cloverdale section preferred." By 1942, however, a more typical ad might have said: "Army officer and wife seek furnished home or apartment" or some variation. While some available apartments carried notations such as "army officers preferred," few landlords welcomed children.[14]

Go Peep rebuked her fellow burghers: "We patriotic soldiers on the 'home front' may give our 10 per cent but the wives of our men on active duty give their men. It seems a pity that our patriotism doesn't include wanting a man to keep his family together until he is sent out there somewhere." Similar appeals from leading citizens and commanders of the bases helped ease the problem for a time. Bachelor officers were more and more lucky in finding rooms for rent in Montgomery homes, sometimes with gentry. Peggy Penton recalled that her aunt and uncle on prestigious Allendale Road took in two officers from Maxwell.[15]

Neither all the young men nor the majority of young women were bound for duty in the armed forces. A small but respectable number attended college as civilians. Those who attended Auburn traveled from Montgomery up the Atlanta highway via Tuskegee by bus or car for about sixty miles or took the train. When Peggy Penton went to Auburn as a freshman in the fall of 1941, the majority of the student body still consisted of civilian males because the drafting of eighteen- and nineteen-year-olds was yet a year away.[16]

The town of Auburn was small. The industry in the area centered in Opelika, seven miles away. Even though it housed a major state institution of higher education, the campus was also small. Its major landmark was the nineteenth-century big red administrative building, Samford Hall, with its white belfry. The on-campus football stadium was barely larger than Cramton Bowl in Montgomery until a building program increased seating capacity to 15,000 in 1942. But no college team had a more devoted following. Fanatical alumni such as Penton's father, the pharmaceutical salesman George ("Doc") Penton, formerly an Auburn player and an assistant coach, were determined that their Tigers would equal the Alabama Crimson Tide with its Rose Bowl tradition.[17]

Peggy Penton was a typical freshman in the fall of 1941. She wrote her mother, Bess Penton: "We've . . . had to go to all sorts of meetings, pay fees, have photographs & fingerprints taken. . . . I'm worn to a frazzle." Social activities came thick and fast: "It's now ten minutes of eleven P.M. . . . . I went to three teas this afternoon, a buffet supper and dinner party tonight." Homesickness crept in: "Cecil [a hometown beau] called me this morning and I sure was glad." Then came the eagerly anticipated news: "I'm so thrilled I don't know what to do. I just got the word this morning—gosh, I'm glad I decided on this sorority." It was Alpha Gamma Delta. Unlike the fraternities, sororities at Auburn had no chapter houses, and Penton, like the other coeds from out of town, stayed in a dorm. She soon grew weary of the academics: "The same old drag day in, day out. These classes are really getting me down to say nothing of the lessons."[18]

By 1943, when Lee Allen from Montgomery entered Auburn as a freshman, the draft included eighteen-year-olds. It soon reduced noticeably the number of civilian male students. The student population for the 1944–1945 school year dropped from 4,000 to 2,700. Still, as Allen later commented, "Staffing classes was an ongoing problem. In part this was because the university had various military programs (such as ASTP and Navy V-5), each of which operated on its own calendar . . . , and teachers were shuffled about." In Algebra 101, Allen "had no less than seven instructors in an eleven-week course." Overall, he was pleased by "a memorable set of teachers," the most memorable of whom was Dr. Fred Allison, "world renowned physicist."

Several times each quarter, Allison "disappeared from campus," after arranging for a substitute to meet his classes. After the war Allen learned that his professor had made "clandestine trips" to Oak Ridge, Tennessee, for work on the development of the atomic bomb.[19]

Allen did not go in for the fraternity culture. He studied hard and found little time for an active social life. He did find time for picture shows at Auburn's one theater, the Tiger, in part because in warm weather only the Tiger Theater offered air conditioning.[20]

The University of Alabama in Tuscaloosa had no direct highway to Montgomery until 1943. Montgomery students who traveled by motor vehicle were forced to ride over a roundabout series of roads, but most students traveled by a train called the Doodlebug. In 1941 Governor Frank Dixon pushed the development of a direct Tuscaloosa connection with U.S. Route 31 a few miles north of Montgomery. The new road was projected to run northwest from Route 31 via Prattville. In eighteen months the main stretches of road had been completed, cutting the distance to approximately 100 miles.[21]

Algie Hill from Montgomery was in graduate school at Tuscaloosa during the school year 1941–1942 pursuing a master's degree in English. She would later recollect that though the campus area had been small, she was awed by several landmarks, including the stately president's white-columned mansion on University Avenue, which was also the highway to Birmingham, and the bell tower across from the mansion at the edge of the tree-lined campus. The town had industry and was much larger than Auburn.[22]

Hill had been aware of the University's most famous professor, the creative writing teacher Hudson Strode, but had no courses with him. His writing students were successful in selling their short stories and novels to leading magazines and major publishing houses, with which Strode had contacts. Before Montgomery's Lonnie Coleman went into the navy as an ensign, he studied under Strode.[23]

Lanier graduate Jean Severence was a freshman at Alabama in 1941–1942. A major in chemistry, she pledged Chi Omega sorority. She enjoyed sorority life and residing in the chapter house, as pledges were required to do. One of her favorite haunts was the "Supe" (Supply)

Store on University Avenue, which sold Cokes and snacks and housed the campus post office. Another favorite was the downtown Bama theater. The university was known as a "party school" and provided a lively social life. Pearl Harbor did not change things overnight. Severence, the daughter of a college football official, loved the game and watched the Crimson Tide play in Denny Stadium near her sorority house. Sisters and pledges came to the games "all dressed up" on Saturday afternoons.[24]

Severence's mother informed her at the end of the school year that her grades did not warrant the expense of a college education and that she would not be returning. Severence was disappointed, primarily because she had a steady boyfriend at the university, but she soon joined in the social whirl of wartime Montgomery. The appeal of college life weakened when Alabama along with Auburn and most other Southeastern Conference teams canceled intercollegiate football in 1943, supposedly for the duration.[25]

Some high school graduates went outside the state for a college education. Dootsie Ball and Isabel Dunn traveled together, sharing a lower berth on a Pullman bound for Hollins in Virginia, an exclusive school for women. Their parents were influential but frugal. After the young women had retired for the night, a drunken soldier came staggering down the aisle, suddenly swayed against their curtain, and sat down on the berth. Ball was fearful, but Dunn, hardly hesitating, pushed against the curtain and shoved him into the aisle. He went away.[26]

Wartime Montgomery affected the two local colleges in different ways because of the makeup of their student bodies. Alabama State was more physically affected by the war as the student body's male complement shrank from the draft. Edward Brown from north Alabama roomed with Fred Burks until Burks volunteered for the army in 1941. Brown continued in school, pledging Alpha Phi Alpha fraternity in his sophomore year. He endured the usual hazing, paddling routine before initiation as a full-fledged member. The college had no fraternity or sorority houses, and Brown continued to live in a dorm. He loved the dances. Student bands furnished music in the tradition of Erskine Hawkins, who had formed an Alabama State student band in the early 1930s before going on to become a famous band leader in New York. Brown was an enthusiastic Hornet football and basketball fan, whose favorite teacher was the basketball coach and social studies instructor Charlie Dunn. In 1943, Brown's college days were temporarily interrupted when he entered the army.[27]

The 1943 Huntingdon annual *Bells and Pomegranates* carried the school's motto, "Enter to Grow in Wisdom; Go Forth to Apply Wisdom in Service." The editors philosophized: "The buildings look on the general disorder of things with tolerance. They were standing with their impenetrable calm before girls were anxious for news of friends and relatives in the services. They will still be standing when peace comes." On Flowers Hall, the administration building, "the spire and the gargoyles were serene up there in the clouds but even higher the planes circled reminding us that all was not as quiet and peaceful as our campus."[28]

Peggy Penton and Jean Severence, having already tasted the social life at Maxwell and Gunter before going to college, were happy to return to that social life on a regular basis. The contacts between local young women and men stationed at the local air bases, Craig Field at Selma, the infantry camp at Fort Rucker near Enterprise, and Tuskegee Army Air Field increased as the number of military personnel multiplied at these posts. In those days before the sexual revolution, young women were still expected to be virgins on their wedding days. But romance and marriage were frequently not the objectives of servicemen. Although many of the "boys" from the various bases were shy, others were womanizers motivated by the prevailing double standard of sexual behavior and eager to cultivate a macho image as soldiers, sailors, and marines. Often they regaled their buddies in the barracks or day room about their sexual encounters of the night before, usually called "pieces." Many married servicemen sought, sometimes successfully, to conceal their marital status. While reported rapes by servicemen in Montgomery were relatively few, undoubtedly some went unreported. Constraints upon young women were weaker than in World War I, in part as a result of the Jazz Age and its assaults upon convention and inhibition. More "girls" dared to experiment in the

Second World War. All too often women were alarmed to discover that they were pregnant. One result was an increase in the number of illegitimate births.[29]

Louise DeShields, daughter of the owner of a leading shoe store in Montgomery, was a state social worker who handled the cases of a number of pregnant unmarried women, all of them white and of limited means. Their dilemma, she observed, was pathetic. Abortions were both illegal and expensive. Many felt shame, for society of the time did not condone extramarital sex or pregnancy outside wedlock. More often than not, DeShields observed, women who turned to their parents were rejected or greeted with scorn.[30]

The men responsible for unwanted pregnancies were in most of DeShields's cases enlisted men from Maxwell or Gunter. Louise made an effort in each case to find the father and tried to persuade him to acknowledge his obligation. Many men fought accepting responsibility and often tried to blame other servicemen. Some men, however, owned up with little pressure. Forced marriages frequently turned out badly.[31]

DeShields helped to arrange a place in town for the lying-in period and hospitalization for the births. Her clients stayed at a boarding-house up the hill on Montgomery Street or in one run by Hank Williams's mother on Bibb Street downtown. DeShields sometimes saw young Hank "picking and singing" on the front steps when she came to check on a client. Babies were either put up for adoption or were placed in foster homes until the women were on their feet.[32]

On rare occasions women from the middle class and even the gentry became pregnant as a result of sex with servicemen in Montgomery. These situations were, at least on the surface, resolved by an abortion or by the involved man's "agreeing to do the decent thing," which was marriage.[33]

The middle class and the gentry gave rise to a bevy of physically attractive and/or accomplished young women, who became the belles of the Second World War. No one rose to the stature of Zelda Sayre, however, the most captivating "belle" of the First World War.[34]

Local women, both black and white, were courted by military men in numbers that began to exceed those seen during any other war, but there were fewer black military personnel stationed in Montgomery. From Tuskegee some black officers, cadets, and men of other ranks came to the capital city. Janis Johnson of Montgomery married First Lieutenant Thomas L. Malone, supply officer with the Ninety-ninth Fighter Squadron, the first all-black combat air unit in the U.S. armed forces. He accompanied the Ninety-ninth to North Africa in 1943.[35] Dorothy Ghent had married Second Lieutenant John T. Moore, whom she met at Maxwell while he was a cadet in training to be a pilot and she was a student at Huntingdon. He departed with a fighter group for the South Pacific in 1943.[36]

During the war, marriages between local women and servicemen from Montgomery and other places began to dominate the society pages. In 1939 only an occasional announcement of an engagement or a marriage by a local woman to a serviceman appeared in the Montgomery papers. By 1943 the majority of such announcements in the society pages involved local women marrying servicemen.[37]

The aviation cadets of class after class at Maxwell and Gunter had the greatest impact on the local young white women. The social high point of each cadet class was its graduation ball. On May 23, 1942, the ball for a graduating class of the preflight school took place at Maxwell in Hangar 6. The *Advertiser* reported a "large vanguard of girl visitors from many parts of the nation . . . arriving in Montgomery last night." Local hotels were filled, and Montgomerians pitched in to put up some of the visitors for the night. It was to be "the largest event of its kind ever to be held at Maxwell Field." The name band for the event was that of Skinnay Ennis, the orchestra for Bob Hope's radio program. Hope himself later put in an appearance at Maxwell for the USO.[38]

Peggy Penton and Jean Severence were at the May 23 ball with cadet dates who were not local. Penton was for the moment playing the field. Both women knew several preflight cadets at Maxwell who were from Montgomery. Silas ("Brook") Nettles, whose class was behind the one graduating, was a close friend of Severence's, but at the time each had a "steady."[39]

A reception line of the senior commanders at Maxwell and their spouses welcomed the cadets and their dates. The women wore corsages, called "Victorages," composed of wire stems with ten-cent war stamps knitted into red, white, and blue ribbons. Under the "Saber Arch" formed by cadet officers of the training wing, couples paraded to the grand march that began the ball. Afterward the dancers foxtrotted and waltzed. The "cats" jitterbugged. Some formed a conga line. Couples crowded around the bandstand to hear Ennis in his breathless style as he sang his current hit, "I've Got a Date with an Angel."[40]

The number of name bands shrank, affected by the magnet of the draft on their musicians. As name bands became rare, the most popular dance orchestra at Maxwell was a fifteen-member group called the Rhythmaires. This orchestra was drawn from the training command marching and concert band. All of its members were enlisted men except for its conductor and the commanding officer. Organizer of the Rhythmaires was Sergeant Gerald ("Jerry") Yelverton, a Montgomery native who as an Auburn student had played in the school's dance orchestra, the regionally famed Auburn Knights. His chief claim to fame, however, was that as a civilian he had played saxophone and clarinet in Glenn Miller's orchestra in 1939.[41]

In December 1942, Yelverton became reunited with his old boss. Captain Glenn Miller was assigned to training command headquarters at Maxwell as assistant special services officer specializing in recreation and entertainment. Miller had disbanded his civilian orchestra in September and had eventually obtained a captain's commission in the U.S. Army.[42]

Arriving on December 7, Miller stayed for only three weeks at Maxwell. But in that time he had the opportunity to test his ambition to organize a super military band that would double in brass as a dance orchestra. His first test vehicle was the Rhythmaires, with which he played his trombone and created some arrangements. He did not, however, try to turn it into a version of his civilian band. Yelverton was the only Rhythmaire who had any name band experience. Miller's arrangements were mostly standard ones. But his presence gave the

Rhythmaires a special appeal. The orchestra and Miller played for aviation cadets at their recreation hall, for officers at the officers' club, and for noncommissioned officers and enlisted men at their recreation halls. Miller was also able to observe the command marching band playing for cadet formations. Although it was one of the finest army bands of the time, Miller believed that the band with a more peppy beat could invigorate the step of young marching men. Primarily he dreamed of boosting military morale with a dance orchestra in uniform made up of former name band musicians under his leadership.[43]

In private Miller was shy, and this was undoubtedly one reason why there was little publicity surrounding his assignment to Maxwell. He did go into the city on occasion. Jean Severence and some friends were sitting at a table in the Beauvoir Country Club bar, when one of them identified Glenn Miller sitting alone at the bar. They hesitantly approached him. He greeted them in a friendly way and stood them to a round of drinks. Jerry Yelverton, who had a crush on Peggy Penton, introduced her to Miller at Maxwell. She recalled that he "was very cordial" to one of his devoted fans.[44]

At command headquarters in Austin Hall, the desk of Captain Frank Hill, training command personnel officer, was next to that of the newly assigned assistant special services officer. The two men soon became friends. Hill and several other Maxwell bachelor officers had managed to rent a house on East Cloverdale Park. Glenn visited there on various occasions, sometimes with his wife, Helen, when she came down from their home in New Jersey. Glenn enjoyed the southern-style meals produced by the officers' black cook and became a devotee of southern cooking. More important, Miller learned a lot about the organization of the AAF from Hill, knowledge that helped him achieve his ambition.[45]

Miller and some of the civilian women aircraft mechanics at Maxwell were featured in a segment of the "Army Hour," an NBC network program broadcast locally over WSFA. But the high point of Miller's assignment to Maxwell came on Christmas Eve. In the afternoon he directed a musical program in a hangar that was broadcast over a regional armed forces network not received in Montgomery.

He led the Rhythmaires in a series of numbers that he had arranged, but the only number in the Miller style was "Alabama Bound." The program also included a choir of cadets and enlisted men singing Christmas carols. That night Miller and the band played for a Christmas Eve dance in the cadet recreation hall.[46]

Major General Walter Weaver had a habit of "raiding" the Southeastern Army Air Force Training Center for personnel for his own Technical Training Command, using his friends and contacts at Maxwell. Weaver ended Miller's stint at Maxwell by arranging for his transfer to the Technical Training Command. It was a fortuitous move for Miller. Weaver, a music lover, made him the Technical Training Command's director of music and cleared the way for Miller to achieve his military ambition as the leader of a super marching band/dance orchestra. The band was eventually based at Yale University, where it became legendary, perhaps the greatest name band ever.[47]

Several other celebrities in uniform visited or were stationed at Maxwell. The great boxer Sergeant Joe Louis came to stage an exhibition for the black soldiers of Maxwell and Gunter. James ("Jimmy") Stewart, a new second lieutenant in the AAF, stopped overnight at Maxwell, breaking his flight from California to Washington, D.C., to attend FDR's Birthday Ball in January 1942 on behalf of the Polio Foundation. He caused a stir among the secretaries in Austin Hall. In the fall of 1942, Captain Clark Gable came to Maxwell for a short assignment. Gable's duty was to produce AAF training films. Maxwell was an ideal base for training orientation. When Corrie Hill Hurt planned a dinner party at her home in Cloverdale, one of the invited guests, the wife of a Maxwell colonel, called to ask whether they might bring along a guest named Clark Gable. Hurt replied, "Why, yes, bring along Ronald Colman, too." To her surprise Gable did in fact accompany the Maxwell couple. She found him to be "good looking, with black hair, tall like Rhett Butler." He was congenial but did not stay long. Gable, who had apparently left Maxwell by the time Glenn Miller arrived, went on to produce training films while flying on several missions over Europe with the Eighth Air Force.[48]

The cadets at Maxwell and Gunter formed their own dance orchestras from talent among their own ranks. These bands had cadet vocalists but recruited female vocalists from the community just as the Rhythmaires had done with a fine singer named June Stanley. Peggy Penton had a good singing voice that she had developed in part in her church choir. She picked up techniques by listening to great female vocalists, such as Helen Forest and Helen O'Connell, and by watching them in movies. When cadet friends from Maxwell discovered Penton's talent, they persuaded her to try out as a vocalist with their orchestra. She always remembered her nervousness at her first guest appearance with the cadet band. The applause banished her anxiety. Afterward, as she later noted, "I sang fairly regularly with the band at the Rec Hall at Maxwell and I was given an official pass designating me Peggy Penton—Vocalist."[49]

In 1943 Peggy dated an officer at Maxwell, Lieutenant James ("Mac") McMillan from New Jersey. She met him at the home of her Aunt Susie Rawlings, where he rented a room. They danced at the Maxwell Officers' Club and the Beauvoir Club but also at road houses and "honkytonks" at the city's edge, where Penton observed daring Huntingdon coeds who had sneaked off with their dates after signing out for a movie or church. Penton and McMillan fell in love. Then he startled her by proposing. Not ready for marriage, she turned him down, ending the relationship. Some months later Penton learned that McMillan was in the Pacific.[50]

Peggy Penton and other young women became members of the USO Girls Service Organization. Two were formed—one for the black Monroe Street USO and one for the white Commerce Street USO. The Catholic USO on Lee Street and the Women's USO on Dexter had their own hostess arrangements. It was not a simple matter for young women to come to the USO as junior hostesses. USO directors had instructions to check out their backgrounds and monitor their on-duty behavior. Servicemen could pick up women in the area around Union Station or in some shabby café with a jukebox or bar off the main drag and even sometimes in places on the main drag, but they quickly discovered that they could not do so at the USOs.[51]

The assistant club directors supervised the junior hostesses. Peggy Penton later summed up the approach of Millie Prentiss of the Commerce Street club: "Miss Millie ruled with an iron hand and saw that 'her girls' came together, left together and were well behaved and well chaperoned while there." Miss Millie had an inflexible rule that a hostess could neither encourage nor accept a serviceman's request for a date after she went off duty. But romance sometimes resulted nonetheless. Mildred Davies, a 1943 graduate of Lanier, met a member of the Maxwell marching band at the Commerce Street club, and soon they were married.[52] Dancing to a band such as the Rhythmaires was a favorite pastime. Peggy Penton remembered, "Someone once said you could cover twenty miles in a night dancing at the U.S.O.!"[53]

At the clubs older volunteers or young women such as Dorothy Ghent Moore whose husbands were away in the service prepared the food, arranged classes in ballroom dancing and bridge, supervised such group games as bingo, and signed out the checkers and Chinese checkers sets, Ping-Pong paddles, and shuffleboard equipment. Mainly women, they set up equipment so that service people could record messages to be sent home. They had towels and soap ready to be used in the showers. Volunteers such as Johnnie Carr of the Monroe Street club put in many hours.[54]

The driving force behind the volunteer groups was the executive unit, the Women's Auxiliary, which worked hand in glove with the paid director and the assistant director. Georgia McGehee, the wife of a druggist, headed the Auxiliary and served as liaison with the local governing board of prominent folk, the USO Council.[55]

The Red Cross/Junior Chamber of Commerce canteen near Union Station functioned most of the time at peak efficiency. In 1944 several hundred U.S. Marines brought their war dogs from a troop train at the station to exercise in the parklike patio behind the canteen. According to the *Advertiser*, a crowd gathered to watch the handlers put the dogs through their paces with "military precision." When dogs and handlers took a break, the hostesses fed the marines soup, cookies, and iced tea. The men shared the food with their dogs. After two

(Left) Margaret "Peggy" Penton at the tennis courts of the Beauvoir Country Club and (right) Dorothy Ghent Moore in the backyard of her parents' home on Cloverdale Road. *Courtesy of the estate of Margaret (Peggy Penton) Cravey and of Dorothy Ghent, respectively.*

hours of entertaining the spectators, the dogs and marines paraded back across to the train shed, where the animals had special kennels on the train.[56]

"V for Victory" became a popular slogan in the course of the war. Two other Vs, however, were seen as negative results of the war on the home front, along with sexual promiscuity and illegitimate births. One was venereal disease, an offshoot of promiscuity. VD at first received little attention from municipal authorities, a legacy of W. A. Gunter's live-and-let-live attitude toward prostitution and gambling.[57]

As the war unfolded, VD became a matter for growing concern that was medical as well as moral. Commanders of the local and nearby military bases pushed civilians into confronting the problem. There was only so much they could do with training films (which enlisted men described as "Mickey Mouse"), lectures by medical officers, and posters depicting the pitfalls of infected prostitutes and "loose" women.

Even courts-martial for those who contracted VD did not slow the rising rate of infection. Beginning in February 1942, a series of meetings in Montgomery featured lectures by both civilian and military experts on the subject. Military authorities blamed city and county authorities for failing to control prostitution. Civilians responded by demanding that the military control the swarms of servicemen who treated the city as if it were one vast brothel.[58]

The Montgomery Ministerial Association issued a series of resolutions to deal with the problem. The preachers spread the blame over both military and civilian authorities, correctly pointing out that the nests of prostitution, hotels and roominghouses, continued to thrive, serving both "amateur and professional prostitutes." Also contributing to prostitution were "unscrupulous taxi drivers" who catered to "adulterers." The solution, proclaimed the preachers, was twofold: a law requiring a test for VD before a couple could be married and more effective Bible instruction in schools.[59]

The VD problem itself finally began to come under control in Montgomery in 1944 when military and local municipal authorities agreed on a city ordinance requiring women convicted of vagrancy to submit to a medical examination. If a woman was found to have VD, she would be confined in city jail while she underwent treatment for the disease. The constitutionality of such a law was apparently not debated. Military personnel found to have VD had long been subject to court-martial. Civilian police and military police crackdowns on the nests and the taxis had already improved the situation somewhat. Taxis, many owned by drivers who evaded the city's regulatory efforts, were harder to supervise because of their mobility. An initial crackdown in 1942 targeted the "Weekend Taxis," vehicles without a taxi license that carried the military johns with weekend passes to the prostitutes who used the taxis, cheaper hotels, and alleyways for stand-up sex. The last large prewar red light district, on Pollard Street, was eradicated by 1944 under a federal law, passed in July 1941, that allowed local authorities to close down brothels near military and naval installations.[60]

The other negative V, vagrancy, became a sensitive issue as civilian labor for farms and factories grew steadily scarcer. Spurred by a state initiative against vagrancy, the county and municipality of Montgomery declared war on draft dodgers, idlers, and tramps. The slogan of the antivagrancy campaign was "Work or fight or work for the city or county." Sheriff Addie Mosley had his deputies tack up posters reading "WORK OR FIGHT" and bearing the signature of Governor Chauncey Sparks. Obtaining a court order against vagrancy, the sheriff maintained that he would proceed in a democratic way. The order would apply to "everybody, men and women, both white and colored." The first persons arrested by deputies were three black males. Mosley appeared in Judge Lomax Crum's Court of Common Pleas to testify against them in August 1943. None got the maximum sentence and one man was released when he produced a letter showing that he was employed. Mosley declared himself pleased with the results of his handiwork.[61]

The city commission passed an antivagrancy ordinance in 1943 that imposed a $100 fine and six months in jail but placed the burden of proof on the city. When the ordinance seemed ineffective, the commissioners in 1944 revised it to put the burden of proof on the accused. The issue of vagrancy became less and less a public concern over time and hence ceased to preoccupy Montgomery officials.[62]

A much more intense public anxiety developed over juvenile delinquency. A sharp increase in juvenile delinquency nationwide joined the home-front crises. The increase was not caused by traditional forces—poverty, a depressed job market, and a lack of opportunity— nor did it reflect simply random acts of vandalism performed as a sort of rite of passage. When windows were broken, tires slashed, or marble lawn statues stolen, property owners became upset and demanded that police track down the culprits.[63]

Initially the public in Montgomery was little concerned about increases in juvenile delinquency. After all, even experts could not agree on the root causes of the wartime phenomenon. And the city had a juvenile court to deal with the problem. The general complacency was slow to subside. About two years after Pearl Harbor, a growing number of white middle-class and gentry families began to discover that their children's behavior had become a part of the national wartime problem.[64]

Eventually, as with the situation nationwide, adolescent girls became the center of attention as a result of the illegitimacy, prostitution, and VD crises. The Montgomery Parent-Teacher Association began a campaign early in January 1944 to prevent girls under sixteen from being out after dark without a suitable chaperon. Police Chief Ralph King had initiated the campaign late in December 1943 by inviting PTA members to accompany vice squad officers on the rounds they made between 3:00 P.M. and 3:00 A.M. The two women of the PTA, who had been accompanied by a newspaper reporter, issued a report to the public. They had "visited night clubs, road houses, cafes, taverns, drug stores, and dance halls. Boys and girls, shockingly young, were patrons." They observed "girls, obviously 'khaki-wacky' on the streets, in 'juke joints,' and at public dance halls." Adolescent boys, driving taxis, stopped at homes with "absentee parents," from which trooped "a bevy of teenage girls, doubtless friends of the adolescent resident, whom recreation leaders call a 'door-key girl.' Into the car they crowded, giggling and snickering." The public tended to view the girls' situation as a moral transgression, but the military and the public saw the servicemen's problem as more medical than moral. Military men, whatever their age, could sin just as long as they did not catch VD. Adolescent girls, on the other hand, could not sin at all.[65]

A single event, also taking place in January 1944, brought to a head the Montgomery public's reaction to wartime juvenile delinquency. On January 8, vandals struck at Sidney Lanier High. At 11:00 P.M. an occupant of a nearby house heard the sound of shattering glass and called the police. A car sped out of the circling drive in front of the school and disappeared before a squad car arrived. The *Advertiser* depicted the damage: "The ornate doors at the front entrance were splintered with an axe. . . . Splintered wood and glass littered the foyer almost all the way to the entrance to the auditorium." Doors of the two wings of the main building and of the gym had also been battered.[66]

The act prompted both despair and a debate in the community.

Rabbi Eugene Blachschlager of Temple Beth Or told the Kiwanis Club that "something is wrong with our people, our homes and our education when such an act of vandalism . . . can happen here."[67] Superintendent Clarence Dannelly called the vandals "American Nazis." He declared that if they were not caught, the community could expect even "greater violence."[68]

What actually lay behind the vandalism? Letters to the local papers offered possible reasons. Parents had become lax, and more old-time discipline should be applied to children "in their early years—and firmness through their later years." The same writer, a woman, singled out mothers. "Motherhood . . . requires patience, endless time, wisdom, understanding, love, and sacrifice of herself." Any woman unable "to give all that is not worthy of motherhood." The writer further advocated that girls "should dress more modestly."[69] Some writers blamed the troubles on a failure to teach and preach old-time religion. Others blamed the war-related absence of fathers. Various writers identified the war per se as the principal cause.[70]

An editorial in the *Advertiser* warned that unless the perpetrators were caught, more similar acts could be expected. What was needed, according to the editor, was "not so much the punishment of the individual as the preservation of respect for law and order."[71]

In March, solicitor Temple Seibels answered a school board plea calling for the apprehension of the guilty: "We have done everything in our power to ascertain who the guilty parties were," and the only hope remaining was for the parents of the guilty to persuade them to confess. A February letter to the *Advertiser* from "A Loyal Poet" had claimed that "we are . . . aware of the fact that certain of the saboteurs are former Lanier students" and eligible for the draft. "We knew who they were," declared Laura Johnston, an English teacher at Lanier, years later. From "very well off families," their parents had the influence to shield them from interrogation. Rewards totaling $600 were all for naught.[72]

The trashing of Lanier had one quick positive result. A downtown club for youth had been in the planning stage since the fall of 1943. Boys and girls had begun to sign up to become charter members, and a building downtown on Washington Avenue was being prepared. But when doors opened two nights before the Lanier incident, its attraction was moderate. After the trashing, members of the club's sponsoring organizations, the PTA and the Junior Chamber of Commerce, beamed as the membership roll soared.[73]

The Youth Club proved a success in helping to curb juvenile delinquency. The first annual report in January 1945 boasted that "since its opening night, one year ago, the club has served thousands of teen-age boys and girls." There were parties, dances, "Youth Club Sweetheart" and "Ideal Boy" contests, Bingo games, and the sponsorship of both a boys' and a girls' softball team. The Youth Club was for whites only, and no equivalent project for black youth was launched. The lost youth joined the lost battalions.[74]

Death on the home front at times overshadowed the debate over VD, prostitution, vagrancy, and delinquency and even momentarily the almost weekly roster of Montgomerians who had died in training accidents or in battle. Front page headlines, eclipsing war news such as the North African campaign, told of a distant fire on the night of November 28, 1942, in a Boston-area nightclub, the Coconut Grove. It was filled with football-weekend merrymakers and service folk. When firemen were finally able to douse the flames around midnight, they saw that almost half of the 1,000 people in the building at the time of the fire had perished from burns, trampling, or smoke inhalation.[75]

The dead included two military Montgomerians—Ensign Charles Norman Albritton, U.S. Naval Reserves, twenty-eight, based at Harvard, who had been studying communications, and army private Albert Clyde Sullivan, twenty-two, stationed at Camp Edwards, Massachusetts. A Montgomery civilian, Osborne Rainer, eighteen, then a student at MIT, also died. A year later, Wesley Newton, an army private and a student in the ASTP engineering unit at MIT, was in the Back Bay area at night and asked directions to the site of the conflagration. He had known Osborne Rainer. Gazing at the boarded-up structure, Newton imagined that he could smell the smoke from the burning interior and charred flesh.[76]

On the home front, death usually occurred under normal circumstances, as in peacetime, arousing widespread interest only when a newsworthy person died or a sensational murder occurred. Mayor Cy Brown died unexpectedly on August 8, 1944. The *Advertiser* of August 11 told of his burial "on a grassy slope in Oakwood Cemetery while hundreds stood with bowed heads." Its editor eulogized him. Brown had "supervised the expenditure of more than a half million dollars to expand our water facilities to meet the [military's] requirements . . . , refinanced the city's bonds at a huge saving in interest . . . , [and] readjusted salaries and city expenses so that tongue and buckle meet for the first time in memory."[77]

Two days after Brown's funeral, David E. Dunn, a World War I veteran with a son who was a B-24 bomber pilot in the Eighth Air Force, announced his candidacy for mayor in the special election of September 5. A state lobbyist for the brewing industry, Dunn had two items in his long résumé that made him seem a shoo-in. First, he stated that Cy Brown had been his "beloved friend of many years," in whose "footsteps" he intended "to follow," and second, he expressed the intention to "resign and declare the office of Mayor vacant" when servicemen and servicewomen returned. Dunn won easily.[78]

At the time of Brown's death and Dunn's campaign and election, the city's most sensational murder during the entire war was under investigation. On June 15 aviation cadet Lynn Drew had kissed his nineteen-year-old wife, Esther, before she boarded a city bus that would take her downtown, where she was to transfer to a Cloverdale-bound bus.[79]

Both the Drews were from Illinois, and Esther had been in training to be a registered nurse. She had taken a break from her studies to come to Maxwell and wed Lynn. Late in the afternoon on June 16, Lynn received a telephone call from Esther's landlady, who told him that his wife had not returned since leaving for Maxwell on the fifteenth. A Maxwell lieutenant accompanied the cadet to Cloverdale in a taxi. While Lynn examined her room, the officer looked about outside. He crossed the street and made his way to a twelve-foot drainage ditch with a concrete bottom. There he saw a naked body with brown hair. He recognized Esther Drew. When Lynn crossed the street, the lieutenant tried in vain to prevent him from looking down. The cadet staggered and almost collapsed.[80]

Chief King and Coroner M. B. Kirkpatrick responded to the call. Gathering dusk left time for only a cursory inspection of the scene. The coroner, saying he had to examine the body as soon as possible, authorized its removal to the White Chapel mortuary downtown. There, however, instead of performing an autopsy, he made only a relatively brief examination, concluding in his report that she had been raped and that a large knife had inflicted the fatal wound. The body was then released to Lynn Drew, who arranged to have it shipped to Illinois by train while he went ahead in an army transport plane.[81]

In late July, his investigation leading nowhere, Chief King requested the aid of state authorities. Dr. N. W. Nixon, the state toxicologist, moved to fill in the forensic gaps. Illinois authorities agreed in mid-August to a request for exhumation and an autopsy. On September 15 the autopsy report was made public. It was inconclusive as to whether Esther Drew had been killed in the ditch or elsewhere. The autopsy was conducted too late to determine whether she had been raped. State Attorney General William McQueen criticized Kirkpatrick without naming him: "Had the examination [autopsy] been made immediately after the body was discovered, we might have something to go on." The state bowed out of the investigation.[82]

When the news of the murder spread in June, panic swept the white sections of Montgomery. The *Advertiser* did not initially help to soothe the anxiety with its image of a "slayer who ravished the cadet's young wife and, after stabbing her in the breast, left her nude in a deep ditch," but the editor soon tried to calm the public. For a time the emotional reaction in its intensity equaled the local response to Pearl Harbor and the recent invasion of Normandy. Rumors about the crime flew like bats in the dark, for a time displacing rumors pertaining to the war. The initial rumor making the rounds was that Esther had met a man in a downtown bar who later raped and killed her. A persistent rumor was that her husband had murdered her in a fit of jealousy. He was cleared, however. Another persistent rumor held that a taxi driver had taken her as a fare to Cloverdale, where he had brutalized her in the cab before dumping the body in the ditch. A woman told of being stalked by a "gorilla-like" black man until she eluded him by hurrying to a nearby house and pounding on the door. A number of versions of this fantasy were reported to police. Chief King assigned extra patrol cars to prowl Capitol Heights, Oak Park, and Cloverdale after dark.[83]

After interviewing various suspects whose names were not released to the public, the Montgomery police department announced on September 2 that it was about to make an arrest. The suspect was Worley James, described in the local papers as "a tall mulatto," age thirty-seven. Recently in the custody of the police in Muncie, Indiana, but currently being extradited to Montgomery, James was the subject of rumors in the black community. Specifically, it was said that recently, while living in Montgomery, he had boasted of raping and killing a white woman. Local authorities already had several outstanding felony charges against him that included rape and grand larceny.[84]

When James returned to Montgomery on September 3, he disappeared behind a curtain of official silence. The panic had ebbed, and public attention focused again on the war. Then the curtain was parted on October 4 when police made the dramatic announcement that James had confessed to the murder of Esther Drew. Knowing its public reputation for beating confessions from prisoners, and in view of the spotlight on this particular crime, the police had James repeat his confession at the station house in the presence of a prominent Montgomery minister, a leading businessman, and a reporter from the *Advertiser,* all of them white. In answer to their questions, James denied being beaten or coerced in any other way. None of the three citizens, however, thought to ask why it had taken a month for James to confess.[85]

James voluntarily took the three to the ditch in Cloverdale, where he described the killing. He had followed Esther onto the Cloverdale bus one night, getting off at the rear entrance after her. From a distance he watched while she entered one of the houses. Later he noted the particular nights of the week when she caught the Cloverdale bus. On June 15 he waited in some trees in a park across from her boardinghouse. She came in from the bus stop on schedule in the dark. He accosted her in the street in front of her boardinghouse, used the knife to force her to the edge of the ditch, and pushed her over when she protested loudly. In the struggle on the concrete bottom he stabbed her. He had wanted, he said, merely to silence her screams, "but I stuck her a little too deep." He denied raping her but said that he had taken her purse and shoes and had placed her clothes, which had torn in the struggle and which he had removed, underneath her.[86]

Legal machinery spun rapidly to indict James and bring him to trial. Trial judge Eugene Carter made the unusual move of appointing not one lawyer but a team of able attorneys to defend James. Immediately he retracted his confession. Apart from the murder of Esther Drew, he had been indicted for the rape of a black woman and carnal knowledge (statutory rape) of a ten-year-old black girl. He pleaded innocent to all three crimes, all of which carried a possible death sentence. Solicitor Temple Seibels chose to prosecute him first on the carnal knowledge charge while claiming that he had fresh evidence in the Drew case and would try it next.[87]

On November 21 the usual all-white male jury found James guilty of carnal knowledge. Carter sentenced him to die in the electric chair. His lawyers filed notice of appeal. When Seibels moved to prosecute James for the murder of Esther Drew, the legal team, to prepare a defense, gained a continuance from Judge Carter until the February 1945 court term. There had still been no retribution for the casualty on the home front.[88]

8

OVERLORD and Aftermath

Private James Donald Godwin (far right) and other U.S. Army infantry replacements in a New York City night club in December 1943 before they shipped to England. *Courtesy of Catherine Cobb.*

Since the early part of the war, the Western Allies had given Europe first priority in their military planning, but British resistance to a direct thrust across the English Channel into France delayed a "second front" for two years. Meanwhile an invasion of Italy via North Africa and Sicily in 1943 proved no substitute.[1]

Captain Peyton Ward Williams wrote his parents in Ramer of seeing the bombing of a German bastion impeding the Allied drive on Rome—Monte Cassino. As German paratroops held the famous abbey in February 1944, "Big and little, our bombers came in steady, slow-seeming waves overhead, swinging over the mountains and hurriedly dumping their loads on the great white building. Suddenly there was no building but a great and growing cloud of dust through which you could see the individual bomb flashes."[2]

When Allied troops attacked up the slopes, the paratroopers came out of cellars and sent a torrent of fire from the ruins down on the advancing troops, like medieval defenders of a monastery on a hill pouring molten lead on besiegers climbing the walls on ladders. It was May before the citadel fell.[3]

In September 1943 the Americans and the British, pressured by Russian dictator Joseph Stalin, made a final agreement on a cross-channel invasion. Operation OVERLORD was scheduled for the late spring 1944. A massive buildup of personnel and material in England began. Men from the Montgomery area, who included parachute artillery (paratrooper) intelligence officer Captain Howard Upchurch, parachute infantry (paratrooper) private Henry Cotten, infantry private James Donald Godwin, and Private First Class Francis David Powell, army ranger, were part of the buildup.[4]

Godwin, eighteen, who preferred to be called Donald, arrived from the states as an infantry replacement in January 1944, eight months after his graduation from Lanier. He wrote home, "I'm stationed somewhere in southwest England. There's a town nearby but I haven't visited it yet. . . . The chow here is good, a lot better than some I had in the states." In February he became a part of a "band of brothers"— Headquarters Company, First Battalion, 116th Infantry Regiment, Twenty-ninth "Blue-Gray" Division, stationed at Salisbury; the Twenty-ninth had been the first large American ground forces combat unit to come to England in 1942. On March 1, Godwin wrote home, "I'll celebrate my 19th birthday in ten days, but it won't be much of a celebration. . . . I saw my first football game"—American style between two service teams—"in over a year last Sunday and I really enjoyed it." Baseball, however, was his favorite sport, as a spectator and as a participant.[5]

The last major military barrier to launching an invasion was German control of the air over Western and Central Europe. In the first three months of 1944, American fighter planes with enough range to fly deep into the Reich—the essential ingredient for victory in the air—arrived in increasing numbers at AAF bases in England. Fighter pilots such as Captain Paul Saffold of Montgomery accompanied the bombers on deep penetration missions. In February and March, two mighty air campaigns took place over Germany itself. When these had concluded, the Americans had wrested daytime air superiority from the Germans—a necessary precondition for a successful landing.[6]

The crucial air campaigns were costly to all participants, including the AAF. The names of Montgomerians appeared on the casualty rolls, and the telegram deliveries increased. An Eighth Air Force B-24 navigator, Second Lieutenant Homer Gentry, Jr., survived the first Ploesti mission only to die in 1944. The strain on affected Montgomery families was heavy. An Eighth Air Force pilot of a B-17, First Lieutenant Leonard Travis ("Tobie") Tobias, who had gone through preflight at Maxwell, flew on two missions to Berlin, on March 6 and 8. The mission of the sixth resulted in the loss of sixty-nine heavy bombers, the greatest number of American heavies shot down on any mission of the war. Tobias survived it. On the eighth, German air defenses brought down thirty-nine AAF bombers, almost half the number felled on the sixth, but Tobias's plane was among these losses. It went down over Magdeburg near Berlin on the return trip. Observers saw him clear the plane and watched his parachute open, but he was not seen afterward and was declared missing. No message of his presence in a prisoner-of-war camp came to comfort his family in Cloverdale for the duration.[7]

In the final phase of the preinvasion air offensive, low-level sweeps by long-range AAF fighters harassed transportation and other targets within the Reich, while the heavy bombers continued to strike Berlin and other deep targets. The panicky German high command began to pull back its fighters from airfields within range of the French channel coast to help defend the German homeland.[8]

A Montgomery airman in England not taking part in the

preinvasion air offensive, C-47 radio operator Sergeant Ralph Teague, twenty, waited for the big day by writing letters. He said little about his military life but instead, like a tourist, described historic sites visited in the British Isles. In Scotland he wrote his mother: "Never did I dream while studying at Sidney Lanier . . . that I'd be standing in [Robert] Burns's home."[9]

In March, Donald Godwin wrote his twelve-year-old niece Catherine ("Kitty") Johnston in Montgomery, "You're getting to be quite a young girl. So you have found you a new boy friend, eh. What's he like?" Godwin had no steady girlfriend. The caption under his 1943 senior class picture in the Sidney Lanier annual called him "Likeable" and "Quiet."[10]

On April 8 he apologized to Kitty for being late in writing again, but "believe me I haven't had the time until today." He could not tell her that his division, the Twenty-ninth "Blue and Gray" (for its shoulder patch), had been undergoing exhaustive training, for it was slated to be one of three American assault infantry divisions to land on the French Channel coast on the day of the invasion. He told her that the roasted peanuts his mother had mailed were "really swell." He had "sent home $70 last Thursday. I got tired of carrying around so much money." On May 9 he wrote home, "I'll be happy when this thing is over and it'll be . . . wonderful when I get home."[11]

On April 30, Alabama, which did not observe the national Memorial Day, had observed Confederate Memorial Day with an official holiday. In Montgomery, first capital of the Confederacy, white schoolchildren made wreaths to decorate the Confederate graves for a solemn ceremony in Oakwood Cemetery, which included the raising of a Confederate flag beside the U.S. flag and the playing of taps. In May three ministers in Montgomery criticized a group of nationally prominent clergymen and writers who had asked for modification of the Allied strategic bombing of German cities, calling the current air campaign "a carnival of death." The Alabama clergymen were resuming a debate that had begun in the summer of 1943 on the local level. On Flag Day, June 13, 1943, federal appeals judge Leon McCord, a Spanish-American War veteran, had told a crowd in front of the Elks Club,

"When you set mercy in front of justice, you mock and break faith with our boys who have died that you might still keep your freedom in this goodly land." Methodist Minister Dan Whitsett, one of the few dissenting voices locally, had answered him in the *Advertiser:* "Vengeance, hatred, and selfishness make an excellent foundation for war No. III," he wrote. "What would justice have done to Pilate and those who nailed Jesus to the cross? Yet Jesus prayed, 'Father forgive them.'"[12]

In answer to the attack on strategic bombing, the three Alabama clergymen, two from Montgomery and Methodist minister Dr. John Frazer from Opelika, addressed an interdenominational audience in Montgomery's First Baptist Church on May 1, 1944. Dr. Frank Tripp, the church's pastor, recently released from the army and with two daughters in the WAC, said that it was the first responsibility of each American to help win the war as soon as possible. Dr. Donald McGuire of the First Presbyterian Church stated that they were gathered to combat pacifism and complacency. He said that the first aim of their movement was to support "our country in accomplishing complete military victory of the Allied nations over Nazi Germany and Japan." Frazer declared, "The Church is at war. Let us who are not permitted the great honor of wearing the uniform keep faith with our men at the front."[13]

Captain Paul Saffold came back to his wife and mother in Montgomery at the end of May. A reporter for the *Advertiser* urged him to tell about his ninety-six missions as a P-47 pilot with the Eighth Air Force spanning the campaigns that gained air superiority and sent the fighters sweeping in low across the German landscape. The "fair-skinned, dreamy-eyed" young captain declined. When asked whether he might visit postwar Europe, he said, "I'll take Montgomery any day."[14]

The Montgomery to which he had returned was affected by the war wherever one looked. A letter to the *Advertiser* in January from Edgar Stuart, official of the Tan-Kar Oil Company, had charged that "black market operations in gasoline have become a very serious problem. Each day the service station operator is approached by some old customer who is trying to get gasoline illegally." The person "attempting to do this may be a very prominent man in the community, a lady of high principles, or a man who has served in the war." The situation had not changed.[15]

A technicolor musical war movie starring Hollywood's ranking "goddess," Rita Hayworth, played at the Paramount from June 4 through June 7. The dazzling beauty, a fine singer and dancer, costarred with Gene Kelly, also a superb dancer and a choreographer. The story was pleasing and trivial, but out of the picture came one of the memorable wartime songs, "Long Ago and Far Away." The Paramount was also the site of a weekly victory prayer meeting, begun in April 1942. A local minister or rabbi or a chaplain from Maxwell—all inevitably white—led the prayers of a segregated audience in support of the armed forces. Few blacks attended.[16]

On June 5, under the large headline "ROME IS CAPTURED," the *Advertiser* carried a war correspondent's account: "As we swept through the outskirts of the Eternal City we saw two dead doughboys lying by the side of the road. Their faces were covered by their jackets. Bunches of red poppies had been placed in their wax-colored hands."[17]

On June 6 the ships of the great invasion fleet were crossing the choppy water of the English Channel in the breaking dawn. The C-47 troop carriers bearing American paratroops had preceded them, flying across in the dark. The airborne force's mission was to seal off the Normandy beach code-named UTAH on the Cotentin Peninsula to prevent German reinforcements once the seaborne assault troops came ashore. The C-47 pilots were mainly new to combat and had first-time jitters. One of the green pilots was Second Lieutenant Harold K. Scarborough, a Lanier graduate, whose C-47 dropped its "stick" of paratroopers over the peninsula, surviving ground fire while flying low over enemy positions.[18]

Montgomerian Captain Howard Upchurch, an intelligence officer in a parachute artillery battalion, jumped into the dark. He was not seen alive again, his body found weeks after D-Day. At home in Montgomery with their two-year-old son, Howard, Jr., his wife endured first the agony of not knowing, then the certainty of loss.[19]

Major Wilson Pelham, whose mother lived on South Perry, jumped and descended in the dark. He landed on a patch of solid ground and managed to keep out of the marshy areas, where a number of paratroopers landed and were drowned, pulled under by their heavy equipment. Pelham moved about under enemy fire, adjusting his parachute infantry regiment's small arms and mortar volleys. He was awarded the Silver Star.[20]

Sergeant Henry Gates, twenty-two, a parachute infantryman from Montgomery County, jumped into the dark. He was wounded and taken prisoner but returned to his waiting mother at war's end.[21] Private Henry Cotten, twenty, also jumped into the dark. He was severely wounded in the fighting on the ground on June 6 and died of his wounds two weeks later. His mother, on Clayton Street, opened the dreaded War Department telegrams, the first about his wounds, the second about her son's death. Each time it was her job to tell his wife.[22] Sergeant Ralph Teague was preoccupied with the radio on a C-47. After unloading the paratroopers and returning to England, his C-47 towed a glider with reinforcements.[23]

The landing craft bearing the assault troops had pushed away from the transports and headed toward the beaches on a restless sea under gray sky. Casualties on UTAH beach were relatively light. It was a different story at the beach code named OMAHA, wreathed in fog and gunsmoke. Shells hit some of the craft. Survivors struggled in the water. William McMillan, twenty-five, whose mother lived on Mildred Street, was a boatswain's mate on a Coast Guard cutter. He helped fish out of the sea those who had not drowned. When Captain Jim Levy, then from Birmingham and later a Montgomerian, came ashore with his mortar team, he had, he would recall, "almost a detached feeling about it. It wasn't happening to me. I didn't really feel a part of it." Yet he earned the Bronze Star for his leadership on the epic day.[24]

Private Donald Godwin, nineteen, was among the assault troops of the first wave who scrambled over the lowered ramps of the landing craft and waded into the water where bullets ringed them with miniature geysers. Acute fear made them want to drop down or turn back. But they had been told to "keep going, keep going," and the "band of brothers" psychology helped stave off fear. The noise grew deafening. Many of the troops slumped in the water, turning it red where the waves lapped at the sand. Many more dropped on the beach. Some had limbs sheared off; others were decapitated. Godwin reached the beach before joining the band of corpses on the sand. His regiment, the 116th, sustained the most casualties of any Allied infantry regiment on D-Day.[25]

Private First Class Francis David Powell, nineteen, army ranger, was killed in action at OMAHA beach. One of three Montgomery brothers in the armed forces, he had at fifteen lied about his age to enter the service in 1939. Corporal Robert Williamson, twenty-three, an alumnus of Lanier, was one of the rangers landing at OMAHA whose task it was to scale the cliff of the Pointe-Du-Hoc straight up, to silence some heavy guns reported to be in a clifftop bunker. He was seriously wounded. The two Montgomerians were among 150 of the 200 elite rangers who landed on June 6 to die or suffer wounds. The guns proved to have been removed to a wooded area inland.[26]

Montgomerian Warrant Officer James Tucker, an army engineer, called up with the Alabama National Guard in 1940, acted under pressure when the assault troops were pinned down on the beach. His Bronze Star citation recorded how he "in the face of sporadic artillery, mortar, and small arms fire . . . personally led his crew onto the invasion beach and supervised the removal of numerous obstacles." Another engineer officer, First Lieutenant Richard Harris, son of a Montgomery physician (and later a physician himself), led his detail to clear a path through a minefield, so that tanks could move in from landing ship tanks and aim counter fire at the enemy above. He received a Silver Star.[27]

It was hours before the bodies could be covered, legs protruding, with shelter halves or blankets. Normandy fishermen came down to the beach to stare and place flowers on some of the corpses. Four decades later their overall ground commander, General Omar Bradley, wrote, "Every man who set foot on Omaha Beach that day was a hero."[28]

First Lieutenant Clement Clapp, Eighth Air Force B-17 navigator, originally from Monroeville, had become a Montgomerian. On the sixth his plane flew to bomb enemy gun emplacements behind the Normandy beaches. Later he told an interviewer in Montgomery: "The invasion is something I'll never forget. . . . We could see the ocean and the beaches. Battleships, cargo ships, and landing barges made the ocean black. There were thousands of them everywhere. The beaches were crawling with Allied troops who had landed and those still coming ashore." With air superiority over the landing area, they were safe from an aerial assault that could have driven them back into the sea with many times the losses.[29]

At dawn on June 6 in Montgomery, it was 71 degrees, and the temperature increased to 90 degrees by the afternoon. The humidity was rising, and the sky was clear. The regular edition of the *Advertiser,* already thrown onto lawns and porches or on newsstands by 5:00 A.M., had a compelling but tentative headline citing a Nazi news source that had announced an Allied landing on the coast of France.[30]

Norma Jean Somerset, Lanier class of '43, recalled half a century later: "My father, Clyde Somerset, who was the bookkeeper and office manager of the Dr. Pepper Bottling Company, always arose early and read the newspaper before he went to work. On that particular day, he awoke everybody in the family with the news of the invasion." They discussed it at the breakfast table. Her father "thought it was the light at the end of the tunnel."[31]

Not long afterward, special bulletins broadcast over WSFA and WCOV confirmed a landing. Soon the *Advertiser* put newsboys on the downtown streets, shouting, "Extra! Read all about it. Allies invade France!" The extra proclaimed "ALLIES STORM ACROSS CHANNEL; LAND IN FORCE ON FRENCH COAST."[32]

The news could be read in some people's faces. The extras quickly left the newsboys' hands, and a few purchasers reacted with obvious emotion. A "woman bound for one of the Army air fields here," reported the *Journal* that afternoon, "began crying as she grabbed a paper. She didn't even read the headlines, but clutched the paper tightly and walked away." Merchants downtown opened their places of business earlier than usual. Not long after 9:00 A.M., American flags began to be unfurled along downtown sidewalks. All in all, the reaction was restrained, as though most people could not fully grasp what had taken place.[33]

A salesman commented: "The full impact of the thing hasn't hit people yet. If it had happened during the day and casualties were heavy, I'd imagine the scene on the streets might have been different." The heavy casualties were censored. At the Veterans Administration Hospital the patients and staff paused at 1:00 P.M. to observe three minutes of silent meditation over the struggle of the new veterans in the making. Veterans of the trenches in the Great War had a sense of the events taking place for the second time in France. Grace Hall Warner driving home from her downtown job was filled with hope because the day had come closer when her husband, A. H. Warner, and her brothers, Jack and Dick Hall, would be coming home to stay.[34]

At 5:00 P.M., according to prearranged plans, police halted traffic downtown. Buglers from Maxwell, Gunter, Hurt Military Academy, and Sidney Lanier sounded the "Call to the Colors." In the neighborhoods sirens called for a moment of silence as police halted traffic on main thoroughfares. The moment hushed most of the city. Then bugles and sirens sounded the end of silence, and traffic moved again. The only businesses slated to stay open after the ceremony were drugstores and theaters.[35]

Picture shows, with only a few viewers as usual on a weekday, stopped the projectors at 6:00 P.M. so that the audience could say a prayer. All sporting events were postponed. At 6:00 P.M. churches over the city were open for brief services and individual prayer. At some attendance was sparse; at others, overflowing.[36]

At Maxwell the troops were assembled in recreation halls or day rooms. They saw ribbons on wall maps stretched across the English Channel to the Normandy coast. Interest was intense, but a calmness prevailed.[37]

A small but serious drama at Gunter diverted the attention of personnel for several hours. At midmorning Aviation Cadet Lawrence Harleston had taken off for his solo in the basic phase of his flight training. As he was preparing to land, his radio informed him that only one wheel was down. Harleston circled the field for two hours, trying futilely to lower the wheel. When most of his gas was gone, an officer in the control tower "talked" the cadet through the procedure of parachuting when his plane was over rural terrain. Harleston floated down safely into a cotton field.[38]

The city would be affected in ways large and small by the launching of the "Great Crusade," as the Supreme Allied Commander General Dwight Eisenhower had termed the invasion in speaking to his troops. But Wednesday, June 7, was a workday and a school day, and most people went to sleep focused on these realities.[39]

The *Advertiser* on the seventh attempted to put things in perspective: "The beginning of the redemption of the conquered lands of Europe is a moment which all the world has waited for. . . . The men who fall today and tomorrow along the Channel beaches are buying victory and peace and security for the rest of the world. The time for rejoicing will come presently when the torch of peace lights the skies over darkened Europe and Asia."[40]

On D-Day plus three, a black Montgomerian, Corporal Henry P. Harvest, landed on OMAHA beach as a member of the 362nd Quartermaster Battalion. His unit's job was to get supplies into the hands of combat troops. With the lodgment expanding, he became a part of what was now the campaign to liberate France.[41]

Montgomerians at home witnessed several war-related campaigns in the city as the summer grew steamier and hotter. The number of servicemen at Maxwell, many with families, had soared with the advent of a new type of training. In 1944 transitional training was offered to pilots assigned for the first time to fly B-24 heavy bombers. The new training was preceded by an expansion of facilities at Maxwell that increased civilian employment opportunities and drew more civilians from outside. The removal of the preflight school elsewhere in November did little to compensate for the recent rise in population, especially as it affected the city, for cadets had been forbidden to live off base, whether with spouses or parents or in a group of peers.[42]

The struggle for housing had commenced soon after Pearl Harbor, then had waned following an appeal by base and municipal authorities asking Montgomerians to open their spare rooms and make available apartments and houses for rent to service people. At first children had been generally unwelcome, but this problem had seemed to ease. An ad in the *Advertiser* for June 5 now dared to ask for "a furnished apartment, 3 or more rooms" for "Officer, wife and 2 year-old baby." Landlords soon proved once again reluctant to accept tenants with children.[43]

Mixed reactions to military and civilian war-worker tenants emerged under the pressure of increased housing needs. In a letter to the *Advertiser,* an anonymous Montgomery woman told of renting her home to a military couple with children when she took her own children to be near her army officer husband stationed in Ohio. Finding no one there who would rent to her because of the children, she returned to Montgomery to discover that her tenants had allowed their children to crayon the walls; jump up and down on overstuffed furniture, breaking the springs; and spill food and drink on the dining room table, which had to be refinished. The experience helped her understand why many people refused to rent to couples with children.[44]

Renters usually blamed the OPA rather than children. R. H. Pippin of West Street in Oak Park complained that "the terrible conditions of the housing situation . . . [are] caused by the fact that people who own property cannot realize a fair return on their investment." The result was that many with rental property preferred not to offer it for rent. It was also objected that rent controls were unreasonable, that requirements for renting were impractical, and that inspectors were rude.[45]

The housing shortage reached crisis proportions as the summer of 1944 neared an end. A sudden rush to sell by owners of houses and apartments meant that existing tenants were threatened with eviction. With the approach of September 1, the usual annual date for signing or renewing leases, the prospect that an estimated 500 families would find housing appeared slim. Most of those facing eviction were long-time tenants.[46]

The city had grown from 78,000 in 1939 to 95,000, but new housing was designated specifically for use by in-migrant war workers. Contractors who wished to build this housing had to stand in the priority line.[47]

Profit was not always the motive for housing transactions. Mrs. Herbert Spencer, who had rented a house, provided an example: "I've lived at 1137 South Lawrence for four years. A lady who used to live out in the country bought this house because she couldn't get enough gas to come to the city." Unable to find an affordable apartment for herself and her two children, Spencer told a reporter, "After 17 years I guess I'll have to go home to mother [in] . . . Russellville, Alabama."[48]

Advocates of the homeless and potentially homeless stepped forward. The *Advertiser*'s renowned cartoonist "Spang" depicted a GI with wife, small daughter, and baby sadly passing a house that advertised rooms for rent but "No Children."[49]

Katherine Cassidy, director of the USO's Travelers Aid Bureau, bluntly ascribed blame for the crisis: "The first to call the Travelers Aid Bureau and ask if they can help ease the room shortage are those people in the low income brackets. . . . Our better off families either don't care or don't feel it their duty to aid the distressed." Her criticism brought angry reactions but also some positive results. Various people who were "better off" called her to confess that they had been unaware of the crisis and to offer rental property to Cassidy's clients. Cassidy disagreed with a move by the airfields' authorities to discourage military people assigned to Maxwell and Gunter from moving their families to Montgomery. "Every wife," she said, "has a right to be with her husband, especially when she knows she may never see him again. If they have a child, they have a right to have their child with them."[50]

The Pilot, Rotary, and Lions Clubs started a drive in August to pressure the OPA into removing rent ceilings and ending the restriction on new housing units to in-migrant war workers. The drive failed in its stated objectives but contributed to an increase in authorizations for new defense housing, which would act to remove some in-migrant workers from the competition for older housing.[51]

After September 1, "moving day," 100 families remained without a place to live. Real estate agents and firms, the Chamber of Commerce, and billeting officers at the fields joined forces to find rental housing for those in need. The crisis faded temporarily.[52]

Taxi drivers feasted on military and civilians. Their reputation had not improved even after the crackdown on "weekend" taxis, yet their power rose as more and more private cars joined the junkyards. Just before D-Day, public and official animosity toward taxis surged because of an increase in "gouging." Chief King vowed to step up enforcement of the ordinance banning overcharging. After D-Day, the Civitan Club joined the crusade, devising a plan for dealing with "rogue taxis." It would require drivers to display IDs inside the cabs (with convicted felons and dishonorably discharged service people prohibited from driving cabs) and to display in full view of passengers a zoning chart with charges fixed by city ordinance. Hailed by public and police, the plan became in July part of the municipal modus operandi.[53]

Both civilians and military personnel began reporting specific instances of gouging to police, and convictions in police court increased, with fines as high as $100. Papers gave a big play to one such fine, levied for charging a serviceman $2 to take him from the bus station on Lee to the Dexter Hotel, a prescribed $0.50 fare. The taxis trouble subsided but did not disappear. The problems with wartime taxis and housing were largely confined to whites. There were few black cabs, and the war did not change a tradition of official aloofness to black housing deficiencies.[54]

On the racial front, six days after the invasion of Normandy, Arthur Madison "invaded" the county courthouse once more. Although disbarred and soon to leave the state, he led a group of blacks to the office of the registrar of voters. Though the group was smaller than in his first such effort, a few of the more prominent members were registered. This incident ended the first modern black voting rights drive in the Montgomery area, but later black voter drives would build on the momentum generated by Madison's leadership.[55]

Another headline-grabbing event the same month as the Esther Drew murder took place at night on June 24. It involved violence and race. City bus driver R. B. Pruitt, trying to break up an altercation among black passengers at a stop on the Washington Park run, was attacked and knifed. An ambulance took him in critical condition to St. Margaret's. Police questioning of witnesses led to accusations against three black soldiers stationed at Maxwell. With the cooperation of the base provost marshal, local police took the three to St. Margaret's. There Pruitt identified two of the men as his attackers, and the police then brought the three back to Maxwell.[56]

Agreement that the accused would be returned to the post guardhouse may have been part of an accord between the city and the airfields discussed in mid-1942. Agreement or not, solicitor Temple Seibels requested that the three men be handed over to civil jurisdiction for trial in circuit court. The acrimony seen in the summer of 1942 resurfaced. Seibels conducted a round of conferences with the Maxwell post commander, Colonel R. E. L. Choate, who recommended to the War Department that the soldiers be tried by court-martial. Seibels then appealed to the War Department, stating that "the negroes would be duly tried, fairly tried, and decently tried." He was informed that "the War Department has concurred in the [post commander's] recommendation."[57]

On October 2 and 3, 1944, the court-martial took place at Maxwell. No representative of the press or other civilian could attend who did not appear as a witness. Pruitt had recovered sufficiently to testify that Private Pontius Flowers was his actual attacker. The court found Flowers guilty and sentenced him to be dishonorably discharged from the army and to serve twelve years at hard labor. The other two soldiers were acquitted.[58]

A War Department mandate in August 1944 intensified discord with local officials and disturbed state officials as well. It decreed that certain eating facilities on army bases were henceforth to be desegregated. Black troops and white troops, however, were not to be integrated in mess halls. Local post authorities interpreted the order as covering only the post exchange cafeteria. Mere rumor of the decree brought from Maxwell and Gunter by white employees touched off a chain reaction of alarm and challenge within the state. Governor Sparks immediately sent a telegram to President Roosevelt protesting the order, fearing it might be extended to include base transportation and recreational facilities such as swimming pools.[59]

The usually moderate editorial voice of the *Advertiser* began by echoing the majority of state newspapers: "Montgomery, a tolerant, liberal, and intensely patriotic city, . . . quickly, firmly, and advisedly wants to let it be known that any efforts designed, directly or indirectly, to impose any form of social equality is something neither this community nor any other Southern community can tolerate." Thus "Army orders, even armies, even bayonets, cannot enforce impossible and unnatural social race relations upon us." Except for the characterization of Montgomery, the editorial to this point might have been composed by Judge Jones. But the judge would likely not have endorsed the rest of the commentary, in which the editor insisted, "We want the Negro soldiers to have the same food, the same pay, the same uniform, the same courts, and the same kind of justice and the same protection as the white race" but no "social equality."[60]

In reply, the War Department told Sparks that it was "not an appropriate medium for effecting social readjustments but has insisted that all soldiers, regardless of race, be afforded equal opportunity to enjoy the recreational facilities which are provided at posts, camps, and stations. . . . Men who are fulfilling the same obligations, suffering the same dislocation of their private lives and wearing the identical uniform should, within the confines of the military establishment, have the same privileges for rest and relaxation." The War Department confirmed that the circular's immediate objective was the post exchange cafeteria.[61]

There were no subsequent upheavals or serious episodes of racially motivated violence at the two Montgomery bases. Any smaller disturbances that might have stemmed from the War Department circular were not reported in the local papers or recorded in available official records. Given the lack of fireworks, it seems likely that only a few blacks, military or civilian, took advantage of their newly granted right. Apparently none tried to desegregate the post theaters or swimming pools. Nonetheless, like the voter registration drive, a desegregation order itself was a harbinger of the future.[62]

Atticus Mullin's column "The Passing Throng" in the *Advertiser* was widely popular in Montgomery. He had a down home approach enlivened by interviews with passing individuals on the street, politicians, businessmen, and service people on leave or stationed in Montgomery. Mullin was free with his opinions about such topics as the conduct of the war and matters of race. Concerning the War Department circular, he commented, "Roosevelt is chuckling almost audibly over protests from the South about his race equality orders at military camps. . . . It merely made the Roosevelts stronger with the negro vote in the North."[63]

For distraction from unpleasantness at home, Montgomerians always had the option of reading about the shooting war. Sometimes the papers carried informative tidbits. Montgomerian AAF staff sergeant Nathan Glick was in London on June 13 when the first of the Nazi "revenge" weapons, the V-1 cruise missile, was "caught in . . . [the searchlights'] glare." He said that the "appearance of the 'planes' reminded me of those little model planes we used in aircraft recognition." The missiles were swallowed in darkness, but one of the explosions killed the first of thousands of English civilians who would fall victim to the V-1 and later to its swifter, unseen, and more deadly fellow missile the V-2 rocket. Another Montgomerian in London, AAF first lieutenant Willie Estes, described the V-1's trajectory and sound: "They came in at 1,000 feet and you listened for their motors like the putt-putt of an outboard motor to cut out. If they do, you've got exactly fifteen seconds to find you a hole—or the robot bomb will make you one."[64]

Sometimes realism was given a poetic touch. One of Montgomery's contributions to the Red Cross was Harriet Englehardt, who had come to France several weeks after D-Day. On August 27, as the Allied drive to the Low Countries and German border was reaching a climax, she wrote to Margaret Booth, her old teacher: "Please don't worry about your France. The war has injured France, but it has not changed it; France will heal. Little gnarled men in sabots still clatter down the cobblestones. . . .There's hay the color of honey piled high in great wheeled blue carts." And "even where the tops of houses have been shelled off, geraniums bloom in the windows and little boys in their checkered smocks tumble out of the doors. Lunch in Cherbourg the other day was characteristic of French food—chock full of onions, herbs, and imagination, really exciting."[65]

Her "home" was "a bed-roll, a canteen, and a helmet, wherever we happen to stop our truck." "Sometimes," Englehardt wrote, "we live in a field, or a barn or a chateau; or, as in Normandy, under a lovely, lovely apple tree," and "often wake in the morning to find ourselves surrounded by smiling old women, offering us hampers of beautiful fresh eggs. . . . The naughty Frenchmen throw kisses to the American girls." But "with something so huge as mass murder at the front and Freedom and Liberation all around, one wants a bit of thought and concentration."[66]

Sometimes a combat veteran could insert a realistic passage in his letter home that would survive the censors. Glider pilot Julius Forest Wade wrote his mother in Montgomery about taking part in Operation DRAGOON, the invasion of Southern France on August 15. With a load of American glider-borne infantry, "in a few moments I could see the plane pulling me leave the ground, and I knew then when I hit the ground again I would be in combat behind enemy lines." As they entered French airspace, tracers streaked up, but none hit them. Julius cut loose at 1,000 feet and circled: "I will never forget the few minutes between the time I cut loose from the plane and that when the glider came to a stop on the ground . . . with a 'small crash.'" It shook up the troops but caused no serious injuries. "It was awful and I hope I will never have to do it again." He did not tell her that there was a high casualty rate from trees and other obstacles to a glider's safe landing.[67]

Fierce battles were taking place in the Pacific in the summer and fall of 1944. In June, with island-hopping in the Central Pacific having reached the Marianas, U.S. Marines invaded the island of Saipan. The Japanese home islands were now within flight range of a new AAF very heavy bomber, the Boeing B-29. Like other marines, Captain Robert Sternenberg had come a long way to reach Saipan. In 1943 he left his wife, Erin, and his son, William, in Montgomery when he went overseas with his artillery battalion, first to Hawaii, where the men spent weeks in training, then into combat on a small island in the Gilberts, where the resistance was light. Afterward came the invasion of Guam in the Marianas, where the resistance was heavy. Sternenberg's battalion had few losses until Saipan, where it suffered 50 percent casualties. Sternenberg was fortunate to be in the surviving half and lived to return safely to his wife and son. The less fortunate included Private First Class Paul Bayne of the marine infantry, who was killed on Saipan. Months later the postman delivered a letter from Bayne's company commander to his mother, Nell Bayne, on Sayre Street. Paul "had knocked out one enemy machine gun nest and was preparing to fire on another when he was hit and instantly killed by an enemy rifleman." (The word "instantly" was automatically used in these letters from commanders.) "Your son is buried in the Fourth Marine Division's cemetery on Saipan Island, alongside other brave Marines who gave their lives for their country."[68]

Navy captain John Crommelin, of the famed Montgomery/ Wetumpka family, helped to direct carrier operations in support of the Saipan landing. He was already legendary. In November 1943, after his light carrier received a fatal torpedo hit, he had hastily left a shower stall to come naked on deck, where he calmly directed the abandoning of the ship. In June 1944, his carrier division took part in one of the most one-sided air-to-air combat engagements of the Pacific War, as two carrier task forces pitted their planes against one another over the open waters of the Philippine Sea. In what became known in American naval lore as "the Marianas Turkey Shoot," U.S. carrier planes destroyed some 400 Japanese planes with small losses of their own, crippling Japan's ability to wage offensive air-to-air combat over the sea.[69]

Late in June, Peyton Mathis, Sr., owner of the Montgomery Marble Works, had a telephone call from Evelyn, his daughter-in-law in San Antonio. She read from a telegram: "We beg to advise that your husband, Major Peyton Mathis, Jr. has been killed in action." Peyton, Jr., had been the commanding officer of an AAF night fighter squadron at the height of MacArthur's triumph in New Guinea. Telephone wires between Texas and Alabama shrank the distance as the family members spoke of their grief.[70]

Second Lieutenant Fred Burks from Mount Meigs sailed for the South Pacific in the late summer of 1944, a member of the Ninety-third Infantry Division's quartermaster company. A long voyage on a troop transport was, he later recalled, "like an adventure to me." Toward the end of the journey his ship picked up a destroyer escort in an area where Japanese submarines were known to hunt. At some point the destroyer dropped depth charges, getting "everyone's attention." They soon put into port at Guadalcanal. There his division staged for combat for several months. Two of the division's quartermaster platoons, including Burks's supply unit, were sent north to Bougainville in the Solomons as part of a regimental combat team. They came ashore from landing craft and immediately pitched tents. The job of the combat team was to capture some Japanese who remained in the thick undergrowth. One of Burks's friends in a cavalry reconnaissance troop was wounded by sniper fire. Ironically, a friend from Mount Meigs, Robert Coprich of the mainly black Twenty-fifth Infantry Regiment, had been killed in the taking of the island earlier in 1944. Burks saw only a few Japanese prisoners of war and some skeletons of Japanese soldiers. A few weeks later his combat team landed on the Treasury Islands, just south of Bougainville, where it encountered no Japanese. Burks was promoted to first lieutenant.[71]

WAVE pharmacist mate Marguerite Sherlock, after finishing boot camp in June, soon saw evidence of the fighting in the Pacific. She was assigned to a naval hospital at Camp Lejeune, North Carolina, as a laboratory technician and was present when a hospital train arrived filled with wounded marines. All hands had to assist with unloading the patients and placing them in beds on the wards. The men seemed incredibly young.[72]

As the war raged on, and as war-influenced disagreements and problems ebbed and flowed or persisted on the home front, war weariness and a concomitant decline in patriotic fervor began to be noticed early in 1944. These feelings lingered, stoked by newspapers' hints of early

Marguerite Sherlock, WAVE
pharmacist mate. *Courtesy of
Marguerite Sherlock.*

victory. The hints also contributed to official overoptimism. Several
months before the Normandy Invasion, Montgomery business execu-
tives met to plan for postwar business activities. This type of meeting
occurred sporadically before there was any real justification.[73]

An alarming trend in a key indicator of patriotic fervor began several months before D-Day when there was a dropoff in volunteers to
prepare Red Cross surgical bandages. The shortage had worsened by
August. On August 30, a reporter for the *Advertiser* stated that "there
is nothing glamorous in sitting at the Beauvoir Country Club making
surgical dressings these days. . . . The ladies just don't come around
much any more. . . . The Beauvoir unit has dwindled to two or three
pairs of hands." He tried a little vinegar: "Instead of folding the dress-

ings, the volunteers appear to have literally folded up themselves." In part, he conjectured, the decline had come about with "the weather turning warmer," and in part with the newspapers' proclaiming "the war about won" as a result of D-Day and the drive across France. In July the local Red Cross chapter had received a copy of a letter in which an army officer overseas told his mother that surgical bandages were being washed, sterilized, and reused because of a shortage. Mrs. Sidney Coleman, director of the chapter's surgical dressing units, warned that unless volunteering picked up, the field hospitals overseas might have to wash and reuse all bloody bandages.[74]

Old volunteers and new recruits responded but not in the large numbers of earlier days. A particularly effective ad of September 26, sponsored by some of the city's best known and least known businesses, carried the headline "The Wounded Need Your Help!" It carried the photographs and names of the women producing bandages at the city centers and at Maxwell.[75]

Other problems cropped up in the same period. The quota for Red Cross kit bags, so popular with service people departing for overseas destinations, went unmet until appeals brought more willing hands. The nurse's aide class scheduled for November 10 had to be postponed when only one volunteer came forward. It was the first time such a class had had to be delayed. A registered nurse commented, "We just couldn't get all our work done without nurse's aides. They carry water, take pulse, temperatures and respiration, give baths, chaperon doctor's examinations." She asked, "You know who my nurse's aides are? One is Mrs. J. Frank Swift, who some times works here all day. She lost a son in France."[76]

Some other Red Cross volunteers kept the faith. At the Veterans Administration Hospital, by late 1944, wounded and injured former servicemen in the ongoing war had joined the veterans of 1898 and 1918. On Thanksgiving, Gray Ladies led by Gypsy Oliver came to cheer up all the veterans, bringing along Staff Sergeant Jerry Yelverton and the Maxwell Field Rhythmaires. The Red Cross Motor Corps women brought twenty Huntingdon College coeds. Some of the vets, young and old, began dancing in their pajamas and gray-striped bathrobes. A reporter from the *Advertiser* was there: "Someone called for a square dance. The old timers grabbed the girls and led them through a square dance. The young vets joined in. Then the jitterbugs went to work. Lads who months ago 'got theirs' in the Pacific or France were dancing for the first time since being wounded. Even those in wheel chairs who'll never walk or dance again jerked their bodies, beat their hands in time with the music."[77]

Disabled veterans of the Great War had received limited disability and vocational benefits. Granted a small bonus in 1924 in the form of bonds payable in 1945, World War I veterans had staged a "Bonus March" in Washington in 1932, during the height of the depression, to pressure the government into permitting them to cash their bonds immediately. Troops had dispersed the marchers, but in 1936 the government gave in and allowed immediate cashing of the bonds. The veterans averaged $1,500 apiece.[78]

In June 1944 Congress passed and FDR signed a "GI Bill of Rights," legislation to ensure that the post–World War I experience would not be repeated. The law dealt with education, home loans, and other benefits. Discharged veterans were to receive mustering-out pay of $300 and a readjustment allowance of $20 a week for fifty-two weeks. By the end of the war, corollary legislation ensured that injured and wounded veterans would receive liberal pensions on a sliding scale that reflected the nature of the disability.[79]

Major General Walter Weaver died from a heart condition in Walter Reed Hospital in October 1944. Bad news from overseas reached local families almost daily. In October, Dorothy Ghent Moore received the dreaded yellow telegram at home on Cloverdale Road. Her husband, Major John T. Moore, a fighter ace and group commander, was missing in action. He had failed to return to his New Guinea base from a mission over the Dutch East Indies as Douglas MacArthur began his thrust toward the Philippines.[80]

Fred Burks had been on New Guinea in the last phase of the MacArthur and Australian victory, but his unit saw no action. His regimental combat team then went to Morotai in the Moluccas, Dutch East Indies, where it helped to flush out Japanese from the bush. Japanese planes dropped a few bombs, but the explosions were not close enough to alarm Burks. With the danger almost gone, Bob Hope brought in his USO show to entertain the Ninety-third Division troops.[81]

In October, Douglas MacArthur returned to the Philippines. The Ninety-third was not among the U.S. troops that landed on Leyte on the twentieth. A great naval battle developed in Leyte Gulf. The Japanese objective was to obliterate the beachhead. The battle went back and forth, but in the end the Japanese fleet was virtually eliminated as an effective force.[82]

Most Montgomerians who were involved in the Philippine campaign lived to tell about it. Navy captain William David Johnson brought his escort carrier safely through heavy fire, receiving the Navy Cross for bravery and the Purple Heart for shrapnel wounds. Some men did not live to tell about it. Army infantry private first class Robert Bailey was killed in December, in the furious Japanese resistance during the drive from the Leyte beachhead. Army infantry private William Collins, wounded on Leyte, later told of Filipino bravery from his ward in the army's Northington General Hospital in Tuscaloosa. Children had taken risks to point out where the Japanese snipers hid.[83]

The Philippines invasion came at a time when Allied momentum had ebbed in Western Europe after the retaking of Paris, the pushing of Germans from much of Belgium, and the penetration of the western edges of the Reich. The plan of Field Marshal Sir Bernard Montgomery for flanking the principal German defenses seemed to offer hope for early victory. In September, in Holland, a British army drove toward the lower Rhine, while Allied paratroops dropped to clear the way. A British airborne division seized but could not hold the key bridge—that spanning the Rhine at Arnhem—upon which all else depended. "The summer's optimism has suddenly given way before spreading pessimism," editorialized the *Advertiser* in October 1944, "as the armies of free nations run up against determined German efforts to save the homeland."[84]

The Philippine landing preserved the illusion at home that V-Day was near. By early winter, this illusion was underscored by the spreading war weariness. Black market and other illegal activity became more audacious. On December 1 the OPA suspended a white Montgomery filling station operator on Bell Street from pumping gas for seven days and put him on probation for sixty days. He had failed to keep required records and had accepted gas coupons before their due date. At the same time, a black janitor at OPA headquarters had stolen almost a thousand gas coupons from his place of employment.[85]

The fall offered Montgomerians opportunities for diversion from negative war news. While Alabama State had continued its football program, Auburn and Alabama had suspended theirs for the 1943 season. The white universities brought the sport back in 1944. With the restoration of this alternative religion, could peace be far behind? Another favorite sport, the presidential election, also offered entertainment. FDR, with Harry S. Truman as his new running mate, swept to a fourth term over Republican challenger Thomas E. Dewey in November. The Democrats had no problems in Alabama. In the same general election, patriotism edged out racism with the adoption of an amendment to the state constitution that exempted veterans of foreign wars from the poll tax, but it was a limited victory for democracy.[86]

A decline in war bond purchases was another index of the optimism that the war would soon end. As the sixth war loan drive cranked up in the fall, Atticus Mullin wrote that "treasury officials are expecting more complacency . . . than . . . in the other five drives due to the belief that victory is just around the corner." In October, holders for the first time were able to cash in their war bonds at local banks without having to go first through a Federal Reserve bank. For a short time the banks had long lines of bond cashers. After the sixth drive began in November, the *Advertiser* reported that "one of Montgomery's firemen using his free time to sell bonds, went into one of the banks this week to purchase bonds for several of his customers and was disgusted to see other men and women in the act of cashing bonds."[87]

The Negro Division of the sixth drive urged blacks to attend a rally in November at the Dexter Avenue Baptist Church. The turnout was respectable but nowhere near the peak attendance during the fourth drive. A speaker reported that Montgomery blacks had thus far in the war purchased a million dollars' worth of stamps and bonds. But it had become progressively tougher for the nation as a whole to meet quotas by the deadline.[88]

As forecast, the sixth drive was especially difficult. The drive began on November 20, with a deadline of December 16. As the deadline approached the drive was so far behind that the *Advertiser* printed a front page editorial on December 14: "The time has come for plain talk. The Sixth War Loan Quotas of this district are not being met. . . . There appears to be a likelihood that Alabama's magnificent record will be broken. Never before has an Alabama county failed to meet an assigned war bond quota." Then the editor threw his Sunday punch: "If you are one of those who think the war is 'just about over,' remember the American soldier who may die . . . doesn't quite understand that if he is willing to risk his life why you decline to lend your dollars. Wake up, Alabamians! We are at war!"[89]

He struck squarely at the apathy of many who had held back, but it was not enough to prevent Montgomery County from being behind in all categories by the official deadline, December 16. The time was extended two weeks, as it had been for other drives. For the first time the E bond category met its quota before the others reached theirs. This fact showed that the editorial's message had moved hoi polloi more than it had Montgomery's more prosperous residents.[90]

By the extended deadline all categories of the drive were subscribed throughout Alabama. Despite the discouraging sales during the early stages, toward the end support for the sixth war loan drive picked up significantly. The Battle of the Bulge, which began the same day that the sixth drive's extension started, may well have acted to spare the state and Montgomery County as well from an embarrassing end to the sixth drive. The chief motivation for the last-minute surge was likely fear.[91]

9

From the Bulge to Victory in Europe

(Left) Infantry Private First Class Neal Howard, U.S. Army, November 1944, and (right) Private First Class William "Billy" Robinson (far right of the three GIs), U.S. Army combat engineer, during a lull in the Battle of the Bulge. *Courtesy of William Howard and Paul Robinson, respectively.*

When Montgomerians in the army left the ports of embarkation for Europe after D-Day, their mental picture of what lay ahead was conditioned by newsreels and *Why We Fight,* the Frank Capra documentary series shown in basic training. The film's images kindled no real fear but only a momentary interest and in some instances a stirring of apprehension. Southern military tradition inspired in some a "let me at 'em" attitude. But films, newsreels, and picture shows were not the same as flesh and blood.[1]

Some men flew to a combat zone. AAF second lieutenant Kalman Shwarts, a navigator, a graduate of the University of Alabama, and a former employee of Klein Jewelers, flew with a B-17 replacement crew to join the Eighth Air Force in the summer of 1944. He left his wife, Gloria, and his baby son in Montgomery. Shwarts, by coincidence the brother-in-law of another AAF navigator, Captain Louis Haas, was soon off on the first of twenty-seven missions against German targets. He was eventually promoted to first lieutenant and survived to bring home a Distinguished Flying Cross after several narrow escapes from flak and German fighters. Private First Class Bobby Young, nineteen, an Eagle Scout, went by sea on June 22, leaving behind a girlfriend in North Carolina. He sailed on *Queen Elizabeth,* one of the prewar luxury liners, in the company of troops such as those in his heavy artillery battalion. On the same vessel was the Glenn Miller AAF dance band, which General Dwight Eisenhower had in May requested be sent to England to bolster troop morale in the pending invasion of France. Miller had already flown to England to prepare for the band's arrival.[2]

Miller had formed his musical unit at Yale University in 1943 three months after his departure from Maxwell. The other band members were all former name band musicians. Miller's band became famous for its sprightly and sometimes controversial march music for AAF cadets at Yale and for broadcasts from CBS in New York City, called "I Sustain the Wings."[3]

On board *Queen Elizabeth,* the musicians practiced in the ballroom and gave concerts to military audiences. Attendance at these sessions was limited. Each soldier was given a pass of a certain color that would admit him to a particular session. Bobby Young and buddies "counterfeited" passes in order to hear the band play more than once. On deck Young watched the blue sky, the dark water, and the whitecaps of a relatively calm sea. *Queen Elizabeth* was too swift for submarines and torpedoes. She docked in Scotland on June 28.[4]

The heavy artillery battalion trained in Wales until August, when it shipped across the channel on landing ship tanks. The personnel landed on OMAHA beach and the equipment on UTAH beach. Except for wrecked landing craft remaining from D-Day, the beaches were virtually clean. Reunited with their eight-inch guns, the artillerymen became part of the liberation of France. In September, with Allied penetration into the edge of the Reich, Bobby's battalion set up its batteries north of Aachen, the first German city of any size to fall to the Allies. Fellow Montgomerian lieutenant colonel Albert Carmichael was the city's military governor. The big guns commenced firing at German positions protecting the dams of the Roer River.[5]

Private Billy Crane, nineteen, who had been an ASTP student and like Bobby a member of Lanier's class of '43, shipped across the Atlantic as an infantry replacement in a convoy in late summer. He had no steady girlfriend. From England he wrote WSFA's *Letter from Home* asking to be put in touch with Neal Howard. After making the rounds of the replacement depots, "repple depples," he became an infantry scout in the Fifth Infantry Division in George Patton's Third Army in Lorraine late in October.[6]

In August, Private First Class Neal Howard, twenty, formerly an ASTP student and a member of Lanier's class of '42, who had studied forestry at Louisiana State University, came home on a final furlough before shipping out. A rifleman in the Seventy-eighth "Lightning" Division at Camp Pickett, Virginia, he had a girl, Dorothy ("Dot") Van Sant, who was a student and member of the choir at Huntingdon. They had fallen deeply in love, and he hated to return to camp. Early in October, Howard's division left New York on an army transport that was part of a huge convoy. The sea was often rough as winter approached, and he spent little time on deck. Instead, he lay in his hammock much of the time, chatting with buddies or writing. A favorite relative was his first cousin Mary Ellen Mathews from Montgomery, who was then attending Mary Baldwin College in Virginia. He wrote her of anticipating "the Great Adventure." He spoke of how sweet, pretty, and fine Dot Van Sant was.[7]

On a different ship in the convoy was combat engineer private William ("Billy") Robinson, nineteen, Lanier class of '43, who wanted to become a commercial artist. A replacement, he was more or less a stranger among other strangers. He had left no girl behind. After two weeks at sea, both Montgomery soldiers struggled down the gang-

Private First Class Robert "Bobby" Young, U.S. Army artillery, provides firing information to his battalion's "big gun" crews near the Roer River, fall 1944. *Courtesy of Robert A. Young.*

plank with full field equipment and a loaded duffel bag onto a dock at Plymouth harbor, where they were greeted by a British army band playing "The Stars and Stripes Forever." They went by train in different directions, Howard with the Seventy-eighth Division eastward along the coast to the southern resort of Bournemouth, where the division was billeted in and around the city, and Robinson and other replacements to a repple depple in west central England near Birmingham.[8]

In England the two men had different personal experiences. Howard for a time enjoyed the sights of the city by the sea and played touch football on a grassy stretch on a cliff overlooking the beach. He and parts of his regiment were billeted in private homes previously taken over by the British army. They performed the manual of arms and bayonet practice in the street in front of the billets. Children watched them and begged for chewing gum. Howard received a pass to London. "That night we went to a stage show, then walked in the moonlight to see the government buildings." But he became acutely homesick and wrote Mary Ellen that he missed Montgomery in autumn. But "another reason I want to be home is, of course, Dot."[9]

In the small village of Sutton Coldfield, Billy Robinson experienced the first of two profound dramas across the sea. He fell deeply in love with a sixteen-year-old girl named Jean Owen, full-cheeked and attractive. Owen clerked in a shop, and as she later remembered, when he was off duty he would "peep his head round the shop . . . all smiles." Robinson at last had a relationship to compensate for all the lonely hours in the repple depples.[10]

The Seventy-eighth packed up late in November. The movement of an American division from England to the western front was now more or less routine. Artillerymen and men of the tank company boarded large landing craft with their equipment at the great naval base of Portsmouth. At the great port of Southampton, Seventy-eighth infantry, combat engineer, and support unit officers and men boarded British troop ships, on whose bulkheads graffiti had been scribbled by GIs taking part in the invasion of southern France. It made the troops of the Seventy-eighth feel more a part of the warrior ethos but also quickened their pulses. Anxiety quickly gave way to boredom, however, as the men found themselves confined below deck on a two-day diet of greasy mutton while they waited to depart.[11]

Finally the soldiers felt the vessels move and traversed the choppy channel to the battered port of Le Havre. It had no remaining serviceable docks, and the troops had to climb down cargo nets with full field equipment into LCIs, which took them ashore. Between piles of rubble they marched to waiting GI trucks.[12]

Bivouacked in a muddy open field, they saw the spires of Rouen Cathedral in the distance. Some of the former ASTP students remembered reading about it in a college history course. The troops were served a Thanksgiving meal with all the trimmings and enjoyed seconds on turkey. They ate from mess kits while they sat on straw in front of their pup tents.[13]

The men traveled aboard the legendary French "forty and eight" boxcars through the gray wintry landscape and blacked-out towns. The urine and feces buckets filled up between stops, and they had to "hold it" until they could climb down and relieve themselves in marshaling yards or at the edge of an embankment. Passing north of Paris, they came near the Somme River and passed places called Cambrai and Mons. Few GIs could have associated these names with the trench warfare and slaughter of the Great War's western front.[14]

Outside the marketing town of Tongeren, Belgium, near the confluence of the Dutch, Belgian, and German borders, small units of the division bivouacked in fields or orchards. During frosty nights they hunkered down in sleeping bags in farmers' haylofts. The Flemish-speaking peasants were friendly but bore the anxious look of a recently liberated people whose enemy was not far off. The front in that area was only twenty-five miles to the east. Companies mounted twenty-four-hour guard around their bivouacs.[15]

Neal Howard wrote to his sister-in-law Margaret on November 29: "We are getting pretty close now and within buzz-bomb range. Day and night they come over, headed for targets beyond. They sound funny, like a motorcycle running fast, and you can see the flame coming out the rear. We can hear the explosion pretty loud." Then he lied gracefully. "There's no danger from them."[16]

Early one morning a V-1 buzz bomb passing over in daylight went silent in clear sight of the American encampments. Howard's rifle company was lined up for breakfast being slapped into mess kits from an outdoor chow table. When the missile plunged, they hit the ground or fled in panic. The explosion shook the earth as if it had occurred in a nearby clump of trees rather than a quarter mile away.[17]

The Seventy-eighth was loaded onto trucks on December 7 and moved southeast in cold rain to a forested area. Bivouacs sprouted among the trees. At the moment weather was the enemy, but the faint rumble of artillery and a briefing that passed down from division headquarters to regiment to battalion to company reminded all of the men that they were not on training maneuvers. A few miles to the east lay the Seventy-eighth's first objective—the largest of two dams on the Roer River. The capture of these dams would, it was hoped, prevent the Germans from unleashing widespread flooding that would indefinitely delay any final drive to the Rhine. South of the Seventy-eighth, the veteran U.S. Second Infantry Division was maneuvering to take the smaller dam. Once the dams were captured, the way was open beyond for a relatively level, forestless run across the Cologne Plain to the Rhine.[18]

The enemy's defenses shielding the dams had thus far proved impenetrable to the assaults of U.S. forces. Rows of concrete antitank "Dragon's Teeth" of the West Wall defensive alignment protected the dams and nearby towns and villages. These defenses were augmented by bunkers and pillboxes, some with interlocking fields of fire. German infantry and artillery waited behind the rows of concrete obstacles in ravines and stands of fir and pine.[19]

Howard and the other GIs understood that they were not far from combat, and they had real and lingering fear. Yet, as a saving grace, few if any comprehended the deadly complexity of the task before them. Snow fell on December 9 and 10, and the temperature dropped to near zero. It was the start of the coldest weather in the region for several decades. A winter wonderland masked what lay beyond the Dragon's Teeth.[20]

On the eleventh the infantry regiments of the Seventy-eighth began to move by foot, and the mobilized tank and artillery battalions and smaller units by wheels and halftracks, in driving snow, to the jumping-off points. German artillery shells exploded here and there.[21]

On the thirteenth began one prong of the most important Allied offensive operation of the moment on the western front. Two villages inside the Dragon's Teeth, Rollesbroich in the center and Kesternich to its southeast, had to be taken and secured to open the way for the seizure of the larger dam. For sixty-odd hours there were noises—the brief, intense whispering sound of an incoming mortar shell, the shrill, arcing whirr of an artillery shell. Explosions left ears ringing. From pillboxes camouflaged in white came the most terrifying sound, the rapid bark of a German machine gun. GIs, advancing in skirmish lines across the snow, were struck before they knew it. Survivors would later wonder why they had been so lucky.[22]

Once the mop-up companies followed on the heels of the assault troops through the villages, the dominant sounds were muffled explosions of grenades tossed through a window or into a cellar and the whine of a sniper's bullet. The pervasive smells of cordite and burning wood hung in the chill air. Green troops had extreme difficulty adjusting to the sight of a corpse wearing their uniform, especially a cluster of bodies. Where bodies had lain for hours, the skin had a waxen pallor. After a day, it began to turn yellowish, as though from jaundice.[23]

Neal Howard's company took part in the assault on Rollesbroich. It was taken and secured with relatively little American loss of life. Just before dawn on the fifteenth, with Howard's fellow Montgomerian infantry scout Private First Class Wesley Newton, nineteen, taking part, the final assault on Kesternich began. Houses and barns blazed from the preparatory artillery barrage. The glow reflected on the dead faces of the first casualties of the assault companies. An officer or noncommissioned officer had to direct traffic: "Come on, move out! Don't pay any attention to them. Move!" In the late afternoon, after heavy casualties among the assault companies, a few of the mop-up company GIs managed to reach the crossroads at the end of the village that led toward the dam. With entrenching tools they hacked out shallow foxholes in the frozen ground.[24]

The Germans did not intend to give up the second village. As dark fell on the fifteenth, fresh assault companies and armor from the area's defending Volksgrenadier infantry division suddenly swept down the crossroads into Kesternich. The fighting for houses and barns and streets raged on until after midnight. Noises ceased when the enemy had most of the village. Much of the opposing American battalion had been eliminated as a fighting force—dead, wounded, prisoners of war. When prisoners were lined up to be led away, some could not walk because of wounds and/or frozen feet. These men had to be carried by comrades. Wesley Newton, wounded and suffering from frostbite, was taken prisoner during the early hours of December 16. The battle for Kesternich would be replayed in place after place farther south in the coming days.[25]

The sudden assault had more than a single purpose. Enemy commanders defending the dams knew of plans, to be implemented on the sixteenth, for a massive German thrust through the Ardennes region, whose forests, wooded ridges, and roads encompassed parts of Belgium, Luxembourg, and France. An American breakthrough to the Cologne Plain would imperil this counteroffensive.[26]

William J. Robinson and Alice Robinson in Riverside Heights in Montgomery drew comfort from the belief that their son, Billy, was still in England. In early December, Private Billy Robinson had been alerted for immediate movement to the Continent. He managed a last pass to see Jean Owen, reaching her house, as she wrote his parents months later, "about eleven-fifteen at night. I walked with him to the bus stop but the last bus was gone so that meant he would have a long walk back." Even though the dark was quite cold, she insisted on walking with him partway. "Bill was very upset that night and hated to leave me. He cried a little to me." Robinson gave Jean Owen his Lanier '43 class ring and "asked me to get engaged. I promised him that I would wait for him."[27]

Robinson began his passage through the replacement pipeline to the western front. Crowded transport and the herding and drilling by callous NCOs on the grounds of the tents and sequestered buildings of the repple depples left him no space, time, or energy to write anybody. He was finally loaded on a forty and eight bound for the front. It was bleak outside the small window of his car. Snow was falling thickly.[28]

"Trace of Snow Lets City Know Winter's Here," declared the *Advertiser* on December 12. The temperature on the thirteenth dropped to 24 degrees. Montgomerians at home were eager for the diversion of Christmas. But the housing shortage deepened with the Christmas season. The Maxwell housing officer appealed for "rooms with a bath and light kitchen privileges for couples with small child. Many of these couples are now living in downtown hotels and the hotel managers would like these rooms emptied for the Christmas rush." Captain Glenn Miller had had to accept a hotel room for himself and his wife during his assignment at Maxwell. In 1944, Miller, now a major with his celebrated AAF band in England, took off as a passenger in a small military plane on December 15, bound for Paris to make arrangements for bringing the band to the continent. Most of the officers caught in the 1944 squeeze in Montgomery were either instructors or students for Boeing Super Fort B-29 transition training to commence at Maxwell early in 1945, replacing the B-24 training. By December a B-29 offensive against the Japanese home islands was well underway from China and soon from bases on Saipan and Tinian.[29]

The news of the campaign heightened the optimism that the war would soon be over. A scrap paper drive in December hit an all-time low, although the press noted that medicine, food, shells, and plasma were often delivered in paper cartons. The armed forces inadvertently encouraged slackness when they announced that their supply of surgical bandages was adequate for the foreseeable future. City bandage centers closed down.[30]

Montgomerians anticipated Christmas of 1944 more eagerly than any since 1941. There was a heightened interest in the traditional caroling in the Square. The *Advertiser* on December 7 commented, "There's excitement in the air on Montgomery's downtown streets these days . . . [and] eager, hurrying crowds, so many that the distance on Dexter from Court Square to Perry Street is traversed with difficulty." The editor had "never seen more package-laden men and women than fill the sidewalks this December. . . . Well, it shows that Montgomery is prosperous and there is money to spend." The depression was past, and on the home front this development was the most positive legacy of the war.[31]

On December 17 the *Advertiser* carried a banner headline, "NAZIS OPEN COUNTER ATTACKS," and a smaller explanatory one, "Germans Blast Way Back into Belgium, Luxembourg." News stories of the eighteenth told of German strikes through the Belgian Ardennes and toward the Meuse River. The objective was the port of Antwerp, held by the Allies and essential for resupplying of the western front. People in the United States did not understand that this was Hitler's desperate attempt to checkmate the western Allies, which in turn would allow the Germans to direct full attention to the oncoming Russians.[32]

The bad news piled up, dampening the Christmas season. The caroling in the Square was canceled. Anxiety was widespread. Few people noticed a short news item in the *Advertiser* on Christmas Day that Major Glenn Miller was missing on the flight from England to Paris.[33]

AAF corporal Bob Lawrence came home on Christmas Eve. Forced by illness to resign as an aviation cadet, he had become a gunner in a B-17 crew, training for overseas duty. He relaxed with his parents and recalled happier Christmases. Christmas night he attended a ball given at the Beauvoir Country Club by the Cotillion Club, whose members were young women of his age group. On such short notice he could not get a date.[34]

At breaks in the dancing, he sat at a table with three couples. One of the young women was Mary Ellen Mathews, whose thoughts now and then strayed to her cousin, Neal Howard. She knew he was somehow involved in the disaster on the western front. Neither she nor his other loved ones, including his girlfriend, Dot Van Sant, had received a letter for three weeks. Across town in Riverside Heights and across the ocean in Sutton Coldfield, England, other loved ones who had not heard from their soldier for weeks wondered if he was involved in the calamity.[35]

Private Billy Robinson had arrived by train in Belgium on December 22. Trucks took him and other replacements across the white landscape with stands of green coniferous trees to the Elsenborn Ridge on the northern shoulder of the Bulge. There Robinson joined a company of the engineer combat battalion assigned to the Ninety-ninth "Checkerboard" Infantry Division. In the distance the noises of battle were like muted thunder. The Ninety-ninth and veteran Second Divisions had met the fury of an SS Panzer column, which had disrupted the Second's drive to take the smaller dam on the Roer River. The Elsenborn Ridge was crucial in the German drive to the Meuse River. From their positions on the ridge, the Americans repulsed the assaults.[36]

Robinson had arrived during a lull in the battle. On the Twenty-third he was able to scratch off a few lines to Riverside Heights and Sutton Coldfield: "We are going to have turkey tomorrow."[37]

Northeast of the ridge and within the West Wall concrete barriers, the Seventy-eighth Division had established a defense line to keep it from being overrun and to prevent a possible German breakout through the Monschau corridor into Belgium. The line ran from Rollesbroich to a point one mile west of German-held Kesternich. The enemy sent out patrols and dropped a few paratroopers behind the line, offering little threat. The line and the German defenses opposite formed the northernmost edge of the Bulge. Neal Howard, who had received a battlefield promotion to sergeant, had time to write. He told each of his correspondents, with some variations, that he was alive and in good shape: "While I could do a heck of a lot better in the good ole U.S., I know I could be a lot worse." To Mary Ellen Mathews, his confidant, he was more frank in a letter of December 22: "It gives you a funny feeling to talk to a buddy you've trained with the whole time one day and find out the next day he's gone." He admitted, "I was hit by a piece of shrapnel when an .88 shell struck a building we were in. It just scraped the skin of my stomach." He yearned for the home fires of Christmas: "It doesn't seem right; everybody was always so happy this time of year. Even if we all can't be with you folks at the Christmas tree we'll be there in our heart."[38]

None of Robinson's or Howard's battlefield letters reached Montgomery before January. Nor did those that Bobby Young wrote to his family on Fairview Avenue. Young's battalion was firing its long-range cannon in support of the northern defenses of the Bulge. Wide of its target, the big guns, a bomb from a low-streaking ME-262 jet fighter-bomber exploded near his observation post.[39]

Harold C. Crane, a pioneer certified public accountant in Montgomery, opened a telegram late in December informing him that his son, Private First Class William Crane, had been wounded on December 22. The telegram did not specify the nature or seriousness of the injuries. Billy Crane had been wounded once before in the shoulder and was out of action for a short time. Later the Cranes would learn that the December 22 wounds had been critical. Their son had been hit by multiple fragments of shrapnel from a mortar shellburst and for a time seemed near death. It was possible that one of his legs would be amputated. Crane, an infantry scout in General George Patton's Third Army, had been wounded on the day Patton began to turn a large part of his army to the north, sending an armored task force racing ahead. The task force had the mission of relieving the Belgian Ardennes town of Bastogne, a communications and marketing center, on which several arterial highways and railroads converged.[40]

With their offensive slowing elsewhere and Bastogne now the major obstacle to a breakout to the Meuse and Antwerp, the Germans had concentrated crack troops and armor around the town. It was defended by the U.S. 101st Airborne Division, the "Screaming Eagles," which had been trucked to Bastogne before the siege to serve as light infantry with other units in support. The desperate clash of arms became the most famous battle of the Bulge. The commander of the 101st, Brigadier General Anthony McAuliffe, had answered "Nuts" when the Germans demanded surrender, but his situation was grim. The 101st had to be resupplied by air, the large bundles of food, medicine, and ammunition parachuted down from C-47s flown by pilots such as Montgomerian first lieutenant James Powell.[41]

Montgomerians were in the midst of the shelling and the German assaults from several directions. The defenders reacted from rubble and foxholes. Sergeant Billy Grant, the son of a popular laundry delivery man in Montgomery, was cited in *Yank,* the army weekly magazine, as typical of the men who "fought out of holes against the big flood of Germans that over-ran them and attacked again and again." He would write his parents of frost-bitten limbs, of the arcing sound of .88 rounds fired one after another, and of piles of enemy dead, the snow dusting their bodies in stark contrast to the congealed blood. Grant cheered Patton's tanks when they broke through to mark the beginning of the lifting of the siege.[42]

Headlines in the *Advertiser* summarized the evolution of the Bulge: "ALLIED PLANES HURL STRATEGIC BLOW AGAINST COUNTER-ATTACK-ING GERMANS" (December 24); "AMERICANS STOP GERMAN OFFEN-SIVE" (December 25); "NAZI ARMOR STAGES NEW ADVANCE, HAMPERED BY ALLIED AIR ARMADA" (December 26); "GERMANS LINK TWO MAIN SPEARHEADS" (December 27); "YANK TANKS SMASH INTO BASTOGNE" (December 28); "NAZI WINTER DRIVE BELIEVED BROKEN BY PATTON'S SAVAGE COUNTER-BLOWS" (December 29); "12 MILE AMERICAN AD-

VANCE NARROWS NAZI ESCAPE ROUTE" (December 30). In January it was a matter of time: "GERMANS FLEE WESTERN END OF BULGE" (January 13); "GERMANS RACING FOR THE REICH" (January 15). On January 9 the *Advertiser* had predicted that "Bastogne will go down with other place-names which are associated with American heroism, places where a few stood bravely against the many."[43]

A half dozen Montgomery area men died in the Bulge. The many GIs who survived in relatively good shape included Montgomerian staff sergeant Luther Hammock, a black former chauffeur. He later told how the Bulge had made him late in sending a crystal ashtray as a gift to a white friend: "I had to leave for Luxembourg for a ten-days trip so I put it in my duffle-bag, thinking I would get to send it, though it might be late for Christmas." But "the breakthrough came early in December, and my bag was lost with . . . everything I had in it. Then for 19 never-to-be-forgotten days and nights I was catching plenty of hell." Months later he recovered his bag and was able to mail the ashtray.[44]

When the Bulge was flattened and the Germans in full, harassed retreat, Billy Robinson found that his "mail still isn't coming through like it should." On January 15, Neal Howard wrote to Mary Ellen Mathews: "I am well and in good health, except being tired and cold. I am filthy dirty, unshaven and in general a rough looking character. I have worn the same clothes about 30 days." But he was "glad to be around and am thankful for every minute I'm still kicking. . . . Nobody will be gladder to see Spring come than me." On January 15, no longer facing a possible leg amputation, Billy Crane wrote from a hospital in England to *Letter from Home* that he had "received the Purple Heart for wounds received in action in Germany."[45]

At the end of 1944, except for the turnaround in the Bulge, Montgomerians at home had little to cheer them. Wartime restrictions continued, and shortages were mounting. Obviously the war would not end overnight. An *Advertiser* editorial tried to put a good face on the situation by emphasizing the military successes.[46]

End-of-the year annual football all-star games had been considerably affected by the war. The Blue-Gray game had been played in

1943 but as a high school game matching two outstanding southern teams, neither from Alabama, where state high school athletic regulations prohibited postseason play. Only 500 spectators had shown up at Cramton Bowl. It had been a cold, rainy night.[47]

In 1944 the game stirred some old-time enthusiasm. Squads for the 1944 game were no longer high school students, but, in line with wartime reality, they included players from various service teams. Most were former collegians; a few were discharged veterans or seventeen-year-olds and 4Fs from civilian colleges, with class status ranging from freshmen to seniors. The weather had gradually warmed after Christmas. Pregame ticket sales were brisk—$3 for the best seats in the west concrete section; $1.50 for the east temporary seats, all reserved for "men in uniform and their dates." A few women in uniform, some with dates, showed up at ticket offices, causing momentary confusion, but they were sold tickets for east side seats. The uncovered part of the north end zone, priced at $1.50 a seat, was reserved for blacks. Montgomery businesses donated $2,576 to a Servicemen's Free Ticket Fund on a first-come, first-served basis.[48]

Returning as part of the extravaganza was the dance for players with belles at the Beauvoir Club. A photographer snapped a Blue player and a Gray player with Betty Holloway and Isabel Dunn, the mayor's daughter. The young women were wearing formal gowns; the young men, the uniform of their respective armed services. There was no parade. The game on December 30, broadcast over the Mutual network, attracted 17,000, shy of the predicted 20,000. Gray fans frequently roared, inspired by the 24-to-7 drubbing the Grays gave the Blues. The Blue team received respectable backing from the sizable number of service people from places outside the South. The game, played in weather the *Advertiser* described as "June in December," resulted in the first clear profit.[49]

Local sports fans also listened intently to the Sugar Bowl broadcast over NBC on January 1. Alabama's Crimson Tide played the Duke Blue Devils. With few exceptions the Tide was composed of seventeen- and eighteen-year-old civilians. The Duke Blue Devils, heavier and composed of service team players, war veterans, 4Fs, and more lettermen, edged Alabama 29 to 26. The game's most outstanding player was Tide tailback Harry Gilmer, eighteen, who had an unusual way of leaping before he launched a pass. He became a home-front hero.[50]

The headlines of the first four months of 1945 remained gloomy about home-front needs and priorities: "MEAT SUPPLY FAMINE FOR THE U.S. LOOMS. . . . Civilian Tire Rations Slashed." The only relief had been that coffee was taken off the ration list. A coal shortage led on February 1 to a brownout of street, shop window, and marquee lights to conserve electricity. Atticus Mullin tried to sound an upbeat note: The dimming "is not going to be as bad as it would have been last September when Montgomery's streets were filled with soldiers," before the preflight school had been transferred from Maxwell to Randolph Field, Texas. Mullin used the occasion to assess the impact on Montgomery's economy: "No class of soldier, not even the commissioned officer, expended as much money as did the thousands of cadets who were individually being processed." But Mullin conceded, "I can get in a place now and buy something. That is . . . , if they have it."[51]

The Civitan Club's proposal to place a marble cenotaph in the plaza formed by the meeting of streets in front of the federal courthouse was the subject of persistent debate. "We believe there should be some sacred spot in our city dedicated solely to those boys and girls who paid the supreme sacrifice in the present conflict," a Civitan member stated. A member of the War Dads chapter countered with the results of a survey taken among veterans and the wounded in military hospitals who asked for "a living memorial—such as a park, swimming pool, library, play ground." The mother of Verbon Sanders, a dead marine hero, disagreed with the War Dad. To walk in a building or playground dedicated to the war dead, she said, would be like "walking over the resting place of my dead son's body."[52]

Coinciding with the needs from the Philippines, Italy, and the global air and sea campaigns, pressure from the many wounded in the Bulge had almost depleted the services' medical supplies. Military chiefs asked the Red Cross to resume its surgical bandage program.

Montgomerians had only to read in the papers the tally of local men wounded in the Bulge alone. The local chapter made an appeal, and the reopened center at Maxwell began turning out bandages in February. Military esprit, however, could not be applied to jump-start the town centers. Two months passed before their work was well underway. The Beauvoir Club had decided to opt out.[53]

Other military crises of the new year exacerbated the need for surgical bandages. The end of the Bulge late in January, along with a failed minor German offensive in Alsace-Lorraine, signaled the end of the defensive stance along the entire western front, which had been in effect since fall 1944. Allied planners now looked toward the Rhine. Both the Seventy-eighth and Ninety-ninth divisions joined in the renewed offensive. The Seventy-eighth finally took Kesternich but was unable to reach the larger Roer River dam before German explosives caused a partial flooding of the Roer Valley, delaying for two weeks a thrust toward the Cologne Plain.[54]

The delay gave Sergeant Neal Howard an opportunity to write letters. He wrote his brother, AAF lieutenant Billy Howard, "I just read in the Stars & Stripes about a tornado which hit Montgomery. I sure hope nobody we know was hurt." After the Ninety-ninth division had pushed forward from the Elsenborn Ridge and paused, Billy Robinson, promoted to private first class, was able to write home. He was impressed that the tornado had "blown a freight train off the track." He wondered "if it hit Riverside Heights, since it isn't far from the tracks."[55]

At about 5:00 P.M. on February 12, an officer at Maxwell Field saw what looked like "a mass of black smoke. Then it seemed to go to pieces." What he had seen was debris from a large tornado that had swept from black clouds to the ground in the H&R Point area. Beginning a fifteen-minute rampage, the tornado smashed several warehouses and carried ten-ton machinery a hundred yards. German prisoners of war on the H&R reservation watched in terror. The twister evoked memories of bombings and bombardments. It missed their compound but leveled a nearby black grammar school, fortunately empty at that late hour.[56]

Then the tornado became a killer. Poor blacks including children died in devastated houses and shacks as the tornado made its way to Bell Street. Sparing both Maxwell and Riverside Heights, it zigzagged about Bell toward downtown, killing more poor blacks before fatally injuring a middle-class white man on Herron Street. A newspaper reporter downtown heard "the roar of the storm . . . , audible on Dexter Avenue, and many people in the heart of town saw the approach . . . and flying debris."[57]

At the railroad bridge over Bell, the killer turned north and moved along the tracks, inspiring a myth that it lifted an entire freight train and then set it back on the tracks. The winds smashed forty-six boxcars. People in the terminal building heard what sounded like a runaway train bearing down. It veered away before crossing the Alabama River.[58]

The greatest damage occurred as the tornado wove a path through parts of north Montgomery, up Lower Wetumpka Road, and into Chisholm. E. H. Barrington was sitting in the living room of his combination house-grocery when the walls and roof blew away. He himself remained untouched. A reporter found him "tall and gaunt . . . still standing on the front room floor, the scene now lighted by moonlight." He had pulled his oldest daughter, alive and only bruised, from the wreckage and saw his wife "get up from behind a meat case. Then I started looking for my littlest girl. I looked at the house . . . , and I said, 'Oh, Lord, I know she's dead.' Just then the child came running down the road. She wasn't hurt a bit."[59]

Before the tornado lifted beyond Chisholm, it severely damaged the white grammar school and destroyed or shattered forty-nine other buildings there. It left a total of twenty-six people dead along its path, together with rubble and the husks of buildings. From the Pacific, Seaman Third Class Lamar Dennis, whose home was in Chisholm, wrote *Letter from Home,* "That will give the folks in Montgomery a little idea of what a place goes through when it is being bombed."[60]

The storm indeed offered Montgomery's civil defense organization its only true test. The air raid wardens had been largely mustered out. Only a few reached the tornado's wake, but 600 auxiliary firemen and 75 auxiliary police, quick to report, had quickly been dispatched to the sites of devastation. CD authorities commended them. The Red Cross sent food and medical teams and found shelter for many of the homeless. B-29s from the pilot transition training school at Maxwell flew overhead after skies had cleared, their roar giving people in the storm's path momentary anxiety.[61]

In the far Pacific, a site was needed for emergency landings of B-29s unable to return from Japan proper to their bases on the Marianas. On February 19, assault marines waited on transports and landing craft in the early morning to invade the small island of Iwo Jima, 700 miles south of Japan. Iwo Jima already had the basis for an emergency landing field in the form of two small airstrips used by Japanese fighters to harry B-29s. Looming at one end was its distinctive small mountain, called Suribachi, which had carpeted the island with volcanic ash and sulfuric sand.[62]

Coast Guard signalman Lamar Best, from Montgomery, overheard the breakfast talk of marines on his landing ship. The men, who were veterans of other landings and campaigns, were speculating that, like felons condemned to die, they might be enjoying their last meal. Lamar watched LCIs carry marines to the black-colored beach.[63]

Awaiting the troops was a defense stronger than anticipated. Aerial reconnaissance could spot pillboxes, bunkers, and caves but not the miles of trenches and none of the hundreds of connecting tunnels. That the battle would be costly became evident when 600 marines died on the first day. The defenders did not resort to their traditional banzai suicidal charges, which were always costly and almost never successful, but instead waited in their various upper and underground locations. Resistance had to be overcome in the latter by satchel charges, grenades, and flame throwers. What had been estimated to be a five-day battle lasted over a month.[64]

The 6,680 marines who died in combat on Iwo Jima, the bloodiest in the Pacific war for the length of the campaign, included Private Louis Kennedy, Jr., a former assistant scoutmaster in Montgomery. Private John D. Smith, Sr., died of his wounds on a hospital ship and was given the traditional burial at sea. His mother resided in the county, his wife in the city of Montgomery. Smith had a baby son that he had never seen and a three-year-old daughter.[65]

Near the end of the campaign, navy Seabees came ashore to prepare for extension of the airfields' runways for B-29s. Seabee enlisted man Robert ("Bobby") Lundquist, an Eagle Scout from Montgomery and a Lanier '43 classmate of Lamar Best, wrote his parents of an experience on the black sand of Iwo Jima. He and his mates "were sleeping in fox holes with bags around us and a pup tent over us. . . . The other day another sniper shot at our group but the Marines in a camp near us went after him and got him. Boy, I really have a lot of respect for the Marines that fought here." The dead sniper was one of 20,800 Japanese who died in a total of 21,000 defenders.[66]

Lamar Best and his landing ship tank participated in another invasion a week after the conclusion of the fighting on Iwo Jima. Northeast of the Philippines lay the island of Okinawa, 500 miles from the Japanese home islands. Because of Okinawa's size, U.S. planners envisioned it as a close-in air base, fleet anchorage, and possible site from which to launch an invasion of the home islands. Best again watched as LCIs took marines ashore on April 1. Army troops participated as assault forces. This time no one expected conquest to be easy.[67]

For a few days the resistance was lighter than it had been in the early stages on Iwo Jima. The kamikaze ("divine wind") was the key to the Japanese strategy. Americans had encountered this aerial strategy off the Philippines. Flown by hyped-up young pilots, with explosives that were designed to go off upon impact, the kamikazes had the suicide mission of driving away the support ships of the landing. A follow-up counterattack on shore was planned to push the invaders back into the sea.[68]

Lamar Best saw the suicide planes come diving through the black splotches of antiaircraft shells and the arcing tracers from the ships. The survivors leveled out and swept over the surface toward a target. Tracers from Best's landing ship tank reached out and downed a kamikaze, which rode the surface of the water in a fiery cartwheel before exploding short of the landing craft.[69]

The air defenses of the German homeland had no kamikazes and were much weakened by 1945. But the flak had been increased and made the skies still deadly. Bob Lawrence was new to the Eighth Air Force. He was now a staff sergeant and gunner on a B-17 assigned to the Ninety-sixth Bomb Group at Snetterton Heath in January. He recalled, "Our guts began to really knot up. The training was over, the fooling around was over, we were getting ready to go to a shooting war." The group's first sergeant paid a visit to a Quonset hut with a "miniscule coke stove" at about three o'clock one chill morning to awake Lawrence's crew for its first mission. They sensed his coming before they heard him. They had an hour to dress and get by truck or foot first to the mess hall and then to the briefing hut. They watched, mesmerized, as the briefing officer motioned with his pointer to the ribbons and described the mission.[70]

These airmen "were never quite comfortable" in what they wore on a mission, for they were padded modern versions of a medieval knight, wearing suits with layers of electrical heating, fleece lining, and flak protection. They plugged in oxygen masks at 10,000 feet. Over flak nests and on the bomb run they wore GI helmets. From the first mission Lawrence felt "something terribly incongruous" about flying over "beautiful landscape" on a mission "to blow part of it away." He had "a lot of time to think" on missions, particularly during the initial, eight-hour round trip. All the flak over the target, the Frankfurt marshaling yards, seemed to be aimed at his plane. A burst of flak out from his waist position sent a fragment through the skin of the plane and, he recalled vividly, "struck me right on the helmet." As a memento he carried "that fragment for a long time. It was so terrifying, when we finally got off the bomb run, I sat down in a corner of the plane by the bulkhead leading to the radio operator's [compartment] . . . , convinced I would never live through that war." He would endure twenty-nine more missions.[71]

The AAF bombers and fighters flying over the Reich to strategic targets could not make out the individual battles taking place along the western front late in February and into March. The landscape below was shades of gray, black, and white. But the push was on to the Rhine. On February 17, Sergeant Neal Howard, waiting with the Seventy-eighth for the Roer River's flooding to recede, wrote Mary Ellen Mathews of his joy that his mail had caught up with him. "I wish you could read some of those sweet letters she [Dot Van Sant] wrote to me." On February 18, his mother wrote him of seeing Dot at their church, First United Methodist. In closing, she told him, "Always remember I am thinking about you all the time and praying for you."[72]

Billy Robinson's Ninety-ninth division was receiving reinforcements, readying to make its run to the Rhine. He wrote home on March 1: "The last four nights we've had motion pictures in a barn and yesterday we had two coca-colas apiece. We've had it easy for about a week now; it can't last much longer."[73]

By February 25 the flooding of the Roer River had receded, and on February 28 the Seventy-eighth and other units in the area jumped off to cross the river. German resistance was at first predictably fierce. Not only was the Cologne Plain an open, level path to the Rhine, it was Germany's breadbasket. By March 2 the entire Seventy-eighth was on the other side. At the northern end of the division's line, Neal Howard's regiment, attached to an armored division, met steady .88 and mortar fire. That day and the next the casualties mounted. In the predawn dark of March 3, Howard was leading his squad on a patrol when enemy fire struck him in the forehead.[74]

At daybreak of March 5, Billy Robinson and his company were constructing a temporary bridge across a Rhine tributary so that the Ninety-ninth's armored battalion could cross for the advance to the great river. German artillerymen, from the east side of the Rhine, inserted shells in the chambers of their cannon and pulled the lanyards. As Billy's platoon leader later wrote Alice Robinson, "Artillery opened up and got a direct hit on us. Robbie was hit instantly—he never knew what hit him."[75]

The telegram arrived first at Riverside Heights. Two of Billy Robinson's brothers, Ray and Paul, were at home with the parents when the delivery boy knocked on the door. John, the brother closest to Billy in age, was downtown playing pool at Willie's. Ray later recalled that "the young man who brought the telegram was an acquaintance. The expression on his face let it be known there was something bad." The father, William J., took the telegram and "went to the back of the house and then told us." Alice's immediate grief was terrible to behold. Ray was eating congealed salad with pineapple. He never ate it again. J. P. Morgan, a neighbor's son, went to fetch John Robinson, who took the news badly, like his mother. Paul, the youngest Robinson son, was sent to bed early. Sensitive and only twelve at the time, he kept the memory of John's crying and talking to William J., the family crisis manager. But like his wife, William J. never got over the death of their oldest son.[76]

There was one notable omission in the communications about Billy Robinson's death. Jean Owen had last heard from him in a letter dated March 1 when he had also written his parents. Weeks passed with no letters. One reason for the omission was that Owen was not in the category of "Next of Kin," but in part it resulted from her sweetheart's reluctance to talk about his love life even with friends and family. No buddy in his platoon or company wrote her. His family did not have her address. Although she had his Montgomery address, she had never written to his parents, perhaps on his instructions. Thus unintentionally Billy Robinson fostered a situation in which his sweetheart did not know of his death for a long time. Finally in the late spring Jean Owen wrote his parents. Already devastated, they had the sad task of informing her that their son had been dead for a number of weeks.[77]

On June 12 she replied: "I received your letter and it was a very great shock to me, and it will be a very long, long time before I make myself realize that it is true." But "it is true enough and I have cried myself to sleep at nights. I just can't stop thinking about Bill. At work I broke down and just sobbed my heart out. I just could not help it. It is such a real loss to you and those others like me who loved Bill." She asked if she could keep his Lanier class ring, for it was all she had of his. The Robinsons honored her request.[78]

Fannie Lee Howard wrote her son on March 15. She had not heard from him since late February: "Well, what I wouldn't give tonight to see you, or even if I could talk to you and know just how you are." The next day a MIA telegram arrived, but hope remained. Then, on March 20, a delivery boy brought a second telegram: "The Secretary of War desires me to express his deep regret that your son Sgt Howard, Neal D was killed in action in Germany 3 Mar 45." The telegram was signed "J. A. Ulio, the Adjutant General."[79]

The Howards received many expressions of sympathy. Dot Van Sant wrote, "Words seem so insufficient to express my deep sympathy for you. . . . I know so little of Neal in comparison with the way that you knew him, but I want you to know that everything I knew of him was good, pure, and fine." Mary Dannelly, whose son Clarence, Jr., had been the first military Montgomerian to die as a result of the war, wrote, "I am so deeply sorry that you have experienced the same tragedy that we have. Life truly isn't fair to mothers—It just ought not to happen!"[80]

Most people were not affected directly by such tragedies. They seemed to have become inured to the accounts in newspapers and magazines and the rare depictions in newsreels, which were sometimes in color but with graphic scenes censored. Most people were more concerned on a daily basis about such troubles as the nationwide brownout, a severe meat shortage in March, and the reduction of the sugar ration by a fourth in April. On May 6 the *Advertiser* reiterated a dreary theme: "City Far Short on Its Surgical Dressings."[81]

The need for bandages seemed on the verge of ending in Europe. As the Western Allies reached the Rhine and prepared to cross to the east bank, the Russians surged to within fifty miles of Berlin. The Germans had blown all the Rhine bridges except, by a fluke, one at Remagen. A small unit of the Ninth Armored Division discovered the bridge and crossed it on March 7. The nearest division-sized unit, the Seventy-eighth, was ordered to cross over on the eighth and to expand the tiny bridgehead on the east bank. The first Seventy-eighth component to reach the east bank was B Company of the 310th Infantry Regiment—the company of Sergeant Neal Howard, killed five days before. Another division that hurried across the Remagen bridge before German shelling and bombing felled it was the Ninety-ninth, but Private First Class Billy Robinson, like fellow Montgomerian Neal Howard, had by then become the responsibility of a graves registration unit.[82]

(Left) Jean Owen and (right) Dorothy Van Sant. *Courtesy of Paul Robinson and Dorothy (Van Sant) Sams, respectively.*

By March 24, employing pontoon bridges, the western Allies had established several bridgeheads, from the south, where Patton's Third operated, to the north where Field Marshal Montgomery's forces prepared to sweep across the Hanoverian Plain. On that day Allied paratroopers and glider-borne troops descended just north of the Ruhr Valley to open the way for Montgomery's breakout to the plain. From the west bank the long-range guns of Bobby Young's battalion fired in support of the airborne operation. In a week's time German defenses on the western front were collapsing.[83]

The taking of territory and swarms of German prisoners in the accelerating advance meant the liberation of Allied prisoners of war in camp after camp. AAF first lieutenant Silas "Brook" Nettles, a POW since October 1943, had spent most of his imprisonment in the notorious Stalag Luft III, forty miles north of Berlin. Evacuated by the Germans in the harsh winter weather of January 1945 to prevent liberation by the oncoming Russians, Brook and the other prisoners journeyed to a camp in Bavaria, partly by foot, partly by unmarked train—the latter under the threat of strafing by Allied aircraft. In Stalag Luft III, Nettles had been consoled by letters from his mother and his girlfriend, Katty Thornton, and by weekly Red Cross food parcels, but he received no letters or parcels in Bavaria.[84]

Existence was grim, with barely a subsistence ration of food daily. Late in April, cannon fire rumbled in the distance and then came closer, encouraging rumors that the Americans were moving in. Artillery shells began to whistle overhead and explode nearby. One night early in May, the senior prisoner-of-war officer and the camp commandant met outside the compound with an American army lieutenant general carrying pearl-handled pistols and a riding crop. The next day a Red Cross sixteen-wheeler full of food parcels drove through the camp gate. Later that day George Patton rode through the gate in a jeep.[85]

First Lieutenant Lola Dickenson, an army nurse from Montgomery, was a member of a mobile hospital in Patton's Third Army. In the rapid advance east of the Rhine, the nurses were constantly on the move. One morning the women in their jeeps became separated from the main column and encountered German soldiers. Forced to leave their vehicles, the Americans with hands over their heads were marched to a hastily constructed prison pen. Sudden prisoners, Lieutenant Dickenson and the other officers were unharmed but anxious. After twelve hours, a relief column of GIs surrounded the camp. The guards surrendered meekly.[86]

When AAF heavy bombers flew to the decreasing number of viable strategic targets in April, the terrain below had a faint green cast—a scene increasingly familiar to Sergeant Kenneth "Peanut" Adcock, a ball turret gunner on a B-17 and a Lanier alumnus. On a mission to the Aussig marshaling yards, his aircraft approached the target, when he glimpsed from his plastic-and-steel-encased bubble a number of ME-262 jet fighters zooming up toward the rear of the bombers. The jets were the only potent air-to-air weapon the Luftwaffe had left. Their speed often got them into and out of a formation before crews knew what had sent bombers spinning down or inflicted damage on others.[87]

"The jets attacked the rear of our formation," Adcock later told his debriefing officer, "and in a few seconds two fortresses . . . on either side of us, went down. I started letting loose with everything I had as six jets came diving at us trying for another kill. One Jerry came in low and the tail gunner and myself started hammering away at it. With all the lead we were throwing he didn't stand a chance and he soon burst into flame and went diving downward." The escort squadrons of P-51 Mustangs, the finest Allied long-range fighter, ganged up on the jets and drove them away. The Fortresses bombed their target. The combat was one of the last between the AAF and the Luftwaffe.[88]

"Allies Racing for the Elbe, Last Barrier to Berlin" read a headline in the *Advertiser.* Bobby Young's family had particular reason to notice. At the end of April, his battalion crossed the Rhine and halted at the Elbe. Young spent a night guarding a flight line of captured ME-262 jets, the same type of plane whose bomb had exploded close to his observation post during the Bulge.[89]

In the morning, having the day off, he walked down to the Elbe. As though he were a spectator at a football game in Cramton Bowl, Young watched from a hillside as a drama unfolded across the river. A large German force was holding a perimeter against oncoming Russians, who made a "semi-circle of 10 miles radius." The "dark green [Russian] YAK fighters were cruising up and down the river. There was a demolished bridge with a single plank treadway across the wreckage and in orderly fashion they fled across." As the Germans retreated, shelled and strafed until they reached the west bank, "most of the officers would throw their lugers onto the rocks. . . . Once across [the troops] . . . would stack their arms and form ranks in their own units" in the surrender to the Americans. Young felt lucky that he had survived unscathed.[90]

April was a cruel month for other Montgomerians. Army medic private first class Jack Merrill and infantry second lieutenant Ronald Daniel were killed in the savage fighting on Okinawa.[91]

Then on April 12–13 the local papers carried large black headlines, as though in mourning, that told of the death of FDR. Harry Truman was quickly sworn in as president. "He died," eulogized the *Advertiser*'s editor, "as gallantly, as bravely and as unafraid as any soldier on the field of battle.... Happily, he lived long enough to see that victory was assured." At Maxwell and Gunter the base commanders made the official announcement before their assembled troops on the thirteenth. Five thousand people gathered on the fifteenth at Cramton Bowl at about the same time that funeral rites were being held in a private ceremony at the White House. White and black clergymen at the Bowl led the segregated assembly in prayer. Tears were common.[92]

The *Advertiser* had other shocking headlines in April. One read: "'Murder Factory' Found near Limburg; British Free 29,000 in Horror Camp." One by one Allied columns captured the scattered concentration camps in Germany and Austria, most of which had become death camps. Bergen-Belsen, characterized as the "murder factory," had been only one such camp.[93]

Late in April a rumor spread that Germany had surrendered. The news touched off a stateside celebration, but it soon proved to be false. The German surrender was actually signed on May 7, and doubts were erased on May 8 when Allied leaders proclaimed the latter Victory-in-Europe Day, or V-E Day.[94]

Montgomery's reaction was relatively low key. As planned, most businesses remained closed, but schools opened with V-E Day observances. All liquor stores were closed that Tuesday. Some Montgomerians got drunk to celebrate, but beefed-up police patrols whisked the few visibly so to Judge Eugene Loe's Recorder's Court, where they were fined five dollars. When the proclamation came at 8:00 A.M., whistles blew and bells rang, but a quiet soon ensued. By noon the downtown streets were all but deserted. One World War I veteran commented, "You would think by the looks of things around here that we were the ones that surrendered."[95]

The deserted look had been deliberately planned. Military police directed all service people downtown to go to one of the four USOs— the three for whites and the single one for blacks. Maxwell and Gunter service people were trucked to their respective bases. Hometown folk in uniform were sent to their residences; others remained in the clubs. Officials of the city bus lines kept their vehicles in the garage, fearing riotous crowds, until Mayor Dunn convinced them by afternoon that the city had to have public transportation.[96]

On the two airfields it was, as the *Advertiser* phrased it, "one part ceremony and two parts work." Gunter base commander Colonel Raymond Winn told his assembled troops, "We must continue working for the last and final victory—the defeat of Japan."[97]

At night, downtown was much brighter with the end of the brown-out. Churches were open. Laura Johnston, an English teacher at Lanier, attended church that night. She remembered fifty years later that her joy was diluted by the sense of what still lay ahead.[98]

10

The End of the War

Enlisted air WACs prepare surgical bandages as volunteers for the Red Cross, summer of 1945. *Courtesy of the Alabama Department of Archives and History, Montgomery, Alabama.*

Montgomerians in the occupation forces perceptively described Europe at the war's end for readers at home. A writer who asked not to be identified wrote a letter to the *Advertiser* from Nuremberg, where "there's a continuous stream of refugees . . . on the main streets. There are DPs [displaced persons], freed Allied prisoners, freed German soldiers, Krauts returning from the countryside where they fled from the bombings, U.S. soldiers, British and American officers, German medical officers. . . . No one smiles." It was, he said, "a lifeless place in spite of the crowds of people and heavy traffic. . . . I passed a cemetery and church that had been plowed up by the bombs."[1]

Major Haynes Thompson, an AAF public relations man and former *Advertiser* journalist, described Berlin: "It isn't laid waste, flat-like. It's just gutted. The buildings . . . [are] hollow, floorless, charred." Touring the city, he thought of the "men who did the wrecking—the boys in the Forts and Libs and Lancasters . . . , those who lived only to see the beginning of their work, not the end. Many of them were Alabamians I knew; some, perhaps, Montgomerians."[2]

Private First Class John Brown wrote home about his tour of a concentration camp. "I saw corpses stacked like cordwood who had died from starvation and thousands . . . who would soon die. Some of the people looked so much like the dead ones that it is hard to distinguish between the living and the dead." He saw "the crematorium where the Nazis burned the victims and . . . the ashes of hundreds. . . . I could go on and on telling about the torture devices, such as whipping posts. . . . Before the Americans came they had nothing to sleep on except wooden racks." If "all Americans could see what I have seen," he said, "they would realize why this fight of right against wrong had to be fought."[3]

The *Advertiser* of May 9 was quick to try to redirect the public's focus to the war with Japan, at the same time reemphasizing the wartime empathy for Russia: "Russia will have every right to slack off her phenomenal war efforts . . . , but Britain and America have another rendezvous with death in the Pacific." Though the United States had "bloodily bought advanced bases from Guadalcanal to Okinawa" and "mopped up the Philippines," it had not yet met "the main armies of these suicidal fighters . . . on soil that they must keep if they are to survive as a national force." The writer sagely warned against a "premature let-down" with the course "so far from being run."[4]

For over a year a "let-down" had been increasingly evident in the population. It had been widespread after the invasion of Normandy but had somewhat dissipated at the onset of the Bulge. Why had there been a general lessening, among Montgomerians and others on the home front, of the fervor that had been evident after Pearl Harbor? Perhaps it was because their courage and stamina had not been tested with a Battle of Britain, the threat of an eminent invasion, a blitz. In spite of motion pictures and newsreels, most people had difficulty imagining the ordeal of the Russians and the horrors of the battle-fronts. After the turning of the tide against the Japanese in 1942, Americans had no doubts that they would win. By June 6, 1944, they had grown impatient for total victory.[5]

Rationing and shortages became harder to tolerate, as did regula-tions with regard to wages, prices, rents, and taxes. An editorial in the *Advertiser* for June 28 spoke of a "Dark Brown Market": "Extortion-ate prices being charged by certain dealers or hucksters for fish, fowl, fruits, and vegetables" were "flagrant violations" of OPA ceilings that allowed "generous profits . . . [on] commonplace items." The writer blamed individuals for "inept purchasing" and enforcement agencies for "deliberate winking."[6]

Many Montgomerians reacted angrily to an announcement from Washington that the United States was going to share its already short meat supply with Europeans on the verge of starvation in many war-ravaged areas. Local residents were not appeased by an editorial in the *Advertiser* noting that the average consumption of meat per person in the United States in 1944 exceeded that in Canada, where meat was not rationed. The federal government moved to ease shortages in some areas but seemed unable to bring relief in others. In mid-June, for example, Senator John Bankhead achieved an increase in pork and lard for Alabama even as the *Advertiser*'s front page headline declared, "Men's Clothing Supplies Drop to New Low." Some bureaucrats be-came weary. On May 15, Clara Kahn, chief clerk of the Montgomery War Price and Rationing Board and a stabilizing presence since Janu-ary 1942, had resigned.[7]

The seventh war bond drive that began nationally on April 9 be-came the longest of the war in the Montgomery area. In a shift from the previous drive, the E bond, or "people's bond," was the last cat-egory to meet its quota. It went over the top on July 4 only after a benefit at Cramton Bowl. The show featured girls waving flags, a parade of 500 cadets from the preflight school that had recently returned to Maxwell, a dance review by students from a local studio, and a jitterbug contest.[8]

The housing shortage, a persistent problem, worsened after V-E Day, intensifying desire for the war's end and a time when material would again be available for normal civilian construction. The *Advertiser* noted that Montgomery had "been spreading out during the war years" and that hundreds of new units had recently been built. The editorial acknowledged that these units were small, and it failed to explain that they were restricted to in-migrant defense workers. Although a few units went up in Capitol Heights, Oak Park, and Cloverdale, most were confined to certain fringe areas such as the extension of Madison Avenue and Upper Wetumpka Road. Constructed hastily, like units of housing projects, they were not dream homes for the postwar era and failed to alter the basic image of the city.[9]

Early in June, Colonel R. E. L. Choate, the commander of the Maxwell base, made a familiar appeal to Montgomerians with rooms and apartments to rent. The staffs of the preflight school and the AAF administrative officers' OCS, both transferred from Randolph Field, desperately needed housing. Choate stressed the plight of couples with children. "There will be a large influx of new personnel within the next three weeks," he said. "Many . . . will be combat returnees, who have not had a chance to be with their families for a long time." He was still appealing in mid-July, when the National Housing Association promised Mayor Dunn 300 house trailers for use at Maxwell and at H&R Point. But it would be sixty days before their arrival.[10]

Dunn's daughter, Isabel, and some of her friends home from college worked on a Red Cross flight line mobile canteen that had opened in May at Maxwell. It served mainly the B-29 crews training for the air offensive against the Japanese home islands. The young women were sometimes greeted by wolf whistles as they handed out coffee, sandwiches, and doughnuts.[11]

As in the summer of 1941, with the effects of the draft and the advent of the flying cadet, uniforms increased on both suburban and downtown streets. The cadets again became a welcome sight. There were more and more men returning from overseas with badges, wings, and multiple ribbons. The men back from the war fondly gazed on the familiar sights of the Square, on Dexter as it climbed to the capitol, and on the area around the intersection of Monroe and North Perry. The returning soldiers helped to crowd the swimming pools and theaters, ignoring the threat of a polio epidemic that seemed mild in comparison to what many had faced not long before.[12]

Those who had returned included AAF lieutenant colonel Claiborne H. Kinnard, Jr., whose wife resided in Montgomery. Kinnard, an eight-victory fighter ace with the Eighth Air Force, joined other military men without prewar ties whose families had moved to Montgomery during the conflict. The area had produced no native-born aces; to be an ace, a flyer had to have five officially credited air-to-air victories. Two men came the closest to acedom. AAF first lieutenant Cleveland ("Jack") Tatum, who grew up in Oak Park, was officially credited with three victories while he served with the Fifteenth Air Force in the Mediterranean. Navy lieutenant Richard Crommelin, before he was killed in an air accident, had scored three air-to-air victories. Kinnard's connection gave the city a slight claim to having an ace. Montgomery had a stronger claim on a second AAF fighter ace in the person of Major John T. Moore, who was missing in action. Moore had received his flight training at Gunter and Maxwell Fields and had later married Montgomerian Dorothy Ghent. Before he was listed as missing, he had destroyed seven Japanese planes with the Fifth Air Force over New Guinea.[13]

Private First Class Billy Crane came home in the summer for a long convalescent furlough from an army hospital in Atlanta. Wearing a metal brace on his right leg, he walked with a cane. The ribbons over the left pocket of his summer "suntans" included the Purple Heart. Above the ribbons shone the coveted blue-and-silver Combat Infantryman's Badge. Around the fringe of his overseas cap was a light blue cord that designated his branch. On his left shoulder was the red diamond patch of the Fifth Infantry Division, which had been Patton's infantry spearhead. He and Private First Class Wesley Newton, a recently liberated prisoner of war, had both been friends of Neal Howard.

Infantry Private First Class William "Billy" Crane, U.S. Army, home on convalescent furlough in summer 1945. *Courtesy of Joanna Breedlove Crane, Billy Crane's widow.*

Though they felt awkward, they visited Howard's parents on Southview. The grieving Howards received them graciously.[14]

With friends and fellow overseas veterans, Crane sampled the city's recreational offerings. The most popular nightclub for whites that summer was Gunn's, a few miles out on the Atlanta highway. While it had an enclosed area for dancing and dining, on clear nights couples preferred the patio, with its surrounding tables under pecan trees. Gunn's did not use any of the local dance orchestras employed by various other nightclubs, relying instead on jukeboxes, one on the inside and one on the patio. They offered familiar selections from name bands. Few who danced to the Glenn Miller theme "Moonlight Serenade" knew that Miller had been stationed at Maxwell Field for a short time or had heard that he was likely dead, a casualty of the war. But "Serenade" remained the wartime generation's favorite.[15]

The majority of the male patrons were military, and Billy Crane felt at ease there. He was unable to dance but did not seem troubled by it. He took a deep pride in his wounds and in the suffering that he had endured as an infantryman. He liked to sit under the pecan trees with a date and his buddies and their dates, chatting mostly about old times. The brutal aspects of the war seemed remote.[16]

Crane and Private First Class Wesley Newton, a buddy with a Purple Heart and Combat Infantryman's Badge, had several double dates that summer. Crane's date was the bright and attractive Virginia Waits, a Lanier graduate from the class of 1943. Wesley's date was the pretty brunette Mary Louise Caton, a Lanier alumna from the class of 1944 and a student at Alabama College in Montevallo. She was an accomplished violinist who played in Fanny Marks Seibels's local symphony orchestra. At Gunn's, Caton told her group of an incident witnessed at the H&R Point, where she had a summer job as a stock clerk. Late one afternoon when she was leaving a warehouse to go home, she watched the contingent of German POWs being marched by guards from the warehouses back to their stockade. A plane from the direction of Maxwell suddenly roared low overhead. All the prisoners of war hit the ground. For the first time, war movies and newsreels notwithstanding, Caton began to understand what combat must be like.[17]

AAF first lieutenant Silas ("Brook") Nettles went to Gunn's. Wearing the shoulder patch of the Eighth Air Force, now called the "Mighty Eighth" for its deeds, he had returned in June from eighteen months as a German prisoner of war. Katty Thornton, his longtime girlfriend, had not come from her job as Red Cross field worker in Florida to be with him. Family and friends were curious but did not probe. He escorted Jean Severence, a friend since junior high. They sat beneath the pecan trees, sipped drinks, and danced under the midnight blue sky that made the stars seem pristine and white.[18]

Nettles and Severence, having grown up in the gross humidity of Montgomery summers, enjoyed sitting together in the dark of air-conditioned theaters. Air conditioning, a new modern luxury, had reached Montgomery theaters, the better restaurants, and many department stores. Severence had broken up with her steady boyfriend of Tuscaloosa days. Like her friend Peggy Penton, she had played the field among cadets and officers at Maxwell and Gunter.[19]

But Nettles was different. In the summer of '45, under the stars and in one another's arms on the patio at Gunn's and in the ballroom of the Beauvoir Club, where a local band played live music, they were drawn together. By August they had acknowledged their love for one another and were planning a September wedding. Before plans were announced, Severence insisted that Nettles go to Florida to break the news to Katty Thornton.[20]

He hitched a ride, flying from Maxwell to Daytona Beach in an AT-6 trainer, a home-front sortie that made him apprehensive even over a peaceful green landscape. When he and Thornton talked privately, she did not act surprised or hurt by his news. For both, absence had altered their feelings for each other.[21]

Such changes of plans and of heart were not unusual in those hectic days of renewal. Romantic musical chairs, in fact, was a common experience over the course of the war, giving rise to the legendary "Dear John" and "Dear Jane" letters that terminated a relationship. Mary Ann Robinson, who had joined the WAC in Montgomery, had been involved in such an episode. As an enlisted woman, she had left behind her boyfriend, an enlisted man in the military police, when she came to Australia with the first WAC contingent in the spring of 1944. She later served in New Guinea and the Philippines, where she suffered through a Japanese air attack and was one of the first WAC enlisted women to enter Manila after its liberation. Although WACs could not be combatants as such, Robinson's company received a Presidential Unit Citation, and she wore two bronze campaign stars on her theater ribbon for having served in a combat area. Her relationship with the boyfriend in the military police did not survive time and separation. In late spring 1945, Robinson, by then a warrant officer, returned to the United States wearing an engagement ring given to her by a lieutenant in the U.S. Navy in the Philippines. She entered WAC officer candidate school and graduated as a second lieutenant.[22]

Word of war casualties continued to arrive. On May 18 at the Baldwin Junior High auditorium, a visiting lieutenant in the Marine Corps presented a posthumous Silver Star to the family of Corporal Paul Bayne, Jr., who had been killed on Saipan. Memorial services for the dead were held from time to time. Army medic private first class Jack Merrill, killed on Okinawa, was memorialized at the First Wesleyan Methodist Church; AAF first lieutenant Frank Harte, killed over Germany, at the Post Chapel, Gunter Field; and AAF first lieutenant J. T. Bryant, Jr., killed over Yugoslavia, at the Cloverdale Christian Church.[23]

News sometimes arrived of those who had been missing. In June, in Belgium, civilians accidentally discovered the grave of AAF first lieutenant Leonard Travis ("Tobie") Tobias. It at least ended the anxiety of his family but raised haunting questions. The grave was several hundred miles from where he had last been reported in March 1944— bailing out of a B-17 going down on the return from a mission to Berlin. How had he traveled so far? Had he made it on his own, been picked up by the German underground and passed along to Belgium, or been brought there for an unknown purpose by captors? Had he died fighting with the underground? Had he been captured and executed in Belgium, or had he perhaps expired of natural causes? The body was identified by dog tags. The cause of death could not be determined.[24]

May 11 saw the real beginning of the season of the new veteran. The War Department, soon followed by the Navy Department, announced a point system for the discharge of troops for other than medical reasons. Males had to have eighty-five points, and females, forty-four. The points were based on certain criteria that included one point for each month served, an additional point for each month overseas, five points for each decoration and official campaign, and twelve points for each child under eighteen years up to a total of three children. Combat troops in the European theater of operations designated for Pacific duty, combat troops already in the Pacific, and certain specialists would be retained "for military necessity" until the end of the war.[25]

In the summer of '45, no flood of discharged service people entered Montgomery. Enough new veterans began to appear, however, for Go Peep to notice them in her June 17 column: "We for one are heartily in favor of the . . . point system. The Beauvoir Club, the corner drug store, the hot dog stand—Montgomery in general seems more familiar, better, because we are beginning to see so many of the boys back at home." She acknowledged that in some cases it was only "thirty days leave before going on to a new assignment."[26]

The bronze battle stars on theater ribbons of some new veterans attested to their participation in some of the early fighting. Technical Sergeant Edward Breedlove wore the European-African-Middle Eastern ribbon over his left shirt pocket. One of his stars, referring to Air Offensive Europe, attested to his participation in the first formation of Eighth Air Force heavy bombers to fly a mission from England to the European Continent—three years past in the summer of '45. The discharge symbol, a golden eagle with a circular shield as background, was worn as a patch sewn over the right pocket of a serviceman's uniform. When he changed into civies, he wore the emblem as a lapel button. Most new veterans did not wear the symbol, which was irreverently called the "Ruptured Duck," for long. Helen Lee Wiley, a former WAC, wore the symbol and was one of the new veterans who joined an American Legion post in Montgomery.[27]

The practical as well as symbolic nature of veterans' clothing became important. For a time the newly discharged wore their uniforms or remnants of them because there was a shortage of civilian clothes until spring 1946. Many found that they had outgrown the old civies hanging in closets or packed in mothballs. Others felt emotionally attached to their uniforms and were reluctant to part with them for good.[28]

Events involving the Pacific fighting, the European occupation, and the Potsdam Conference dominated the news in the summer of '45. The last act of a local drama momentarily diverted attention in July. The lawyers for Worley James had succeeded in postponing his execution for carnal knowledge (tantamount to rape) of a black child; a clemency hearing took place on July 18. Standing before Governor Chauncey Sparks, defense attorney John Sankey charged that the trial jury had in reality recommended death because of the Drew murder but had masked its true intention behind the carnal knowledge verdict. Hinting that James might have been involved in the Drew murder, Sankey asked Sparks not to allow his client to die in the chair, since his early execution would leave the Drew case "unsolved." Two hours before James was to be executed, the governor commuted his sentence to life in prison, calling execution "under the facts . . . excessive." A few days later, B. Frank Noble, the foreman of the jury that had convicted James of carnal knowledge, wrote Sparks that "this fiend had an absolutely fair and impartial trial in every respect and his conviction met the general approbation of members of his race." James spent the rest of his life in the penitentiary.[29]

Many Montgomerians knew but cared little about a group meeting in San Francisco to create a second world peace organization to be called the United Nations (UN). Some were cynical, in view of the precedent set by the League of Nations. Dr. John Frazer, who had become the pastor of Dexter Avenue Methodist Church, was the spokesman for those in favor of the UN. A letter writer for the *Advertiser*, reflecting the "Bible Belt" disposition of the state, charged that the first act of the body "stamped it as the most colossal farce." The opening ceremony was begun with "a moment of silent meditation." "Why," he asked, "was God barred from the conference? Apparently to appease atheistic Russia."[30]

A few savvy Montgomerians understood the significance for the city's future of a new passenger and mail service inaugurated by Eastern Airlines on June 1. An *Advertiser* reporter described the ceremony: "Three Eastern Airline planes arriving almost simultaneously at Dannelly Field from as many points of the compass, were met by a representative group of State, city and county officials, members of the press and city business men." All flights employed the twenty-one-passenger DC-3, the first great modern American airliner. The military version had dropped paratroopers over such crucial battlegrounds as Normandy and the Philippines. The flight of one of the airliners had originated in New York and ended in New Orleans. The mail part of their route had been available in Montgomery since 1932 and the passenger part since the late 1930s. The other planes were inaugurating the new service, one from Miami bound for Chicago and one from Chicago to Miami.[31]

The *Advertiser* reiterated the ambition of the late Mayor W. A.

Gunter, who had paved the way for the city's first airline service and had been confident that Montgomery would become a major center for commercial aviation. The paper predicted that the "new service will make Montgomery and Atlanta the two hubs of the Eastern Air Lines system in the South and will give this city more stops than any other in the system except Florida." Additional good news came when Atlanta-based Delta, though not yet Eastern's equal, began to investigate Montgomery as a stop for its service.[32]

The majority of Montgomerians had never flown in an airliner and were unaware of Eastern's new service. The automobile, the train, and the bus, despite wartime inconveniences, were still the transportation of choice for Americans. Montgomerians were elated to read in June that the first new automobiles for civilians after three and a half years would soon go into production. It would, however, be over a year before enough cars would appear in dealers' showrooms to satisfy the demand.[33]

Such optimistic news helped to cool patriotic fervor. The *Advertiser* tried to reverse a trend, in which sewing and surgical bandage production had gotten increasingly behind their quotas. The paper observed that "other cities, too, have found interest lagging in phases of voluntary war work since the victory in Europe." On June 1 the *Advertiser* stated, "We are pleased to report that Montgomery women are responding handsomely to the appeals by the Red Cross." The paper again noted that the war with Japan was far from over.[34]

That the nation remained at war was evident from the fact that the transition training of crews in B-29s was at its peak at Maxwell. Some of the trained men soon joined Major Elmer Ambrose, the commander of a B-29 squadron based on Guam, whose wife and son rented lodging on Southview Avenue. One of the bombers on Guam was named the *City of Montgomery* because its pilot had trained there. Ambrose and Major Robert D. Luman had piloted B-29s in raids on Tokyo. Their formations had "poured thousands of tons of incendiary bombs on congested areas," according to a wire service story in the *Advertiser* of May 30, leaving "more than 51 square miles surrounding the imperial grounds . . . , a great mass of gray ashes marking the site of thousands of buildings and residences." Virginia Welch Luman, a Montgomerian, had met Idaho native Robert Luman while he was stationed at Maxwell. Early in July she received a telegram at her mother's house on West Fifth Street that he was missing in action. The last message from Major Luman's plane had been "We are ditching." The aircraft had failed to reach Iwo Jima.[35]

Montgomery had contributed its share of general officers to the armed forces. Some of them, such as Major General Curtis LeMay, a key figure in the B-29 campaign, were connected with the city because their families resided there temporarily during the war. Others, such as Brigadier General Nicholas Cobbs, fiscal director of army operations in the European theater of operations, were native sons. Marine Corps lieutenant general Holland M. "Howling Mad" Smith came to the city late in July to be with his sick mother. The controversial architect of amphibious operations in the Pacific, such as those at Tarawa, Iwo Jima, and Okinawa, the Auburn graduate had once coached football at Starke School and had briefly practiced law in Montgomery before deciding to join the Marine Corps. On July 28 he predicted to a reporter for the *Advertiser* that the Japanese would "fold up" in six months or less. "They haven't any fleet . . . [or] any merchant marine, and their cities are being systematically destroyed one after the other." Knowing that Japan's industry depended heavily on electrical energy, the United States "was rapidly knocking out their dams, their factories, their power plants and industries." When the Japanese saw the powerful force assembled for invasion, it would "give them a pretty weak heart."[36]

First Lieutenant Fred Burks had gone with the Ninety-third Infantry Division from Morotai, Dutch East Indies, to Mindanao in the Philippines in late February 1945. The campaign there was essentially over, and the Ninety-third saw no action. The destruction was extensive, forcing the Ninety-third to live in tents. While the division trained for an invasion of Japan, Fred took time to interact with the Filipinos. No local priest was left to minister to an overwhelmingly Catholic population. Not himself a Catholic, Burks attended a mass celebrated by a black chaplain of the Ninety-third. Afterward people flocked around to kiss the chaplain's hand. When Burks realized that no dogs were anywhere to be seen, he did not have to ask the Filipinos why. Their hungry faces and gratitude for food brought by the Americans gave the answer. For recreation the Ninety-third troops watched nightly movies and divided into teams for sports. Burks played basketball in an officers' league. The white Thirty-first "Dixie" Infantry Division, the Alabama Nation Guard unit federalized in 1940, was stationed on Mindanao but not close enough for much contact with the Ninety-third.[37]

Navy quartermaster third class John Sawyer had his last leave in the fall of 1944 before shipping out to the far Pacific. As a special treat he took his young son and daughter to the Peking Theater. His family went to see him off when he left Union Station to return to base. Parting was hard. From Hampton Beach, Virginia, he traveled with other black service people by segregated day coach to Chicago. From Chicago to California, Pullmans were available for blacks, and Sawyer had a berth. Blacks were allowed to eat in the diner but behind a screen that separated them from the white section. During one of his meals, Sawyer noticed that some German prisoners of war were being served in the white section.[38]

Sawyer boarded his ship at Oakland. It was a refrigerated food ship with a crew of 300 whose mission was to provision the fleet. In a Navy Department experiment, Sawyer was the first of eighteen black seamen to be absorbed into the crew with various duties. The others were to be picked up at a station in the Pacific. Sawyer was not segregated when he went aboard, but unlike the whites who held the same rank, he had no command authority over seamen who worked around him.[39]

In November the ship sailed for Pearl. On the voyage Sawyer worked on the bridge and noticed no hostility from the skipper. At every opportunity he sent his wife V-Mail letters, but censorship was tight. He saw the watery image of *Arizona* at Pearl Harbor. From Pearl, his ship sailed to Eniwetok in the Marshalls, where the other seventeen black sailors joined the crew. At that point the black sailors were assigned segregated facilities for berths and at the chow table. Representing the other blacks, Sawyer went through channels to seek redress. The ship's executive officer told him that the officers—all white—had decided that the arrangement was best for the crew in general. Sawyer and the other black sailors felt betrayed and "dehumanized."[40]

The ship went south to New Zealand for several months' stay. There Sawyer appreciated the respectful and even friendly treatment that he received from the white population. His ship arrived off Okinawa in late May while the kamikazes were still harassing the fleet. His ship was protected by smoke screens laid by a "smokeboat." "We could see them [the kamikazes]," he recalled, "but they could not necessarily see us." His skipper decided to make sure they continued unseen by rewarding the crew of the smokeboat with five gallons of ice cream for every day they remained unscathed. When Sawyer's ship was ordered to another side of the island, the cruiser that took its space was soon hit by a suicide plane.[41]

Organized Japanese resistance came to an end on Okinawa on June 21. In July, Corporal Aaron Harris, Jr., arrived on the island after a month's voyage from Seattle. He had left a girlfriend behind in New Jersey. His journey on a transport in a convoy had been both tedious and interesting. "Wherever we wanted to sleep on the ship," he recalled, "we slept." Soldiers became seasick when they encountered heavy seas, but he did not. They played cards and rolled dice, little aware of the threat of Japanese submarines. Sirens and loudspeakers eventually generated excitement. They went back to their games after learning that the alarm had been only a drill.[42]

On Okinawa Harris heard the distant fire of small arms, a sign of scattered resistance, mainly from individuals. He saw a few dead Americans and Japanese, the latter the target of flies, the former covered by shelter halves. Harris felt fortunate that he was not under one of the shelter halves. His prime duty was to guard Japanese prisoners of war, who wore special uniforms stamped POW. Sullen and banding together, they were kept in a hut with a shower outside and were allowed to make saki. Armed with a service .45 automatic pistol, Harris accompanied the prisoners for work such as KP. No one tried to escape.[43]

Corporal Aaron Harris, Jr., U.S. Army,
1944. *Courtesy of Aaron Harris, Jr.*

Harris and his buddies lived in tents but ate cooked meals. As the
fighting petered out, WACs, in both white and black companies, came
to Okinawa as stenographers and clerks. Harris saw black American
commissioned officers but was not involved with them. He encountered no obvious racism from white troops.[44]

Ralph Loeb, Jr., electrician's mate third class (for interior communications), joined the crew of a new destroyer, U.S.S. *Hanson* (D.D.
832), early in 1945 in Boston. One of his first duties was to repair faulty
bearings in a motor. Since his training had been all theoretical up to
that point, the chief electrician's mate had to give him on-the-job training. The shakedown cruise was from Boston to Cuba. Loeb was for a
time quite seasick. In the blue and turquoise waters of the Caribbean,
he saw battleships and carriers like *Hanson* engaged in various training exercises, including the dropping of depth charges.[45]

Hanson returned to Boston for supplies and then left again for the
Caribbean and the Panama Canal, where the ship joined a destroyer
flotilla bound for Pacific combat. The men were informed that the

ship would have picket duty off Okinawa. The kamikazes had at first ignored picket ships, but the situation changed in the summer of 1945. The Japanese had learned that the pickets alerted the fleet when the suicide planes were on the way. Before putting in at San Diego, *Hanson's* crew learned that the danger from kamikazes had ended.[46]

Loeb's crew had a black sailor, but he was not segregated. The trip to the far Pacific was wearing. The ship encountered heavy seas, but Loeb adapted. He averaged five to six hours of sleep out of twenty-four and stood watches of four hours on, six hours off. Between watches, he had other chores. On watch he was often overcome by grief. His father, Loeb's best friend and counselor, had died just before he shipped out, and Loeb had obtained emergency leave to attend the funeral. He tried to write his mother every day and postdated an extra letter for days when he could not write. Loeb had no steady girlfriend to occupy his thoughts.[47]

As the war seemed to be nearing some kind of climax, people whose loved ones were prisoners of war in Japanese camps became more anxious. News about one prisoner increased their foreboding. In September 1944, regular army major James C. Knowles, captured on Corregidor, had been permitted to send a message over shortwave radio that a ham operator relayed to his family in Montgomery. "I am in good health. Hope to be home soon, then we can have a reunion. God bless you all." His mother and sisters did not hear of him again until Japanese records were uncovered in the Philippines after the liberation. These records revealed that Knowles had been aboard a Japanese merchantman taking prisoners of war to the home islands in December when it was sunk by Allied aircraft. The family learned late in July 1945 that Knowles had been one of 942 POWs who had died.[48]

The Crommelins had their own tragedies to bear. The family had lost Charles, a navy dive-bomber pilot and air group commander, over Okinawa in March 1945 in a collision with another American plane. Fighter pilot Richard died over Japan in June in a similar accident.[49]

With the end of the main fighting on the Pacific islands by July, an expectant waiting gripped many on the home front, while others no longer paid much attention to the world far away. In Montgomery, after a brief pickup in the production of Red Cross surgical bandages, volunteering hit rock bottom late in July. No quota had been met since April. The local chapter reported that the entire daily output from the three centers left open—Maxwell, the Elks Club, and the Capitol Heights Church of Christ—was enough to supply only one seriously wounded soldier with bandages during his hospitalization. The Maxwell center's output was primarily produced by WACs who volunteered to turn out bandages during off-duty hours or while they were patients in the base hospital. On August 4 the Red Cross chapter announced that most of its volunteer structure seemed to be collapsing—sewing, knitting, the motor corps, the canteen corps, and the Gray Ladies as well as surgical bandage wrapping. In desperation, the organization turned to black volunteers, at segregated centers in the Paterson housing project and the newer Cleveland Avenue project, but this move was too late.[50]

The especially bloody and protracted nature of ground combat on Iwo Jima and Okinawa worried the Allied high command in the Pacific, and U.S. president Harry Truman, as they planned for an invasion of Japan. Censorship prevented telling the home front that the planners estimated that an invasion and the conquest of the Japanese home islands would bring casualties of more than 200,000. But the media wasted no time in reaching such a conclusion; they did so on the basis of comparisons with Okinawa, where fierce enemy resistance had brought thousands of civilian and military casualties. The home islands had more organized defense and a much larger population. Privately, a few experts believed casualties might exceed a million.[51]

Censorship likewise kept the public from hearing of the successful test of a "Super Bomb" in New Mexico in mid-July. The delivery of an operation-ready atomic bomb to the Marianas in late July was veiled in secrecy.[52]

One of the first uses of the term V-J Day in Montgomery came in a headline of an *Advertiser* editorial on June 4, 1945: "V-E DAY—AND V-J DAY." The editor predicted "one of these days we shall have occasion to celebrate final and complete victory." When the day came,

Montgomery would greet it either "happily but soberly" or with a "spontaneous celebration such as greeted the armistice in 1918." Municipal and military officials decided that the V-E Day scheme with modification would be applied when V-J Day dawned. Police and military police patrols were to be larger.[53]

Early in the morning of August 6, a B-29 named the *Enola Gay* appeared over the Japanese city of Hiroshima, near the inland sea on the southern coast of Honshu. It released an atomic bomb, producing a soaring, mushroomlike cloud and clear-air turbulence. In Montgomery, radios told of the event, and the evening *Journal* had a banner headline—"U.S. TURNS ATOM BOMBS AGAINST JAPAN"—but the accompanying story had sparse details. The *Advertiser*'s headline of the seventh was dramatic: "Deadliest Bomb of All Time Erases Jap City of 318,000 on Inland Sea." An article analyzed the bomb's workings and traced some of the scientific efforts that had produced it.[54]

The local papers had more details on the eighth. The *Advertiser* editorialized that if Japan had received and ignored an ultimatum, "then the Japanese will . . . face extermination." But the editor warned that "the force American scientists have discovered is so terrible in its potentialities that it could, improperly used, mean the end of civilization."[55]

The *Advertiser* had a banner headline on the ninth: "RUSSIANS ATTACK JAPS IN MANCHUKO." Besides the account of the Russian action of the eighth, an article with a smaller headline reported a military development of the ninth: "Second Atomic Bomb Dropped on Nagasaki, 12th Largest Nip City." The accompanying article reported, "Crew members radioed that results were good."[56]

Former Eighth Air Force B-17 gunner staff sergeant Bob Lawrence, on a Victory Ship transport headed for New York City, heard the announcement about Nagasaki over the ship's loudspeaker system. He was happy; he would not go to the Pacific. Details about the second A-bomb explosion followed in the papers on the tenth.[57]

A story published on the eleventh got more attention in Montgomery and set off some celebrations elsewhere. The Japanese had offered to surrender on the condition that Emperor Hirohito be allowed to stay on the throne. Americans were so jumpy on the twelfth that a "False V-J Day" occurred when a wire story inaccurately announced that Japan had accepted all Allied peace terms. In Montgomery, a correction headed off a possibly wild celebration.[58]

On the thirteenth the city bus drivers' union announced that drivers would stay home on V-J Day. Immediately Mayor David Dunn declared that this would amount to a strike. O. O. Martin, chairman of the local union, responded by saying that many of the drivers were veterans of overseas service or fathers with sons overseas and were entitled to a day off. The two sides met to seek a compromise.[59]

On the fourteenth, a Tuesday, at 7:00 P.M. President Harry Truman announced that the Japanese had agreed to the Allied terms of unconditional surrender. Montgomery, according to the *Advertiser* for the fifteenth, "erupted with joy and from then on until far into the night the city's business section was a place of joy and celebration." Night businesses closed, and only vital businesses, such as drugstores, planned to open the next day. For "a hour and a half after the surrender was announced, horns and all kinds of noise makers were sounding loudly on the main thoroughfare and Dexter Avenue was a mass of streaming cars, oblivious to all traffic signals." Along Dexter "from the Capitol to the Exchange Hotel . . . , confetti, streamer tape and torn paper strips" littered the ground and floated "from passing cars and upstairs windows." Fireworks exploded, and "many wondered where such a multitude of explosives had been cached since Montgomery had voted it unlawful some years ago within the city limits."[60]

To head off violence, Chief Ralph King and Commissioner W. P. Screws had consulted a few moments after Truman's announcement and dispatched police patrols and civil defense auxiliary police onto the streets. Beefed-up military police patrols came from the air bases and began to order military personnel off the streets into the USOs and hotels or back to the bases. Chief King told law enforcement officers that they should act with restraint, making arrests only to prevent property damage or injuries. Immediately after Truman's announcement, all liquor stores were ordered to close. In line with an agreement made between the city and the union, the buses made one more run after the word of surrender came, then headed for the garage. They resumed their schedules on the fifteenth.[61]

Contrasting scenes took place at each end of Dexter. On the corner of Bainbridge and Dexter, "seven or eight small boys and girls, five or six years old, had gathered with flags and improvised noise makers. While some of the children waved their Stars and Stripes, the others beat upon kitchen pans with spoons in an ecstacy of joy." At the Square several young men scaled the fence around the fountain, climbed the statue, and jumped in the water. Police watched and deterred others but did not arrest the swimmers. One youth who climbed the statue placed a small American flag in the goddess's hand. Ushers at the Strand Theater on the Square beat on garbage cans and joined a "snake dance" that had originated on Commerce and wrapped itself around the fountain. The *Advertiser* reported that "even the newly arrived Chinese [aviation] cadets joined the milling crowd. They might not understand the language, but they understood the celebration."[62]

Reporter Charles Harbin, Jr., interviewed various celebrating people. One new veteran said, "Listen, mate, tell 'em that a discharged Marine calls it a day for celebrating. I'm tight but I still know what's going on." A gray-haired white woman said, "I'm so happy I could cry. This is the second World War I've been through but this is the first time I've had a son in one." Harbin saw a black woman "trying to jump up and down with glee."[63]

Service people began to return to the streets as the night wore on, some with spouses or sweethearts. "Three gobs" on Dexter told Harbin, "We're really getting drunk. It's wonderful and it really hit us nice. The women here just won't leave us alone. What a town!" A Montgomerian, army medic corporal Leon Shirley, who had been wounded in the Bulge and had been decorated with a Silver Star, told him, "I think it's perfectly all right. Too bad it took so long."[64]

A small number of military people did not join in the celebration but instead watched it soberly. Other reporters saw a marine with overseas ribbons standing apart: "His face was unlined, but as he glanced our way when a tire blew a short distance from us, the pain and emptiness of his eyes shocked us into realizing that this boy's reaction was

Petty Officer John Sawyer, U.S. Navy.
Courtesy of John Sawyer.

not that of the crowd. . . . Tarawa was his background. Or maybe Iwo Jima."[65]

At the local airfields most personnel were at supper when the news came. At Maxwell the announcement came over the extensive public address system. Troops rushed from mess halls, barracks, and day rooms whooping and waving their arms. The same thing happened at Gunter. The troops were told that the news did not mean immediate demobilization. No organized celebration took place that night, but on the seventeenth, troops assembled at the flight lines to hear the official declaration of peace from the base commanders.[66]

At Alabama State and Huntingdon, students cheered and danced with one another in the dorms and on the campuses. Religious services, previously arranged, soon took place.[67]

Firecrackers popped about the city almost until dawn. Throughout this Wednesday, an official holiday for state and federal employees, the city was largely quiet. Businesses were closed unless they were regarded as essential, but the yellow city buses made their regular runs. City street-sweeping machines cleaned up the debris downtown. Apart from this relatively brief activity, the day seemed like some normal tranquil Sabbath. The next day was just another weekday in peacetime.[68]

The ships of John Sawyer and Ralph Loeb put in at Japanese ports and were among the first to arrive after the signing of the peace treaty in September on the battleship *Missouri*. Sawyer went with a truckload of shipmates to Hiroshima, which they surveyed from the truck. The city was still charred and desolate. Loeb soon saw vivid evidence of B-29 incendiary bombing. From the vantage point of ground zero, he also observed the wasteland of Nagasaki.[69]

Epilogue

Retired college administrator Frederick D. Burks at the site of his
boyhood home in Montgomery County. *Courtesy of Frederick D. Burks;
collection of Wesley Newton.*

A nationwide coal strike diverted attention from events overseas in late 1945 and the first half of 1946. Such events included the
Bikini Atoll A-bomb experiments, the beginning of the Nuremberg
and Japanese war crimes trials, the crisis affecting the British and the
Jews in Palestine, U.S. involvement in the Chinese civil war between
the Nationalists and the Communists, and the widening split between
the western Allies of World War II and the U.S.S.R.[1]

But the effects and echoes of the Second World War lingered

throughout 1946. One of the biggest items of unfinished business was demobilization. The War and Navy Departments speeded up the implementation of plans to discharge most of their wartime host of 15 million men and women only after there had been several demonstrations by servicemen overseas, and female relatives had exerted pressure, with the power of the vote, on Congress. The bulk of the downsizing took place starting in September 1945 and lasting until the summer of 1946.[2]

Fred Burks, Aaron Harris, Ralph Loeb, and John Sawyer returned home across the Pacific. Bob Lawrence and Bobby Young crossed the Atlantic to reach Montgomery. Marguerite Sherlock arrived with a discharge from Camp Lejeune, North Carolina. Each had suffered recurrent and sometimes acute homesickness.[3]

These seven had homecoming experiences that were at once universal and personal. Bob Lawrence was the first of the seven to reach Montgomery. When his transport arrived off New York City late in August 1945, boats and ships sprayed water into the air, blared horns, and blew whistles. Before docking, Lawrence's ship passed downtown Manhattan, where confetti streamed from windows and people cheered, waved flags, and held up welcoming banners. Lacking sufficient points for discharge, Lawrence was sent to Fort McPherson in Atlanta for reassignment after a thirty-day furlough. On a Greyhound bus and "growing more excited with every passing mile," he experienced "a surge of nostalgia as the bus drove by Gunn's where we used to gather in high school days on Friday and Saturday nights."[4]

The reunion with his parents was especially emotional because Bill Lawrence was confined to a wheelchair after a major heart attack. The depression and the war had combined to take their toll in the ranks of middle-aged males on the home front.[5]

At the end of the century, no longer living in Montgomery, Lawrence would recall his impressions of the city: "Home at last! Or was I home? Everything looked the same but somehow it wasn't. Yet was it that I had changed or was it home?" He went to see whether Lanier looked the same. Were the halls, as in the alma mater's lyrics, "hallowed?" Lawrence quickly realized, "I didn't belong there any more. . . . I left my boyhood somewhere on a bomb run over Germany." Eventually he came to the conclusion that "no, I wasn't the same and neither was anybody else. Nor was Montgomery."[6]

The immediate happiness of homecoming was universal. Bobby Young, after seven months with the occupation forces, willingly endured the stormy North Atlantic of January 1946. During the voyage he "collected many francs" from other GI's as a result of the Crimson Tide's upset victory over Southern California in the Rose Bowl, a victory sparked by Alabama tailback "leaping" Harry Gilmer. He arrived home with a Ruptured Duck, and "Union Station did not seem different after three years' absence." As a boy he had spent "a lot of time" there, where his grandfather, Frank Young, had been chief dispatcher for the L&N railroad, a position he held when the station first opened in 1898. Frank had watched young men depart and return from the Spanish American War and World War I. The first change Bobby Young noticed was not a structural one to the city itself. Meeting his family at the station, he saw that his "bratty" little sister, Betty, had become "a grown woman . . . , graduated from Lanier, and was a draftsman for the [state] highway department."[7]

In its physical aspect, Young saw little change in Montgomery as a whole. And the racial scene remained the same. In 1947 the public swimming pool at the lovely city park in Oak Park, which he managed that summer, was still for whites only.[8]

Marguerite Sherlock was exceedingly happy to come home with a discharge in April 1946. She had missed her family and friends more than she had thought possible. When she had settled in at home and had had a chance to look around the city, she concluded that downtown "looked the same" except that the crowds were fewer than before the war because of a continued shortage of goods. It would be a year before the crowds seemed normal. By the mid-1950s population growth had accelerated, contributing to the postwar suburbia phenomenon as the commercial center had begun to shift away from downtown to outlying shopping malls.[9]

In 1946 Sherlock noticed that within her social circle—the middle class and gentry—people were feeling "a loss of freedom." Economic controls since 1942—rationing and resultant shortages, war taxes, and wage and price ceilings—had limited individual choice. The sense of loss persisted because the effects of rationing and the shortages of such things as clothing, liquor, and automobiles persisted. Though rationing ended soon after the war, food was not abundant in the immediate postwar years because it had to be shared with impoverished non-Communist Europe. The postwar low morale was also evident, Sherlock noticed, in the failure of people in her circle to show the zest for partying that they had had before the war and even during it. Bob Lawrence had noticed the same phenomenon on a broader scale: "The days of wine and roses were gone for good—if they ever existed."[10]

Sherlock also observed that, even in her circle, mothers continued to be the parent primarily responsible for raising the children, as they had been during the war. Families had to readjust as fathers returned. In time the male parent regained his traditional status as the head of household and the final arbiter. By the same token, war industry changed over to peacetime production, and women war workers relinquished their jobs to make way for males returning from the service. Still, war workers appeared more reluctant than mothers to return to the old ways of doing things. Feminism in the future would have much to say about women in both categories.[11]

Young, Sherlock, and Lawrence quickly grasped one prime factor that contributed to the civilian malaise. Young found civilian clothes "very hard to buy." Sherlock, off to Auburn in the fall of 1946 to finish her degree on the GI Bill, had to supplement her wardrobe with navy blouses and skirts. Lawrence, discharged in November 1945 after the point system was canceled, located only one available white shirt—the principal piece of clothing that for many veterans symbolized liberation from the uniform. Unable to find presentable civilian slacks, Lawrence was fortunate in being able to purchase a sports jacket that went with his GI pants. Ties "were outlandish," but veterans "bought them anyway" to indicate their civilian status. The three veterans shared a desire for new cars or at least cars that looked like new, but many months passed before new ones appeared in dealers' showrooms in adequate numbers. When Sherlock was finally able to buy a new car, she found that, like other women, she could not get credit in her own right. She had to buy on her father's credit. Feminism later addressed this subject as well.[12]

Ralph Loeb, Jr., who was discharged in May 1946, recalled the "long waiting lists for cars at the time. . . . It was virtually impossible to get a car, if you didn't have one to trade in." Some dealers expected bribes as part of the deal, but "many of the dealers who used such tactics went out of business as soon as new cars began to really roll off the assembly lines."[13]

Loeb and many others who had just been discharged assembled once a week at the state employment office on Clayton Street downtown to collect their readjustment pay. The sum was twenty dollars a week for a total of fifty-two weeks, or until a veteran found a job or went back to school. When asked by a clerk at the employment office what he was qualified to do, Loeb replied, "Shipboard electrician." After three years in the navy, he had no ambition to work that summer. He planned to attend college at Alabama on the GI Bill. He collected his twenty dollars per week until September. "Even though there was some criticism of it," he later reflected, "even the wealthiest returning veterans took it, because they earned it."[14]

Bob Lawrence did not take it. Having been admitted to Auburn beginning with the January 1946 term, he decided that the money was not worth the red tape necessary to get it for such a short time period. After spending several months courting his girlfriend in North Carolina, Bobby Young enjoyed part of the summer of 1946 as a "beach bum" at Panama City. With his mustering-out pay of $300, he had purchased a 1940 Plymouth. Its "tires were missing large amounts of rubber," but he made the round trip to Montgomery each week to collect his twenty dollars at the required office in his hometown. After abandoning his courtship as unsuccessful, Young joined the college-bound veterans in the fall and enrolled in Centenary College in Louisiana for the fall term. There he eventually found his future wife.[15]

Marguerite Sherlock, looking back in 1998, did not remember ever being briefed about her rights to readjustment pay. Aaron Harris, Jr., collected his twenty dollars for a few weeks until he went to work at his father's dry cleaners. The disbursement offices for black and white veterans were separated.[16]

Along with streets, theater lobbies, and social occasions, the benches in the employment office on Clayton Street frequently witnessed reunions between old friends who not seen each other for what felt like an eternity. There were vigorous handshakes or hugs and rapid-fire exchanges of news in the ritual of renewal. Occasionally the conversation touched on recent bulletins related to the war, such as word of the death of army private Douglas Kittrell and the torture of AAF first lieutenant James Tucker Fite, both survivors of the Bataan death march, before the liberation of Japanese prisoner-of-war camps. The newly reunited men and women exchanged other information: "Did you hear that Harriet Englehardt was killed in a Jeep accident in Europe?" "I dropped by to see Mr. and Mrs. Robinson. It was hard to keep from busting out crying."[17]

Not long after the war, in 1947, the Robinsons, Howards, Godwins, and other next of kin had to decide where their loved ones were permanently to be buried. Both Billy Robinson and Neal Howard lay in the U.S. military cemetery at Henri Chapelle, Belgium, that had been created in 1944 to accommodate the anticipated casualties from the final assault on the Reich. Donald Godwin was buried in the U.S. military cemetery overlooking the Normandy beaches and the English Channel. Families could choose to leave a loved one's body in one of the well-tended military cemeteries overseas, with their orderly rows of white crosses and Stars of David, or, as soon as practicable, could have the body brought back and buried in a family plot at government expense.[18]

The Howards chose to have their son brought back and buried in Greenwood Cemetery. They simply wanted him home so that they could put flowers on his grave and pray there. The Godwins made the same choice for the same reasons and buried their son in the smaller Memorial Cemetery not far from the H&R Point. The Robinsons agonized over their decision. In the end they decided to leave their son's body in Belgium. Alice felt that to bring him back for a second burial would be like having him die all over again. The Robinsons later learned that a Belgian family visited Billy Robinson's grave periodically and placed flowers by the white cross.[19]

Dorothy Ghent Moore did not have a choice. In January 1946 the War Department notified her by form letter that her husband, AAF major John T. Moore, missing in action in the Pacific for almost two years, was now presumed dead. Similarly, Sherman White, Sr., and his wife had no decision to make about their son, AAF first lieutenant Sherman, Jr., who had been shot down over the Mediterranean and was never found. Peggy Penton learned that a former sweetheart stationed at Maxwell, Mac McMillan, whose offer of marriage she had rejected, had died in the Pacific and had been buried in the U.S. military cemetery at Manila.[20]

Veterans were for the most part ready to put the war behind them. Some were taking important steps for the future. AAF first lieutenant Brook Nettles married Jean Severence in September 1945. Peggy Penton was Jean's maid of honor. Billy Crane and his former Lanier classmate Virginia Waits were married in June 1946. In general new veterans had confidence in the future. While they may not have consciously thought about it, they were appreciated, more than any other generation of recently demobilized American veterans except possibly those of the Civil War. Some could return to the jobs they had had prior to military service. Tacky Gayle, on leave for three and a half years, resumed his place on the Montgomery City Commission. John Sawyer regained his job with the Montgomery Post Office. But Bob Lawrence later recalled that "the job you had before you left might not be waiting on you."[21]

The new veterans had the GI Bill with its educational, loan, and other benefits. Enrollment in U.S. colleges jumped from 1.6 million in 1945 to 2.1 million in the fall of 1946. Of those enrolled in 1946, 48.7 percent were veterans. Though the books and fees were underwritten by the government, the monthly seventy-five-dollar stipend for living expenses was not designed for luxurious living.[22]

Huntingdon College had admitted a few "town boys" in the 1930s. The Huntingdon administration announced in 1946 that it would admit more males if they were Montgomery veterans. Huntingdon

AAF First Lieutenant Silas "Brook" Nettles and Jean Severence Nettles on their wedding day. *Courtesy of Silas and Jean Nettles.*

thereby helped to relieve a severe rooming and housing shortage at the state's colleges with the influx of veterans as students. A minority of veterans attending college soon quit or "horsed around" and flunked out. Bob Lawrence spoke for the serious majority of veterans. "There was this anxious feeling that life had run off without me and I had to catch up. Many of us broke our backs going year 'round in college in order to graduate in three years."[23]

The many veterans across the land who benefited from the GI Bill became essential to a nation that was prosperous as well as powerful. After adjustments at the end of wartime controls, the United States began to develop into a superpower. As a future historian of the GI Bill put it, veterans who were able to take advantage of the legislation's benefits were "about to get a new life, and the lives of all Americans would be transformed as a result."[24]

Billy Crane became a certified public accountant; Wesley Newton, a college professor who specialized in history; Bobby Young, an entrepreneur in the oil industry (and eventually, fulfilling an old ambition, a Texas cattle rancher). Bob Lawrence was ordained a Presbyterian minister after studying to be an architect. Ralph Loeb became an electrical engineer; Marguerite Sherlock, a medical technician. Crane, Loeb, Newton, and Sherlock in time became permanent residents of Montgomery.[25]

But the majority of veterans, in Montgomery and elsewhere, did not attend college. Bobby Young encountered Talmadge Lambert, who had been a cannoneer in his artillery battery overseas. A driver for the Red Taxi Company, he was more nearly representative of Montgomery veterans in the immediate postwar period than were college students Young, Crane, Lawrence, Loeb, Newton, and Sherlock.[26]

Former merchant marine seamen, such as Tommy Oliver, received no government benefits despite the vital service they had rendered. Oliver worked to help put himself through Auburn and graduated a veterinarian. The percentage of merchant seamen who had lost their lives when submarine warfare was at its worst was higher than that for the armed forces. In the 1980s, four decades after the end of World War II, Congress finally gave the conflict's merchant marine veterans the status of war veterans.[27]

One of the war's more positive legacies, in part a product of the GI Bill, was to raise the standards of lower-class whites. As historian J. Wayne Flynt described it, across the South, "thousands of poor people were absorbed into the lower middle class." Locally the effect among whites was at first felt most in West End, north Montgomery, Boylston, and Chisholm. Still, the elite continued to dominate politics and business. A fair number of the lower-class veterans now entering the middle class found employment elsewhere with skills acquired in the services.[28]

Across the classes, as Bob Lawrence later observed, "Many of us who went away [to war] and returned did not stay." There was, however, no decrease in the population. Many of the people who had become residents during the war, swelling the prewar population, remained as permanent residents after the war. Ralph Loeb, who was in and out of Montgomery during the postwar decade, observed that as some residents left, "more new people" moved into the city, repeating a phenomenon seen after World War I. War may have made profound change inevitable, but Lawrence was not certain: "Places where I once went hunting are suburbs. Urban sprawl invades the old neighborhoods. The quiet streets are jammed with traffic.[29]

"The quiet southern town of the 40s I loved so dearly is no more. Would it have survived without the war? Probably not. Still, sometimes in my dreams I go back to how it was and wonder if my old home town is better now or worse. . . . But one thing is certain: Whatever Montgomery was it's different."[30]

Some changes brought by the war were heartening. The Standard Country Club removed the restriction that limited its membership to Reform Jews. The revelations of the Holocaust's horrors brought Jews together. Neither the Standard nor the Beauvoir Club ceased to deny membership to blacks, however, and notwithstanding the Holocaust, the Beauvoir Club waited five decades before it began to admit Jews, and the Jews would reciprocate by admitting Gentiles. The bulk of business and governmental leadership remained concentrated in these country clubs for a time. But of greater consequence was the fact that whites across the board in the old Confederate South, including the majority of white World War II veterans, had no intention of tolerating integration of the municipal swimming pools, their churches, civic clubs, motion picture theaters, water fountains, and, more important, public schools and judicial and criminal justice systems. And they intended to keep access to the voting booths as restricted as possible.[31]

While war wrought or accentuated some social, psychological, demographic, and economic changes in Montgomery, the city's physical image, as returning service people discovered, was largely unchanged. Ralph Loeb noticed practically no changes in his city's physical appearance, "perhaps," he would later comment, "because of a wartime restriction against any construction that did not directly concern the war effort." The yellow city buses remained the cheap and reliable chief form of municipal transportation. The older regular taxi companies had survived their wartime image.[32]

With war's end, however, physical change was now possible. At the city commission meeting of August 6, 1945, the postwar resumption of street improvements began with approval of the paving of several streets in Capitol Heights and Oak Park. The streets of chiefly black areas came up short as in the past. The housing shortage had not vanished with the war, and construction of new houses and apartments for the general population depended upon scarce materials that only gradually became available. For a while the garage apartment was the leading postwar type of newly constructed housing. The city received federal funds for two veterans' housing projects that contained, respectively, 274 units for whites and 75 for blacks. Montgomery had resumed a regular pattern of paving and construction by 1948, extending the city primarily eastward.[33]

The majority of returning veterans overlooked one major physical change within the city limits. Maxwell Field, a relatively small military airfield at the beginning of the war, had swelled both in acreage and in physical plant. A few returnees recognized this change because they had taken phases of their training at the base. Some Montgomerians who remained in or rejoined the service were stationed at Maxwell soon after the war.[34]

The Montgomery area's civilian population, black and white, by the war's end had a much greater appreciation for a military base that had given many of them employment. Some people understood that Maxwell's wartime growth had helped end the depression. Certainly many local businesses comprehended its role. A special event at Maxwell in September 1946 ensured that the base would remain prominent in Montgomery's economy as well as in its social and cultural life. With both military and civilian dignitaries from far and near in attendance, the Air University was launched in a special ceremony that was appropriately held in one of Maxwell's hangars. The Air University was designed to provide the AAF's most promising company grade, field grade, and staff officers with an advanced military education. Senator Lister Hill, the "Godfather of Maxwell," was largely responsible for this new educational institution located in his hometown. The hallowed tradition of the Air Corps Tactical School at Maxwell and the base's prominence as headquarters of a major wartime training command also figured in the choice of Maxwell for the Air University. In 1947, when an independent U.S. Air Force supplanted the AAF, and blue uniforms replaced brown ones, Maxwell acquired even higher status.[35]

Civil aviation was boosted by the War Department's return of Dannelly Field to the city in 1946. But Dannelly was not destined to live up to expectations for its postwar future. It came in second behind the airport not only of Atlanta, which in time became one of the nation's leading terminals, but also of Birmingham. Montgomery leadership would bear much responsibility.[36]

Sports in Montgomery in the postwar era remained a form of religion, and Cramton Bowl its major temple. The local event with national appeal, the Blue-Gray game, did not again have players all of whom were civilian college seniors until the 1947 game. The teams remained all white until 1964, when the game began to reflect the racial integration of college sports.[37]

In March 1946, Mayor David Dunn retired from office to go into private business, keeping his promise to give the returning veterans a chance to take part in the selection of a mayor after the war. The Machine selected city attorney John L. Goodwyn to succeed Dunn. Goodwyn, a cousin of the wife of the late W. A. Gunter, had solid Machine credentials. But the rise of the white lower middle class after the war with lower middle-class leadership effected the displacement of the older elite leadership along with the Machine, and Capitol Heights, Chisholm, and Dalraida became key districts. The impact of white rural emigration on the city, which swelled in the war, led to the growth of white Pentecostal churches with poorer congregations that followed the different leadership. The elite eventually made a comeback under new leadership, however. City hall became the headquarters of another long-ruling mayor named Emory Folmar, who followed in the footsteps of W. A. Gunter and whose automatic following was the old elite and its progeny. Folmar became equally dominant.[38]

The distance in miles across the Pacific for Aaron Harris, John Sawyer, and Fred Burks had been much longer than the journey across the Atlantic had been for Bob Lawrence and Bobby Young. The psychological and legal distance that the three black veterans would have to travel in Montgomery was even greater. As before the war, Montgomery's black citizens would continue to reap the least benefits socially, economically, educationally, politically, and demographically. West Montgomery was still a vast area of wretched housing with little modern sanitation, electricity, or paving. No in-migrant worker housing had been constructed there.[39]

But the war had nonetheless raised black expectations. When would blacks see the justice for which they as well as whites had fought? Women such as Idessa Redden, Jo Ann Robinson, Johnnie Carr, and Rosa Parks grew increasingly discontented. In 1946 E. D. Nixon and Rufus A. Lewis headed a voter registration drive, picking up where Arthur Madison had left off in 1944. After failing to take over the local chapter of the National Association for the Advancement of Colored People in 1944, Nixon succeeded in 1945. In that year the number of black voters in the county increased, but it was still proportionally a small fraction of the black citizenry of voting age. In August 1946 the *Advertiser* printed an article that summarized black voting gains in the South. About Alabama it reported: "Alabama was the first state of the deep South to open the door to Negro voting. But Alabama has strict voting requirements, including a drastic cumulative poll tax."[40]

A football coach at Alabama State, Lewis was employed in 1946 by the county board of education to teach returning black veterans. Many had returned to Montgomery with hopes that their dignity as human beings and their broader rights as citizens would be recognized. Nixon began to conduct voter registration classes among black veterans. Some individuals, such as John Sawyer, were allowed to register and vote, but otherwise, as Sawyer later commented, "there was very little effort to show any respect for the Negroes who had served their country." Black veterans suffered acute disappointment.[41]

The relatively few houses in the new black subdivision of Mobile Heights were available under a loan program authorized by the GI Bill. A comparatively small number of black veterans attended college under the GI Bill. Fred Burks was able to complete his degree in 1949 at Alabama State with this aid. Between terms and during holidays, he traveled to Cleveland, Ohio, to be with his closest relative, a brother. Like Bobby Young, Burks had signed up for the unorganized Army Reserve. Like Young, he was later called for active duty at the outbreak of the Korean conflict in 1950. Returning to Montgomery, Burks married a local woman and became first a schoolteacher and then a college administrator. He, Sawyer, and various other black veterans persevered and were at the core of a larger and more self-sufficient black middle class of the future.[42]

A large number of Montgomery veterans joined the continued postwar flow of blacks northward. A friend urged Aaron Harris, Jr., to come with him to Detroit. Harris was tempted but decided to stay, for he had a good job in the family dry cleaning business.[43]

The seeds of profound change had nonetheless been sown by Madison, Nixon, and Lewis. The need for change was apparent from an incident that occurred in the spring of 1946. The Civitan Club held the dedication service for a cenotaph it had erected in the square where Washington, Church, and South Court came together. Chairs were set up in a blocked-off area reserved for the loved ones of Montgomery area service people who had died in the war. Sherman White, Sr., and his wife, whose aviator son had been killed in action, came to be seated. As White later wrote in a letter to the *Advertiser,* "The Civitan Club had sent me an invitation which read 'Present this invitation for reserved seat.' When I presented this card and it was ascertained that I was a Negro I was refused a seat and was told that I would have to stand." He and his wife "did not choose to stand because we had an invitation for seats. . . . Our son was one of the 99th Pursuit Squadron. . . . He paid the supreme sacrifice over or near Sicily." They left before the ceremony commenced.[44]

In 1946 the editor of the *Advertiser* was the moderate liberal Charles G. Dobbins. He printed White's letter and commented: "The experience of these Negro parents of a dead American soldier is an unhappy commentary upon Democracy." Dobbins reminded his readers that "even in slavery days, white owners gave their Negroes seats in church."

He offered the Civitan Club space to explain its action, but no explanation was forthcoming.[45]

The dedication ended, and the chairs were removed. When vehicular traffic resumed, on the city buses it was still whites to the front, blacks to the rear.[46]

Notes

1. THE CITY AT THE START OF THE WAR

1. *Montgomery Advertiser,* September 1, 1939.

2. Charles Wampole, Jr., interview with the author, November 13, 1987.

3. *Montgomery Advertiser,* September 1, 1939.

4. Ennels and Newton, *The Wisdom of Eagles,* 41–68.

5. *Montgomery Advertiser,* September 1–4, 9, October 24, November 1, 1939; Stokesbury, *A Short History of Air Power,* 194–195; Sherry, *The Rise of American Air Power,* 76–79.

6. Ralph Loeb, Jr., interview with the author, June 13, 1991.

7. Ibid.

8. John Sawyer, interview with the author, September 10, 1991.

9. *Montgomery City Directory,* 1939, preface, 11–18; *Montgomery Advertiser,* September 1, 1940.

10. *Montgomery City Directory,* 1939, pp. 716–720, 726–728.

11. Ennels and Newton, *The Wisdom of Eagles,* 77; *A History of Montgomery in Pictures,* 152.

12. Rogers, Ward, Atkins, and Flynt, *Alabama,* 190–191.

13. *Montgomery Advertiser,* November 26, December 4, 17, 19–20. 1939, November 10, 19–20, 1940.

14. *Montgomery City Directory,* 1939, p. 930; Branch, *Parting the Waters,* 1–5; *Montgomery Advertiser,* March 16, 1945.

15. *Montgomery Advertiser,* May 6, 1898; *Montgomery City Directory,* 1939, pp. 776, 845; Greenhaw, *Montgomery,* 12, 24.

16. *Montgomery City Directory,* 1939, pp. 795–796, 811–812.

17. Ibid.

18. Coleman, *Escape the Thunder,* 9–10.

19. *Montgomery City Directory,* 1939, pp. 797, 929.

20. Ibid., 727–728.

21. Ibid., 728.

22. Ibid., 712–714, 720.

23. Ibid., 712, 797–800; Connor, *Remember When. . . ?* 21; *The Story of WSFA,* 4, 7–8, 20, 30, 32, 34.

24. *Montgomery Advertiser,* December 14, 1939.

25. *Montgomery Advertiser,* January 16, 19, 20–21, 23, 28–29, 1940.

26. Sawyer, interview with the author, September 10, 1991.

27. *Montgomery City Directory,* 1939, pp. 780–782. See *Montgomery City Directory,* 1939, for North Perry, North Lawrence, and North McDonough and intersecting streets Jefferson, Columbus, Randolph, and Pollard for the composition of the industrial park.

28. *Montgomery City Directory,* 1939, pp. 931–932.

29. Ibid.; Loeb, interview with the author, June 13, 1991.

30. Ennels and Newton, *The Wisdom of Eagles,* 57, 94.

31. Ibid., 67.

32. *Montgomery City Directory,* 1939, pp. 818–819; Ennels and Newton, *The Wisdom of Eagles,* 66.

33. Ennels and Newton, *The Wisdom of Eagles,* 54; *Montgomery City Directory,* 1939, p. 958; oral history statements by Johnnie Carr and John Sawyer at a meeting of One Montgomery, an interracial group, September 15, 1998.

34. *Montgomery City Directory,* 1939, p. 958; *Montgomery Advertiser,* June 23, 1940.

35. *Montgomery City Directory,* 1939, p. 811.

36. Thornton, "Challenge and Response," 464; *Montgomery Advertiser,* December 5, 1940.

37. J. Mills Thornton, interview with the author, July 27, 1992; *Montgomery Advertiser,* December 5, 1940.

38. Thornton, interview with the author, July 27, 1992.

39. *Montgomery Advertiser,* September 4, 1940, July 3, 1942; Sawyer, interview with the author, September 10, 1991. Sawyer did not experience police brutality but heard it described by other blacks. On the condition of blacks in the U.S. on the eve of World War II, see Polenberg, *One Nation Divisible,* 24–30.

40. *Montgomery Advertiser,* October 11–12, 1939.

41. *Montgomery City Directory,* 1939, p. 428.

42. *Montgomery Advertiser,* November 6, 13, 20, December 4, 11, 18, 1939, January 22, September 23, November 12, 17, 1940.

43. Idessa (Taylor) Redden, interview with the author, September 22, 1991.

44. *Montgomery City Directory,* 1939, pp. 427–428.

45. See Minutes of the Meeting of the Montgomery City Commission [Office of the City Clerk, City Hall] for 1938 and 1939 for the paving and water extension patterns, and the means and methods of financing these, in the city by the outbreak of World War II. (The minutes are hereafter cited as Minutes, MCC.)

46. Minutes, MCC, 1938–1941.

47. Greenhaw, *Montgomery,* 64. Paul Robinson observed the West End environment as a boy in a middle-class family in Riverside Heights. See Paul Robinson, interview with the author, March 24, 1991.

48. *Montgomery City Directory,* 823–824; Minutes, MCC, April 23, 1940.

49. *Montgomery Advertiser,* November 6, 1940; Ennels and Newton, *The Wisdom of Eagles,* 71.

50. *Montgomery Advertiser,* September 29, 1940, June 27, 1999.

51. Montgomery County Probate Judge's Office, Tax Assessment Records, Alabama Department of Archives and History, Montgomery, Books LG 675, 684, 686, 691–692.

52. Key, *Southern Politics in State and Nation,* 36–44, 56; Schulman, *From Cotton Belt to Sunbelt,* viii; Thornton, "Alabama Politics," 349–358; Flynt, *Dixie's Forgotten People,* 74, 95. For an analysis of the South for much of the first half of the twentieth century, see Tindall, *The Emergence of the New South.*

53. Kohn, *The Cradle,* 98. The *Montgomery City Directory* for 1939 reports on occupations and streets of residence and identifies blacks and whites by class, although the term "class" is not used. A useful source mainly for the gentry is the column "The Promenader" by Go Peep that appeared each Sunday in the *Advertiser*'s society pages.

54. Robert Lawrence, interview with the author, November 4, 1995.

55. Ibid.; Wampole, interview with the author, November 13, 1987.

56. Sadie (Gardner) Penn, interview with the author, August 13, 1991; Sawyer, interview with the author, September 10, 1991.

57. Penn, interview with the author, August 13, 1991; Sawyer, interview with the author, September 10, 1991.

58. Mary Louise (Caton) Weed, interview with the author, January 7, 1994.

59. Ibid.; Polenberg, *One Nation Divisible,* 15–24.

60. *Montgomery City Directory,* 1939, 22–676; Sadie (Gardner) Penn, interview with the author, September 17, 1991.

61. Idessa Redden, interview with the author, September 22, 1991; Loetta (Gardner) Haynie, interview with the author, March 24, 1994.

62. *Montgomery City Directory,* 1939, 22–276; Dorothy Ghent, interview with the author, April 2, 1994; *Montgomery Advertiser,* May 25, 1944, May 26, 1945.

63. Lois W. Banner, *Women in Modern America,* 183.

64. Ghent, interview with the author, April 2, 1994; *Montgomery Advertiser,* November 7, 1943; *Montgomery City Directory,* 1939, pp. 2, 210, 576, 940, 967–969, 981–982.

65. *Montgomery Advertiser,* October 11, 1939.

66. *Montgomery Advertiser,* April 30, 1943, October 15, 1944; *Montgomery City Directory,* 1939, pp. 176, 434.

67. *Montgomery Advertiser,* March 22, 1942; Paterson, *Sweet Mystery,* 207.

68. *Montgomery City Directory,* 1939, pp. 949, 951. The *Montgomery City Directory* for 1939 indicates that more than a few women held jobs in the WPA. Most of these women were white.

69. Montgomery County Board of Education, History of Black Schools in Montgomery, 8–9; *Montgomery Advertiser,* September 24, October 1, 1939, August 22, 1999.

70. *Montgomery City Directory,* 1939, p. 994; *100 Years, 1863–1963,* 44–45; *Montgomery Advertiser,* June 23, 1940.

71. Loeb, interview with the author, June 13, 1991; Robinson, interview with the author, March 24, 1991.

72. *Montgomery City Directory,* 1939, p. 993; Benton, "Lanier's South Court Building"; Loeb, interview with the author, June 13, 1991; *Montgomery Advertiser,* November 25, 1939, November 3, 1940, February 22, May 27, 1942.

73. Ellison, *History of Huntingdon College,* 152–154, 240–244; Bibb, "A Brief History of Alabama State University," 9–11; *100 Years, 1863–1963,* 45, 48–49.

74. *Remember When. . .?,* 58; *Montgomery Advertiser,* December 10, 1939, September 27, 1940, July 5, 1942, July 7, September 16, 1943.

75. *Montgomery Advertiser,* November 18, 25, 1939; Loeb, interview with the author, June 13, 1991.

76. *Montgomery Advertiser,* March 18, 1942.

77. *Montgomery Advertiser,* July 5, 25, 1942.

78. *Montgomery Advertiser,* July 25, 1942; Newton, "The Blue and Gray Game," 11–12.

79. Newton, "The Blue and Gray Game," 11–14.

80. Ibid., 14; *Montgomery Advertiser,* December 27–30, 1940, December 11, 1944.

81. Minutes, MCC, meetings of November 23, 1939, and July 7, 1940; Newton, "The Blue and Gray Game," 14; and Robbins, "Blue-Gray Colonels," 17–18.

82. *Montgomery Advertiser,* November 24, 30, 1939, December 1, 1940.

83. *Montgomery Advertiser,* November 19, 1939, March 27, 1940, May 27, 1945.

84. Williams, "The Dixie Art Colony," 6–15; Ausfeld and Neal, "The World of Kelly Fitzpatrick," 16–19; Sarah (Woolfolk) Wiggins, memorandum to the author, September 28, 1994.

85. *Montgomery Advertiser,* March 31, 1940; "Fine Folk: The Art of Bill Traylor," 66–71.

2. THE ADVENT OF PEARL HARBOR

1. Weinberg, *A World at Arms,* 113–131, 208–210; Stokesbury, *World War II,* 89–114, 137.

2. Paramount Theater's newsreel *Paramount News,* June 1940.

3. Ibid., August 1940.

4. Ennels and Newton, *The Wisdom of Eagles,* 69–70.

5. Ibid., 70–71.

6. Ibid., 71–74; Stokesbury, *World War II,* 114.

7. Ennels and Newton, *The Wisdom of Eagles,* 77; Walter Weaver, Diary, entries for June 24 and July 2, 1940, file 286.106, Historical Research Agency, Maxwell Air Force Base; *Montgomery Advertiser,* November 27, 1940.

8. Ennels and Newton, *The Wisdom of Eagles,* 77–78; *Montgomery Advertiser,* November 2, 1940.

9. Ennels and Newton, *The Wisdom of Eagles,* 77–78, 83.

10. Ibid., 73; Weaver, Diary, entries for July 2, 9, 1940.

11. Ennels and Newton, *The Wisdom of Eagles,* 76–77; *Montgomery Advertiser,* June 23, 29–30; Weaver, Diary, entries for July 2, 8, 12, 31, August 6, 1940.

12. *Montgomery Advertiser,* June 29–30, 1940; Weaver, Diary, August 6, 10, 1940; Minutes, MCC, August 6, 13, 1940. In the lease agreement was a clause that involved certain sections of the right-of-ways of the highway to Wetumpka and of the Seaboard Airline Railroad; these sections together were leased for the army flying field for $1 a year for five years, and then the fee was to become $5,000 a year for the next thirty years. See Minutes, MCC, August 13, 1940.

13. Minutes, MCC, July 16, August 13, 1940; Crist, "An Army Camp."

14. *Montgomery Advertiser,* November 2, 10, December 13, 25, 1940; Minutes, MCC, November 19, 1940, January 7, February 11, March 20, 1941.

15. Millett and Maslowski, *For the Common Defense,* 118–119; *Montgomery Advertiser,* November 28, 1940.

16. *Montgomery Advertiser,* September 21, October 17, 22, 29, 1940; April 23, 1942.

17. *Montgomery Advertiser,* October 30, 1940.

18. *Montgomery Advertiser,* October 30–31, November 9, 14, 1940; Minutes, MCC, November 5, 1940.

19. *Montgomery Advertiser,* November 20, December 6, 1940.

20. *Montgomery Advertiser,* December 12, 1940.

21. *Montgomery Advertiser,* December 15, 1940.

22. Ibid.

23. *Montgomery Advertiser,* December 12–13, 1940.

24. *Montgomery Advertiser,* November 10, December 19–20, 1940. For correspondence, statistics, and other data on the draft in Alabama, see the administrative files of Governors Frank Dixon and Chauncey Sparks, in the Alabama Department of Archives and History.

25. *Montgomery Advertiser,* September 16, 1939; Crist, "Fear Stalks Nazi Refugees."

26. *Montgomery Advertiser,* July 28, 1940, August 6, 1944.

27. Frederick D. (Fred) Burks, interview with the author, July 24, 1991.

28. Ibid.

29. Newton, My Short Military Career.

30. *Montgomery Advertiser,* December 5, 1940. From March to December 1940, Gunter was absent from the majority of commission meetings. See Minutes, MCC, for these months.

31. *Montgomery Advertiser,* December 5, 7, 20, 1940.

32. *Montgomery Advertiser,* December 17–19, 23–24, 1940.

33. *Montgomery Advertiser,* January 7, 10, 1941.

34. *Montgomery Advertiser,* January 10–15, 1941.

35. *Montgomery Advertiser,* November 23, 1940.

36. Minutes, MCC, January 7, 21, 28, February 20, 1941; *Montgomery Advertiser,* June 9, December 7–10, 17, 1940, January 1, 12, 15, February 18–19, 1941.

37. *Montgomery Advertiser,* November 24, 1938, November 1, 3, 1940.

38. *Montgomery Advertiser,* November 8, 1940.

39. *Montgomery Advertiser,* November 29, 1940.

40. *Montgomery Advertiser,* March 16, 1941, February 1, April 24, 27, August 9, 1942, August 1, 6, 1943; Minutes, MCC, August 19, October 21, November 12, 25, 1941.

41. *Montgomery Advertiser,* September 21, October 22, 24, 1941, February 1, March 1, April 24, 1942, October 24, 1943, April 19, 1944.

42. *Montgomery Advertiser,* March 22, 29, April 5, 12, 26, May 3, 1942, June 6, 1943, February 6, March 5, 1944.

43. *Montgomery Advertiser,* January 12, 22, 1941; June 14, 1942.

44. McEnnels and Newton, *The Wisdom of Eagles,* 74–75.

45. Ibid., 75.

46. Ibid.

47. Carter, "Little Generals," December 15, 1940.

48. Ibid.; Carter, "Little Generals," November 17, 1940.

49. Loetta (Gardner) Haynie, interview with the author, March 24, 1994; Dorothy Ghent, interviews with the author, October 27, 1991, and April 2, 1994; Col. Hubert K. Anderson USAF (ret.) and Jeanne (Walker) Anderson, interview with the author, October 25, 1996.

50. *Montgomery Advertiser,* August 10, 1941.

51. Lee Allen to the author, September 29, 1995; *Montgomery Advertiser,* September 2, 9, 1942, August 31, 1943.

52. Ennels and Newton, *The Wisdom of Eagles,* 75–76.

53. Ibid., 82–83.

54. Ibid., 87–88.

55. Ibid., 83.

56. *Montgomery Advertiser,* March 7, 1942; Stokesbury, *World War II,* 151–158.

57. Stokesbury, *World War II,* 161–167.

58. Minutes, MCC, May 27, 1941.

59. Morris, *Encyclopedia of American History,* 367.

60. *Montgomery Advertiser,* November 9, 12, 1941.

61. *Montgomery Advertiser,* November 12, 1941.

62. *Montgomery Advertiser,* December 6, 1941.

63. Ibid.

64. *Montgomery Advertiser,* December 7, 1941.

65. Ibid.

66. Ibid.

67. Ibid. I was the football player who responded to the news with little interest. Of the more than two dozen people I interviewed who were in Montgomery on December 7, 1941, none recalled the headlines, but several recalled going to see *Sergeant York* that afternoon, and all have vivid memories of where they were and what they were doing when they heard of the Pearl Harbor attack. None knew where Pearl Harbor was, and few understood the implications of the attack until some hours later. For a short, graphic description of the attack on Pearl Harbor, see Spector, *Eagle Against the Sun,* 1–8.

68. Jean (Severence) Nettles, interview with the author, August 30, 1994; Algie (Hill) Neill, interview with the author, March 20, 1995.

69. Ennels and Newton, *The Wisdom of Eagles,* 84–85.

70. Ibid.

71. Aaron Harris, Jr., interview with the author, March 16, 1995.

72. *Montgomery Advertiser,* December 8, 1941.

73. *Montgomery Advertiser,* December 9, 1941.

74. Margaret "Peggy" (Penton) Cravey, interview with the author, September 10, 1991; *Montgomery Advertiser,* December 9–10, 1941.

75. Ennels and Newton, *The Wisdom of Eagles,* 85.

76. *Montgomery Advertiser,* December 11, 1941.

77. Minutes, MCC, December 9, 1941.

78. *Montgomery Advertiser,* December 10, 1941; minutes of the meeting of the Montgomery County Civilian Defense Council, December 9, 1941, Folder 33, "Montgomery County Defense Council," SG19877, Alabama State Council of Defense Program Administrative Files, 1941–1946, ADAH. The national, state, and county-municipal civil defense organizations used the term "civilian" before "defense" in their titles, but during the war the term "civil defense" was most commonly employed. In this book I use "civil defense," or CD.

79. *Montgomery Advertiser,* December 9–10, 28, 1941.

80. John Sawyer, interview with the author, November 18, 1997.

81. *Montgomery Advertiser,* December 8, 1941, January 23, 1942.

82. *Montgomery Advertiser,* December 7, 1994.

83. Ennels and Newton, *The Wisdom of Eagles,* 84.

84. *Montgomery Advertiser,* December 8, 10, 1941; January 18, 1942.

85. *Montgomery Advertiser,* December 9, 16, 1941, April 12, 1942, September 8, 1943, July 29, 1945.

86. *Montgomery Advertiser,* December 9, 1941. I was one of the Lanier students who "enlisted" in ROTC under pressure, then returned to physical education and football at the first opportunity.

87. *Montgomery Advertiser,* December 10, 1941; Ennels and Newton, *The Wisdom of Eagles,* 85–86.

88. Ennels and Newton, *The Wisdom of Eagles,* 86.

89. *Montgomery Advertiser,* December 22, 1941.

90. Ennels and Newton, *The Wisdom of Eagles,* 86; *Montgomery Advertiser,* December 24–25, 1941.

91. December 25, 1941, was the first Christmas Day since about 1935 that I did not take out my skates, from a Christmas past, and join the skaters or set off fireworks.

92. Ennels and Newton, *The Wisdom of Eagles,* 86; *Montgomery Advertiser,* December 26, 1941.

93. *Montgomery Advertiser,* December 28, 1941.

94. Ibid.; *Montgomery Advertiser,* January 4, 1942.

95. *Montgomery Advertiser,* December 31, 1941; *Alabama Journal,* December 31, 1941.

96. *Montgomery Advertiser,* January 2, 1942.

97, *Montgomery Advertiser,* January 7, 1942.

98. Ibid.

3. THE CREATION OF CITIZEN ARMED FORCES

1. *Montgomery Advertiser,* April 10, May 3, June 30, 1942.

2. *Montgomery Advertiser,* April 17, 19, 23, 28, June 30, July 2, September 4, December 30, 1942; Newton, My Short Military Career; Sawyer, interview with the author, September 10, 1991.

3. *Montgomery Advertiser,* May 17, June 28, 1942.

4. Newton, My Short Military Career.

5. *Montgomery Advertiser,* November 29, 1942.

6. I was one of the Lanier students who retreated from Pollard Street.

7. Newton, My Short Military Career; *Montgomery Advertiser,* March 26, 1944.

8. Caroline ("Dootsie" Ball) Matthews, Isabel (Dunn) Hill, and Betty Baldwin, interview with the author, December 3, 1991; Newton, My Short Military Career.

9. *Montgomery Advertiser,* May 3, 1942.

10. Ibid.

11. Robert ("Bob") Lawrence, audiotape, 1992.

12. Ibid.

13. Ibid. See Fussell, *Wartime,* chap. 7, for a classic interpretation of "chicken shit."

14. October 27, 1943.

15. *Montgomery Advertiser,* September 14, 1942; Manchester, "The Raggedy Ass Marines," 367–371; Newton, My Short Military Career.

16. Neal Howard to Fannie Lee Howard, August 9, 23, and 29, 1943 (all of Neal Howard's correspondence and other relevant documentation is in the collection of William Howard, Jr., in Montgomery).

17. Harris, interview with the author, March 16, 1995.

18. Ibid.

19. Ibid.

20. Robert ("Bobby") Young, interview with the author, November 10, 1997.

21. Ibid.

22. William S. ("Billy") Robinson to Alice Robinson, November 7, 1943, and to William J. Robinson, March 22, 1944. (William S. ["Billy"] Robinson letters and other documents are in the collection of Paul Robinson in Montgomery.)

23. Ralph Loeb, interview with the author, July 26, 1991.

24. Sawyer, interview with the author, September 10, 1991.

25. Robert Sternenberg, interview with the author, August 9, 1999.

26. *Montgomery Advertiser*, October 26, 1943, December 31, 1944. I was in the Lanier class of '43 and, after infantry basic training at Camp Fannin, Texas, attended ASTP (engineering) at M.I.T. and Rhode Island State.

27. William ("Billy") Crane, interview with the author, 1991; Neal Howard to Fannie Lee Howard, October 6, 1943, William Howard Collection.

28. Loeb, interview with the author, July 26, 1991.

29. Sawyer, interview with the author, September 10, 1991.

30. Fred Burks, interview with the author, July 31, 1991.

31. Fred Burks, John Sawyer, and Ralph Loeb were some of the men who traveled across the western part of the United States in World War II. Aaron Harris felt awed by the skyscrapers of New York City. Neal Howard was awed by the beauty of New England in the fall.

32. Hartmann, *The Home Front,* 32; *Montgomery Advertiser,* December 7, 1941.

33. Hartmann, *The Home Front,* 34–36.

34. Ibid., 36–37; *Montgomery Advertiser,* May 13, 15, 1942.

35. *Montgomery Advertiser,* July 12, 28, 1942.

36. *Montgomery Advertiser,* September 6, 13, 1942, October 15, 1944.

37. *Montgomery Advertiser,* June 6, August 15, December 5, 1943, October 6, May 7, 1944.

38. Hartmann, *The Home Front,* 41; *Montgomery Advertiser,* January 3, September 19, October 3, 1943, May 9, 1944.

39. *Montgomery Advertiser,* October 10, 1943.

40. *Montgomery Advertiser,* March 22, 1944; Sherlock, interview with the author, June 21, 1991.

41. *Montgomery Advertiser,* June 3, 1945.

42. *Montgomery Advertiser,* October 15, 1944.

43. Dorothy Ghent, interview with the author, February 1, 1995; *Montgomery Advertiser,* May 9, 1944.

44. *Montgomery Advertiser,* April 28, June 17, 1943; Ennels and Newton, *The Wisdom of Eagles,* 103; Ghent, interview with the author, February 1, 1995.

45. Hartmann, *The Home Front,* 39–40.

46. Ennels and Newton, *The Wisdom of Eagles,* 103; *Montgomery Advertiser,* June 11, November 16, 1943.

47. *Montgomery Advertiser,* November 23, 1943.

48. *Montgomery Advertiser,* February 11, 17, 1944.

49. *Montgomery Advertiser,* December 2, 1943, August 12, 1945.

50. *Montgomery Advertiser,* December 3, 1943, January 18, February 3, 8, 1944.

51. *Montgomery Advertiser,* April 1, 1944.

52. Newton, My Short Military Career.

53. Ibid.

54. Ibid.

55. Letters of the following to WSFA Radio, *Letter from Home:* Private Jerome L. Carter, n.d.; Seaman Second Class Edward Chambless, December 20, 1944; and Pharmacist Mate First Class Thomas H. Cox, January 30, 1944 (all in box 2); Sergeant G. P. Gardner, n.d., and Lieutenant Colonel Edward A. Galt (both in box 3).

56. Newton, My Short Military Career. From early 1942 on, the *Advertiser* published the section called "Alabama at the Front" in the Sunday edition.

57. Burks, interview with the author, July 31, 1991.

58. Margaret (Peggy Penton) Cravey, account of a wartime train trip, n.d., Margaret Cravey Papers.

59. Ibid.

4. MONTGOMERIANS HEAD OVERSEAS

1. In wartime the U.S. Army had three main components: army air forces, army ground forces, and army service forces. The U.S. Navy had its fleet and shore installations. The U.S. Marines provided the ground troops for the U.S. Navy, but some marines served on navy cruisers and battleships in such capacities as guards and antiaircraft gunners. Both U.S. Navy and Marine Corps planes and personnel carried out the various missions of naval aviation as part of the fleet and supported Marine Corps ground troops and navy construction battalions.

2. Compare the experiences of William ("Billy") Robinson and Neal Howard in Chapter 9 for the differences between being a replacement and a member of an existing organization or ship.

3. Newton, My Short Military Career.

4. Ibid.

5. Ibid.

6. Ibid.

7. Ibid.

8. *Montgomery Advertiser,* May 24, 1942. I was Nelson Van Pelt's roommate at the University of Missouri.

9. Ford, *Chennault,* 27, 36–39, 157–158; *Montgomery Advertiser,* September 7, 1941, April 17, 26, May 3, 1942. I quote the *Advertiser* for April 26, 1942.

10. Ford, *Chennault,* 334–335 (quoted), 387; *Montgomery Advertiser,* May 24, 1942.

11. *Montgomery Advertiser,* May 17, 1942.

12. Spector, *Eagle Against the Sun,* 154–155; *Montgomery Advertiser,* July 11, 1942.

· 13. Spector, *Eagle Against the Sun,* 156–162; *Montgomery Advertiser,* October 27, 1943, January 23, 1944.

14. Spector, *Eagle Against the Sun,* 166–178; *Montgomery Advertiser,* January 23, April 8, 1944.

15. *Montgomery Advertiser,* December 6, 1942, January 23, April 8, 1944. "Torpedo Eight" lost all its attacking planes at Midway and all but one pilot and became legendary in naval aviation annals.

16. Spector, *Eagle Against the Sun,* 185–192; *Montgomery Advertiser,* January 2, 1942.

17. *Montgomery Advertiser,* March 7, 1943.

18. *Montgomery Advertiser,* April 11, 1943.

19. *Montgomery Advertiser,* April 29, 1943.

20. Spector, *Eagle Against the Sun,* 192–194; *Montgomery Advertiser,* June 20, 1943, December 10, 1944.

21. Spector, *Eagle Against the Sun,* 211–213.

22. Ibid., 213; *Montgomery Advertiser,* October 14, 1943.

23. *Montgomery Advertiser,* October 14, 1943.

24. Spector, *Eagle Against the Sun,* 214; *Montgomery Advertiser,* August 2, October 14, 1943.

25. *Montgomery Advertiser,* April 9, 1944.

26. Ibid.

27. Spector, *Eagle Against the Sun,* 216–217; Stokesberry, *Air Power,* 242; *Montgomery Advertiser,* May 30 (quoting McCord), December 15–16, 1943.

28. Stokesbury, *Air Power,* 243; Spector, *Eagle Against the Sun,* 258.

29. Spector, *Eagle Against the Sun,* 259–266; *Montgomery Advertiser,* August 6, 1944.

30. *Montgomery Advertiser,* July 1, 1944.

31. *Montgomery Advertiser,* August 19, 1945; Stokesbury, *Air Power,* 196.

32. Millet and Maslowski, *For the Common Defense,* 423–425; *Montgomery Advertiser,* October 24, 1943.

33. *Montgomery Advertiser,* January 14, December 3, 1943.

34. *Montgomery Advertiser,* August 1, 1943.

35. *Montgomery Advertiser,* July 25, 1943.

36. Stokesbury, *Air Power,* 196–197; *Montgomery Advertiser,* August 1–2, October 10, 1943.

37. Stokesbury, *World War II,* 292–293; *Montgomery Advertiser,* January 23, 1944.

38. Stokesbury, *World War II,* 293–295; *Montgomery Advertiser,* July 13, August 8, 1943.

39. *Montgomery Advertiser,* December 6, 17, 1943.

40. *Baltimore Afro-American,* September 11, 1943.

41. Stokesbury, *World War II,* 297–299; January 2, 1944.

42. Stokesbury, *World War II,* 299, 302–304; *Montgomery Advertiser,* October 13, 1944.

43. Stokesbury, *Air Power,* 197–200.

44. *Montgomery Advertiser,* July 11, 1943.

45. *Montgomery Advertiser,* July 11, November 1, 1943.

46. Ennels and Newton, *The Wisdom of Eagles,* 60–65.

47. *Montgomery Advertiser,* November 1, 1943. The account of Brook Nettles's being shot down over Germany and captured is based on an article that I wrote for the *Advertiser* of March 4, 1994. The Eighth Air Force's operations in the European theater until to the invasion of Normandy are described in McFarland and Newton, *To Command the Sky.*

48. *Montgomery Advertiser,* March 4, 1994.

49. *Montgomery Advertiser,* October 19, 1943.

50. *Paramount News,* Paramount Theater. The account of the merchant marine is in part based on an article that I wrote for the *Advertiser* of December 17, 1995.

51. Newton, My Short Military Career; *Montgomery Advertiser,* May 6, 1945.

52. *Montgomery Advertiser,* October 4, 1942.

53. Thomas W. Oliver, Jr., interview with the author, November 27, 1995; Robert C. Holmes, interview with the author, December 3, 1995; and John H. Stovall, interview with the author, December 6, 1995.

54. *Montgomery Advertiser,* December 17, 1995.

55. *Montgomery Advertiser,* June 4, 1944; Bese Stovall to John H. Stovall, July

29, 1944, in the collection of the Stovall family, Montgomery.

56. Chuck Holmes, interview with the author, November 27, 1995.

57. *Montgomery Advertiser,* October 21–23, 1943.

58. *Montgomery Advertiser,* October 27–28, 1943.

59. Thornton S. Cody to WSFA, January 29, 1944 (in box 2 of *Letter from Home*).

60. Ibid.

5. THE EMERGENCE OF THE HOME FRONT

1. Thomas, *Riveting and Rationing,* 19; *Montgomery Advertiser,* January 18, 1942. See Neeley, *Montgomery,* 8, for a succinct characterization of the rural-urban nature of Montgomery County and city at the time of World War II.

2. Walter Weaver to Lister Hill, May 19, 1943, file 168.7027.5, Historical Research Agency.

3. Goss, "Air Defense," 290–295; Cronenberg, *Forth to the Mighty Conflict,* 21–22. The planning for a civil defense organization and CD activities in Montgomery began early in 1941, when a federal mandate prescribed the formation of state and county-municipal CD committees, but little in the way of action took place until after Pearl Harbor. See Frank M. Dixon to L. D. Rouse, December 15, 1941, and other documents in folder 33, "Montgomery County Defense Council," SG19877, Alabama State Civilian Defense, 1941–1946, Alabama Department of Archives and History.

4. *Montgomery Advertiser,* January 13, 21, February 14–15, 17, 28, March 1, 1942; Minutes, MCC, February 27, 1942.

5. *Montgomery Advertiser,* April 8, May 7, 1942; Margaret (Peggy Penton) Cravey, untitled paper presented at the Architreats Program, Alabama Department of Archives and History, Montgomery, October 8, 1993.

6. *Montgomery Advertiser,* April 8, 19, May 7, 9, 14, June 1, 1942; Cravey, paper presented at the Architreats Program, October 8, 1993.

7. *Montgomery Advertiser,* January 26, 1942.

8. *Montgomery Advertiser,* July 31, 1942.

9. *Montgomery Advertiser,* February 25, March 4, 8, 12, 16, 1942.

10. *Montgomery Advertiser,* March 15, 17–18, 1942; Captain C. W. Crabb to W. P. Screws, March 18, 1942, folder 34, "Montgomery County Defense Council," SG19877, 1941–1946, Alabama Department of Archives and History.

11. *Montgomery Advertiser,* March 18, 1942.

12. *Montgomery Advertiser,* June 19, August 2, 18–19, 1942.

13. *Montgomery Advertiser,* December 3, 1942, May 6, July 25, August 15, 27–28, 1943.

14. Pat (Caton) Ireland, interview with the author, October 15, 1993; Mary Louise (Caton) Weed, interview with the author, November 8, 1994.

15. *Montgomery Advertiser,* January 31, 1943.

16. *Montgomery Advertiser,* October 30, 1943; Cravey, paper presented at the Architreats Program, October 8, 1993.

17. *Montgomery Advertiser,* December 26, 1942.

18. *Montgomery Advertiser,* August 23, 27–28, October 31, 1943. *Montgomery Advertiser,* June 20, 1944, contained a list of the block leaders as of that date.

19. Blum, *V Was for Victory,* 94, 226–227.

20. *Montgomery Advertiser,* January 1, 3–4, 21, 1942.

21. *Montgomery Advertiser,* January 2, 1942.

22. *Montgomery Advertiser,* January 15, July 1, 1942.

23. *Montgomery Advertiser,* March 18, 23, April 18, May 29, 1942.

24. *Montgomery Advertiser,* March 3, 1942; June 2, 1943.

25. Blum, *V Was for Victory,* 226; Thomas, *Riveting and Rationing,* 94; *Montgomery Advertiser,* May 1, 1942.

26. *Montgomery Advertiser,* July 29, November 26–27, 1942, January 6, 1944. I rode as a passenger in a car that raced up and down Fairview.

27. *Montgomery Advertiser,* May 30, 1943.

28. *Montgomery Advertiser,* January 25, May 3–6, 1942.

29. *Montgomery Advertiser,* February 27, May 12, 1942.

30. Thomas, *Riveting and Rationing,* 94–96; Cronenberg, *Forth to the Mighty Conflict,* 33.

31. *Montgomery Advertiser,* May 8, 1942.

32. *Encyclopaedia Britannica,* 1965 ed., s.v. "rationing."

33. *Montgomery Advertiser,* June 27, 30, December 27, 1942, June 6, 20, July 4, 1943.

34. *Montgomery Advertiser,* February 22, August 1, 1943.

35. *Montgomery Advertiser,* June 27, 1943.

36. Blum, *V Was for Victory,* 227–228; *Montgomery Advertiser,* April 29, May 17–18, 1942.

37. Blum, *V Was for Victory,* 228.

38. Ibid., 228–230; *Montgomery Advertiser,* June 30, 1943, December 31, 1944.

39. *Montgomery Advertiser,* April 18, 27, May 5, August 11, 25, 1943.

40. *Montgomery Advertiser,* June 13, 1943, May 5, 1944.

41. Florence Newton, oral statement to the author, 1946.

42. Margaret (Peggy Penton) Cravey, interview with the author, September 10, 1991; Mary Henrie (Harris) Borders, interview with the author, August 9, 1993.

43. *Montgomery Advertiser,* May 5, 1943.

44. Ibid.

45. *Montgomery Advertiser,* February 3, 1942.

46. *Montgomery Advertiser,* March 27, 1942.

47. Cronenberg, *Forth to the Mighty Conflict,* 26; *Montgomery Advertiser,* February 3, April 5, 22, May 17, 1942.

48. *Montgomery Advertiser,* April 26, 1942.

49. *Montgomery Advertiser,* May 27, June 5, 16, 1942.

50. *Montgomery Advertiser,* June 17, 23–24, July 2, 1942.

51. *Montgomery Advertiser,* July 1, 19, December 6, 1942.

52. *Montgomery Advertiser,* October 1–2, 4–8, 10, 13, 16–18, 20, 1942.

53. Cronenberg, *Forth to the Mighty Conflict,* 25–26; Thomas, *Riveting and Rationing,* 88–89; *Montgomery Advertiser,* December 19, 1941.

54. Mrs. Ralph Loeb, Sr., interview with the author, February 2, 1988; *Montgomery Advertiser,* July 24, 1942, March 4, July 17, August 8, 10, November 14, December 25, 1943, October 13, 1944.

55. *Montgomery Advertiser,* July 21, 24, 1942.

56. Marguerite Sherlock, interview with the author, August 18, 1998; *Montgomery Advertiser*, July 1, 1942.

57. *Montgomery Advertiser,* January 19, July 1, 1942, July 18, 1943; February 21, 1944.

58. *Montgomery Advertiser,* May 11, August 9, 1944; February 4, 1945.

59. Allen Cronenberg, *Forth to the Mighty Conflict,* 100; *Montgomery Advertiser,* June 23, 1942, June 4, August 6, September 2, 8, 1943.

60. *Montgomery Advertiser,* January 12, 19, 1941, May 23, August 26, 29, 1943.

61. *Montgomery Advertiser,* March 1, August 9, 1942, April 3, 1944, March 4, 1945.

62. *Montgomery Advertiser,* February 12, March 4 (quoting Lobman), April 5, 10, July 7, 10, October 2, 1942.

63. *Montgomery Advertiser,* April 29, 1942; January 31, 1943.

64. *Montgomery Advertiser,* January 22, April 5, 26, 1942.

65. *Montgomery Advertiser,* January 31, 1943.

66. Maj.-Gen. Ralph Royce to Mrs. Fred Ball, April 6, 1943, in the collection of Caroline "Dootsie" (Ball) Matthews; *Montgomery Advertiser,* September 18, 1943.

67. *Montgomery Advertiser,* October 29, 1943.

68. *Montgomery Advertiser,* October 31, 1943; Matthews, Hill, and Baldwin, interviews with the author, December 3, 1991.

69. Caroline "Dootsie" (Ball) Matthews, note to the author, February 15, 1995; *Montgomery Advertiser,* August 23, 1944.

70. Newton, My Short Military Career.

71. *Montgomery Advertiser,* November 21, December 1, 20, 1940, January 8, 1942, February 18, March 22, 1944, February 8, 25, 28, March 4, 11, 18, 1945; Annual Report of Montgomery County Red Cross Chapter, December 1, 1943–November 30, 1944.

72. Blum, *V Was for Victory,* 16.

73. *Montgomery Advertiser,* January 15, March 20, May 24 (quoting Strassburger), June 3, 14, July 12, 1942.

74. *Montgomery Advertiser,* July 8–12, 15, 17–18, 1942.

75. *Montgomery Advertiser,* July 11, 1942.

76. Ibid.

77. *Montgomery Advertiser,* December 1, 1942, April 11–12, 15, 20–26, 28, 30, 1943.

78. *Montgomery Advertiser,* April 22 (advertisement for second war loan), April 30, November 9, 1943, Blum, *V Was for Victory,* 19–21.

79. *Montgomery Advertiser,* July 25, August 19, 25, September 2, 5–9, 11–13, 15, 17–19, 21–26, 28, 30, October 2–3, 1943; January 4, 16–31, February 1–28, 1944.

80. *Montgomery Advertiser,* January 25, 1944.

81. *Montgomery Advertiser,* April 26, 1943.

82. *Montgomery Advertiser,* September 11–12, 15–17, 1943.

83. *Montgomery Advertiser,* September 27–30, November 25, 1943.

84. *Montgomery Advertiser,* July 14, 1942, October 10 (quoting Go Peep), 1943, February 1, 1944.

85. *Montgomery Advertiser,* September 26, October 1, 6–7, 10 (quoting Go Peep), 1943.

86. *Montgomery Advertiser,* October 7, 1943.

6. THE BLACK COMMUNITY IN MONTGOMERY AND ABROAD

1. Blum, *V Was for Victory,* 182; Polenberg, *One Nation Divisible,* 24–33.

2. Blum, *V Was for Victory,* 184–188, 218–219; Polenberg, *One Nation Divisible,* 69–77; *Montgomery Advertiser,* January 12, 1942.

3. Colonel William Welsh, Command Diary, entries for July 13 and 14, 1942, file 286.26–106, Historical Research Agency.

4. Ibid.

5. Ibid.

6. Ibid.

7. Ibid.

8. Ibid.

9. Ibid.

10. Ibid.; *Montgomery Advertiser,* November 7, 1940. I have combed records at Maxwell and Gunter and the *Montgomery Advertiser* and *Alabama Journal* for the period in which the episode occurred and on through September 1942 as well as Minutes, MCC, for the period July 12 to September 30, 1942. Apart from the entries made in Colonel Welsh's diary for July 13 and 14, 1942, these sources do not mention the police actions, the negotiations, or any agreement.

11. *Montgomery Advertiser,* March 28, 1943.

12. *Montgomery Advertiser,* August 10, 1943.

13. *Montgomery Advertiser,* September 11, 1943.

14. *Montgomery Advertiser,* March 25, 1942.

15. Ibid.

16. *Montgomery Advertiser,* November 3, 1940, July 13, 1942, July 12–16, 20, 22–23, 1943, May 25, 1944, June 6, 1945.

17. See Chapter 2.

18. E. D. Nixon, interview with Randall Williams, n.d.

19. Ibid.

20. *Montgomery Advertiser,* June 21, 1942, January 8, 1943.

21. Matthews, Hill, and Dunn, interviews with the author, December 3, 1991.

22. *Montgomery Advertiser,* March 18, 1945.

23. Ibid.

24. *Montgomery Advertiser,* February 1, October 18, 1942; Johnnie Carr, interview with the author, August 1, 1997; Newton, My Short Military Career.

25. *Montgomery Advertiser,* March 25, 1942, February 1–2, May 3, March 28, May 29, 1943, February 4, 1944; Warrant Officer Frank Weirauch, "Maxwell Field's Bands, 1 October 1941 to 1 February 1944," 4, Microfilm Copy at Historical Research Agency.

26. News Release of April 1942 and Annual Report, December 1, 1943–November 30, 1944, of Red Cross, Montgomery Chapter, in chapter files, Montgomery; *Montgomery Advertiser,* January 7, 1943. Johnnie Carr and Sadie Penn, as young women in Montgomery in World War II, were never aware that any

black women took part in Red Cross sewing, knitting, or surgical bandage wrapping. Red Cross Records for the period do not reveal any black involvement in these activities. Carr and Penn, Montgomery, interviews with the author, both August 19, 1997.

27. *Montgomery Advertiser,* October 4 and 6, 1942.

28. *Montgomery Advertiser,* March 7, 1943.

29. *Montgomery Advertiser,* February 3, 1944.

30. Ibid.

31. Ibid.

32. Ibid.; Spector, *Eagle Against the Sun,* 388–389; Burks, interview with the author, July 31, 1991.

33. *Montgomery Advertiser,* February 3, 1944; *Nashville Globe and Independent,* November 13, 1942.

34. *Montgomery Advertiser,* February 3, 1944.

35. *Montgomery Advertiser,* February 12, 13 (quoted), 14, 1944.

36. *Montgomery Advertiser,* February 7, 1944.

37. See the *Advertiser* and the *Alabama Journal* for 1941–1945.

38. See "Alabama at the Front," *Montgomery Advertiser,* 1941–1945.

39. See the *Advertiser* for 1939–1945.

40. *Montgomery Advertiser,* May 29, 1943.

41. Ibid.

42. *Montgomery Advertiser,* March 28, 1945.

43. *Montgomery Advertiser,* March 5, 1945.

44. WSFA, *Letter from Home,* July 1943–August 1945.

45. Ibid.; Captain Francis Thigpen, letter to WSFA, n.d., 1945, box 3, *Letter from Home.*

46. Johnnie Carr, interview with the author, April 25, 1995.

47. *Montgomery Advertiser,* November 1, 1943.

48. *Montgomery Advertiser,* December 31, 1943; April 20, August 5, 1944.

49. *Montgomery Advertiser,* April 9, May 23, 1944.

50. *Montgomery Advertiser,* February 9, 1944; J. Mills Thornton III, interview with the author, July 27, 1992.

51. *Montgomery Advertiser,* April 9, 15, 20, 1944.

52. *Montgomery Advertiser,* May 24, 1944, January 15, 17, 1945.

53. Idessa Redden, interview with the author, August 25, 1991.

54. *Montgomery Advertiser,* May 30, June 6, 1943, February 7, 1944.

55. *Montgomery Advertiser,* May 14–15, 1944.

7. LIFE AND DEATH AT HOME

1. Lingeman, *Don't You Know There's a War On?* 173.

2. Ibid., 173, 190, 205–206.

3, *Montgomery Advertiser,* February 15, 19–21, 1943.

4. Newton, "Montgomery and Hollywood," 6–7.

5. Newton, "Montgomery and Hollywood," 7.

6. *Montgomery Advertiser,* March 18, April 1 and 17, June 17, 1942; March 14, 1943.

7. Ennels and Newton, *The Wisdom of Eagles,* 100; *Montgomery Advertiser,* February 7–8, March 6, April 15, September 1, 1942.

8. Redden, interview with the author, August 25, 1991; Mary Lett Neeley, interview with the author, August 4, 1992; Ennels and Newton, *The Wisdom of Eagles,* 101–102.

9. *Montgomery Advertiser,* August 26, 1944; Neeley, interview with the author, August 4, 1992; Hartmann, *The Home Front and Beyond,* 77.

10. *Montgomery Advertiser,* January 2, 8, 14, 22, 24, February 5, April 22, May 15, 1942, January 12, June 24, September 15, 22, 30, 1943, February 16, June 2, 16, 1944.

11. Minutes, MCC, June 30, 1943; *Montgomery Advertiser,* July 10, 1942, May 27–28, 1944.

12. *Montgomery Advertiser,* November 15, 1942, June 23, 1943.

13. *Montgomery Advertiser,* June 27, July 1–2, 4, 1943.

14. *Montgomery Advertiser,* May 1, 29, June 12–13, 21, 28, 1942.

15. *Montgomery Advertiser,* July 8, 1943; Margaret (Peggy Penton) Cravey, interview with the author, September 10, 1991.

16. Cravey, interview with the author, September 10, 1991.

17. Ibid.

18. Peggy Penton, letters to Bess Penton, September 16, 22, 30, and October 6, 1941, Margaret (Peggy Penton) Cravey Collection, Montgomery.

19. Allen, "Auburn Fifty Years Ago," 8–9; *Montgomery Advertiser,* July 30, 1943.

20. Allen, ""Auburn Fifty Years Ago," 10.

21. *Montgomery Advertiser,* January 22, March 17, May 27, 1942, July 30–31, August 1, 1943.

22. Algie (Hill) Neill, interview with the author, March 20, 1995; *Montgomery Advertiser,* December 19, 1944.

23. Neill, interview with the author, March 20, 1995.

24. Jean (Severence) Nettles, interview with the author, August 30, 1994.

25. Ibid.

26. Baldwin, Hill, and Matthews, interviews with the author, December 3, 1993.

27. Edward G. Brown, interview with the author, August 2, 1991; Brooks, *Swing Time!* 28–29.

28. *Montgomery Advertiser,* August 1, 1943.

29. Dorothy Ghent, interview with the author, April 2, 1994; Cravey, interview with the author, June 3, 1991.

30. Louise DeShields Larson, interview with the author, July 23, 1991.

31. Ibid.

32. DeShields Larson, interview with the author, March 28, 1995.

33. The sources for this information were my mother and some of the friends with whom she played bridge.

34. Cravey, interview with the author, August 4, 1988; Ghent, interview with the author, February 6, 1995.

35. *Atlanta Daily World,* January 3, 1944.

36. Ghent, interview with the author, February 6, 1995.

37. *Montgomery Advertiser,* December 31, 1939, March 30, 1941, March 1, 7, 15, 18, 29, May 10, 17, June 7, 28, November 1, 1942, May 30, September 16, October 3, 10, November 7, 14, 1943.

38. *Montgomery Advertiser,* May 22–23, 1942; Ennels and Newton, *The Wisdom of Eagles,* 108.

39. Cravey, interview with the author, June 3, 1991; Silas "Brook" Nettles and Jean (Severence) Nettles, joint interview with the author, August 30, 1994.

40. "Graduation Ball at Maxwell Field," 8–9; *Montgomery Advertiser,* May 23–24, 31, 1942.

41. Newton, "Launching a Legend."

42. Ibid.

43. Ibid.

44. Ibid.

45. Ibid.

46. Ibid.

47. Ibid.

48. Ennels and Newton, *The Wisdom of Eagles,* 106–107, 110; *Montgomery Advertiser,* January 28, February 1, November 22, 1942; Corrie (Hill) Tankersley, interview with the author, October 23, 1993.

49. Cravey, interview with the author, June 8, 1991; Cravey, "Cadet Widow," unpublished narrative, n.d., Margaret (Peggy Penton) Cravey Collection.

50. Cravey, interview with the author, June 8, 1991.

51. Ibid.; Carr, interview with the author, April 25, 1995; *Montgomery Advertiser,* August 26, 1943.

52. Cravey, interview with the author, June 8, 1991.

53. Cravey, interview with the author, June 8, 1991; Mildred (Davies) Smith, interview with the author, January 29, 2000.

54. *Montgomery Advertiser,* January 25, February 15, 28, March 22, 29, June 28, July 19, December 27, 1942, February 2, July 4, September 19, October 24, 1943, April 19, January 30, November 11, 1944; Carr, interview with the author, April 25, 1995.

55. *Montgomery Advertiser,* November 11, 19, 1944.

56. *Montgomery Advertiser,* September 22, 1944.

57. Thornton, "Challenge and Response," 464.

58. *Montgomery Advertiser,* July 17, 1942, July 1, 10, 22, 1943.

59. *Montgomery Advertiser,* June 2, 1943.

60. *Montgomery Advertiser,* June 17, 1942; October 20, 1944; Polenberg, *War and Society,* 151.

61. *Montgomery Advertiser,* July 21, 29, August 12, 14, 1943.

62. Minutes, MCC, July 20, 1943; *Montgomery Advertiser,* September 17, 1943, May 24, 31, October 20, 1944.

63. Polenberg, *War and Society,* 149–150.

64. Ibid., 150; *Montgomery Advertiser,* October 22, 1943.

65. Polenberg, *War and Society,* 149–150; *Montgomery Advertiser,* January 1–2 (quoting the PTA report), 9, 1944.

66. *Montgomery Advertiser,* January 10–11, 1944.

67. *Montgomery Advertiser,* January 15, 18, 26 (quoting Rabbi Blachschleger), 1944.

68. *Montgomery Advertiser,* January 11, 16 (quoting Superintendent Dannelly), 1944.

69. *Montgomery Advertiser,* March 17, 1944.

70. *Montgomery Advertiser,* January 21, February 9, 20, March 12, 1944.

71. *Montgomery Advertiser,* March 17, 1944.

72. *Montgomery Advertiser,* January 11, 18, February 2, March 11, 14, 1944; Laura Johnston, interview with the author, July 23, 1991.

73. *Montgomery Advertiser,* January 7, 9, 31, August 15, November 26, 1944, January 6, 1945.

74. *Montgomery Advertiser,* January 6, 21, 28, February 4, 11, March 11, 18, April 15, 1945.

75. *Montgomery Advertiser,* November 29, 1942.

76. *Montgomery Advertiser,* November 30, 1942; Newton, My Short Military Career.

77. *Montgomery Advertiser,* August 8–12, 1944.

78. *Montgomery Advertiser,* August 14, September 5–6, October 10–12, 1944.

79. *Montgomery Advertiser,* June 17, 1944.

80. Ibid.

81. *Montgomery Advertiser,* June 17–19, 1944.

82. *Montgomery Advertiser,* June 22, August 15, September 15, 1944.

83. *Montgomery Advertiser,* June 18–21, 23, 1944.

84. *Montgomery Advertiser,* June 20, September 2–3, 1944.

85. *Montgomery Advertiser,* September 4, October 4, 1944.

86. *Montgomery Advertiser,* October 4, 1944.

87. *Montgomery Advertiser,* November 12, 14, 1944.

88. *Montgomery Advertiser,* November 22–23, 25, 1944.

8. OVERLORD AND AFTERMATH

1. Stokesbury, *World War II,* 184–186, 310–311.

2. *Montgomery Advertiser,* August 13, 1944.

3. Ibid.

4. Stokesbury, *World War II,* 311–313.

5. James Donald Godwin to Melba and Kitty Johnson, January 29, 1944, Godwin to Melba, March 1, 1944, both in the collection of Catherine ("Kitty" Johnson) Cobb, Montgomery. All of the letters of Godwin that I quote are in Catherine Cobb's collection.

6. McFarland and Newton, *To Command the Sky,* 157–237.

7. Eleanor ("Tobie" Tobias) Hopper, telephone statements to the author, October 5, 1995, and January 20, 1996.

8. McFarland and Newton, *To Command the Sky,* 236–237.

9. *Montgomery Advertiser,* July 30, 1944.

10. James Donald Godwin to Kitty, March 30, 1944; *Lanier Oracle,* 27.

11. James Donald Godwin to Kitty, April 8, Godwin to Melba and Kitty, May 9, 1944.

12. *Montgomery Advertiser,* June 14 (quoting McCord), August 17 (quoting Whitsett), 1943, March 6 ("carnival of death"), April 26, May 1, 1944.

13. *Montgomery Advertiser,* June 1, 1944.

14. *Montgomery Advertiser,* June 2, 1944

15. *Montgomery Advertiser,* January 6, 1944.

16. *Montgomery Advertiser,* April 9, 1942, June 4–7, 1944.

17. *Montgomery Advertiser,* June 5, 1944.

18. Stokesbury, *World War II,* 314; *Montgomery Advertiser,* August 27, 1944.

19. *Montgomery Advertiser,* November 12, 1944.

20. *Montgomery Advertiser,* May 13, 1945.

21. *Montgomery Advertiser,* May 20, 1945.

22. *Montgomery Advertiser,* September 16, 1944.

23. *Montgomery Advertiser,* July 30, 1944.

24. *Montgomery Advertiser,* July 23, 1944, June 6, 1999.

25. *Montgomery Advertiser,* July 30, 1944; Catherine (Kitty Johnson) Cobb, interview with the author, November 13, 1998: Ambrose, *D-Day,* 581–582.

26. *Montgomery Advertiser,* June 29, August 6, September 3, 1944; Ambrose, *D-Day,* 417.

27. *Montgomery Advertiser,* November 9, 1944; February 9, 1945.

28. Ambrose, *D-Day,* 434. I have seen photographs of Normandy fishermen sitting on debris near the water's edge surrounded by the partly covered corpses of GIs. Some of the bodies have flowers on them. I have no source for the photographs.

29. *Montgomery Advertiser,* December 17, 1944; Stokesbury, *World War II,* 315–317.

30. Newton, "News of Assault Brought Tears, Prayers."

31. Ibid.

32. Ibid.

33. Ibid. I quote p. 23 of the *Advertiser* supplement on D-Day, in which "News of Assault Brought Tears, Prayers," is found.

34. Newton, "News of Assault Brought Tears, Prayers." The quoted copy appears on p. 23 of the supplement.

35. Newton, "News of Assault Brought Tears, Prayers."

36. Ibid.

37. Ibid.

38. Ibid.

39. Ibid.

40. *Montgomery Advertiser,* June 7, 1944.

41. *Syracuse Herald-Journal,* July 7, 1945.

42. Ennels and Newton, *The Wisdom of Eagles,* 100, 102, 112; *Montgomery Advertiser,* November 28, 1944.

43. *Montgomery Advertiser,* June 5, 1944.

44. *Montgomery Advertiser,* August 19, 1944.

45. *Montgomery Advertiser,* August 24, September 6 (quoting Pippin), 1944.

46. *Montgomery Advertiser,* July 25, August 22, 1944.

47. *Montgomery Advertiser,* July 8, October 6, 21, 1944.

48. *Montgomery Advertiser,* August 22, 1944.

49. *Montgomery Advertiser,* August 25, 1944.

50. *Montgomery Advertiser,* August 18, 20, 23, 24–25 (quoting Cassidy), 31, 1944.

51. *Montgomery Advertiser,* August 24, 26, 1944.

52. *Montgomery Advertiser,* August 27, September 2, 6, October 11, 1944.

53. *Montgomery Advertiser,* June 17, 1942, May 21, June 5, 24, 29, July 26, 1944.

54. *Montgomery Advertiser,* July 1–2, August 4, 1944.

55. *Montgomery Advertiser,* June 13, 1944; Thornton, interview with the author, July 27, 1992.

56. *Montgomery Advertiser,* June 25–26, 1944.

57. *Montgomery Advertiser,* September 12, 1944.

58. *Montgomery Advertiser,* September 23, October 2–4, 1944.

59. *Montgomery Advertiser,* August 24, September 6, 1944.

60. *Montgomery Advertiser,* August 25, 1944.

61. *Montgomery Advertiser,* September 6, 1944.

62. Ennels and Newton, *The Wisdom of Eagles,* 11.

63. *Montgomery Advertiser,* August 30, 1944.

64. *Montgomery Advertiser,* August 4, October 8, 1944.

65. Stokesbury, *World War II,* 317–324; *Montgomery Advertiser,* September 17, 1944.

66. *Montgomery Advertiser,* September 17, 1944.

67. *Montgomery Advertiser,* October 15, 1944.

68. Stokesbury, *World War II,* 336; Robert Sternenberg, interview with the author, August 9, 1999; *Montgomery Advertiser,* January 5, 1945.

69. Scott, "The Crommelin Brothers," 14; *Montgomery Advertiser,* December 28, 1944.

70. *Montgomery Advertiser,* June 18, 1944.

71. Fred Burks, interviews with the author, August 7, September 4, 1991.

72. Marguerite Sherlock, interview with the author, June 21, 1991.

73. *Montgomery Advertiser,* January 9, 25, 1944.

74. *Montgomery Advertiser,* February 21, April 13, July 9, August 30, 1944.

75. *Montgomery Advertiser,* June 30, September 26, October 29, 1944.

76. *Montgomery Advertiser,* August 27, November 6, 1944.

77. *Montgomery Advertiser,* December 3, 1944.

78. Bennett, *When Dreams Came True,* 57–67.

79. Ibid., 181–192.

80. *Montgomery Advertiser,* October 29, 1944; Ghent, interview with the author, April 2, 1994.

81. Burks, interview with the author, September 4, 1991.

82. Stokesbury, *World War II,* 339–345.

83. *Montgomery Advertiser,* January 28, April 15, May 6, 1945.

84. Stokesbury, *World War II,* 324–326; *Montgomery Advertiser,* October 2, 1944.

85. *Montgomery Advertiser,* December 1, 1944.

86. *Montgomery Advertiser,* September 30, October 28, November 9–10, 1944.

87. *Montgomery Advertiser,* October 3, 19, November 26, 1944.

88. *Montgomery Advertiser,* November 22, 1944.

89. *Montgomery Advertiser,* December 14, 1944.

90. *Montgomery Advertiser,* December 16–17, 27, 1944.

91. *Montgomery Advertiser,* January 23, 1945.

9. FROM THE BULGE TO VICTORY IN EUROPE

1. Newton, My Short Military Career.

2. Kalman Shwarts, interview with the author, August 1, 1999; Bobby Young, interview with the author, November 10, 1997; Newton, "Launching a Legend." Shwarts's brother-in-law Louis Haas is also living.

3. Newton, "Launching a Legend."

4. Ibid.; Young, interview with the author, November 10, 1997.

5. Young, interview with the author, November 10, 1997; *Montgomery Advertiser,* October 29, 1944.

6. William ("Billy") Crane, interview with the author, 1991; Crane to WSFA, *Letter from Home,* October 1 and November 11, 1944, Box 1, WSFA, *Letter from Home.*

7. Neal Howard to Mary Ellen Mathews, posted on troop ship, n.d., William Howard Collection; Newton, My Short Military Career. I was an enlisted scout

in a rifle company of the Seventy-eighth. Neal Howard and I were friends and, although in different battalions of the 310th Infantry Regiment, had similar experiences from Camp Pickett to the Bulge. We did not, however, see each other overseas.

8. Newton, "Death of an Alabama Soldier"; Newton, My Short Military Career.

9. Neal Howard to Mary Ellen Matthews, November 5 and 20, 1944, William Howard Collection; Newton, My Short Military Career.

10. Newton, "Death of an Alabama Soldier."

11. Newton, My Short Military Career.

12. Ibid. The account of the 310th regiment's movement to the western front and its early combat is told in *Roer, Rhine, Ruhr,* the official history of the 310th Infantry Regiment, Seventy-eighth Division (Berlin: Seventy-eighth Infantry Division, 1945), 16–46.

13. Newton, My Short Military Career.

14. Ibid.

15. Ibid.

16. Neal Howard to Margaret Howard, November 29, 1944, William Howard Collection.

17. Newton, My Short Military Career.

18. Ibid.

19. Ibid.

20. Ibid.

21. Ibid.

22. Ibid.

23. Ibid.

24. Ibid.

25. Ibid.; Miller, "Kesternich," 30–34.

26. Miller, "Kesternich," 33.

27. Newton, "Death of an Alabama Soldier."

28. Ibid.

29. *Montgomery Advertiser,* December 12, 15, 1944; Ennels and Newton, *The Wisdom of Eagles,* 112; Newton, "Launching a Legend."

30. *Montgomery Advertiser,* November 21, December 19, 1944, January 10, 15, 1945.

31. *Montgomery Advertiser,* December 6–7, 1944.

32. *Montgomery Advertiser,* December 17–18, 1944; Stokesbury, *World War II,* 352–353; MacDonald, *A Time for Trumpets,* 10–11.

33. *Montgomery Advertiser,* December 25, 1944.

34. Robert Lawrence, memorandum to the author, 1992; *Montgomery Advertiser,* December 26, 1944.

35. Lawrence, memorandum to the author, 1992.

36. Newton, "Death of an Alabama Soldier"; MacDonald, *A Time for Trumpets,* 92–93, 116, 160–183, 207–210, 391–411.

37. Newton, "Death of an Alabama Soldier."

38. I tell the story of Neal Howard in the Bulge in "Soldier's Letters Tell of WWII Life."

39. Young, interview with the author, November 10, 1997.

40. Crane, interview with the author, 1991.

41. MacDonald, *A Time for Trumpets,* 488–513; *Montgomery Advertiser,* February 4, 1945.

42. *Montgomery Advertiser,* July 22, 1945; *The Time-Life History of World War II,* 325–329; McDonald, *A Time for Trumpets,* 514–533.

43. *Montgomery Advertiser,* December 24–31, 1944, January 9, 13, 15, 1945.

44. *Montgomery Advertiser,* July 31, 1945.

45. Newton, "Death of an Alabama Soldier" and "Soldier's Letters Tell of WW II Life"; Crane to *Letter from Home,* January 15, 1945, box 1, WSFA, *Letter from Home.*

46. *Montgomery Advertiser,* December 31, 1944.

47. Newton, "Blue-Gray Game," 14.

48. Ibid.; *Montgomery Advertiser,* October 31, December 23, 26, 28, 1944.

49. *Montgomery Advertiser,* December 28–31, 1944, January 3, 1945.

50. *Montgomery Advertiser,* January 2, 1945.

51. *Montgomery Advertiser,* October 2, 1944, January 31 (Mullin quote), February 11, March 18, 1945.

52. *Montgomery Advertiser,* January 27, February 2, 4, 1945.

53. *Montgomery Advertiser,* January 10, 28, March 15, May 9, 1945.

54. Miller, "Kesternich," 33–34; *Lightning,* 79–122.

55. Neal Howard to Billy Howard, February 14, 1945, William Howard Collection; Billy Robinson to William J. and Alice Robinson, March 1, 1945, Paul Robinson Collection; Newton, "Twister," 8.

56. Newton, "Twister," 8.

57. Ibid.; *Montgomery Advertiser,* February 13, 1944.

58. Newton, "Twister," 8.

59. Ibid., 8–9; *Montgomery Advertiser,* February 13, 1944.

60. Newton, "Twister," 9; Seaman Third Class Lamar Dennis to *Letter from Home,* February 26, 1945, box 2, WSFA, *Letter from Home.*

61. Newton, "Twister," 9; *Montgomery Advertiser,* February 13–15, March 6, 1945; W. P. Screws to Haygood Paterson, February 19, 1945, on Montgomery tornado, folder 3, "Montgomery County Correspondence," SG19852, Alabama State Civilian Defense, 1941–1946.

62. Stokesbury, *World War II,* 367–368.

63. Lamar Best, interview with the author, February 28, 1995.

64. Stokesbury, *World War II,* 368.

65. Ibid., 368–369; *Montgomery Advertiser,* March 18, 25, 30, May 4, 1945.

66. Stokesbury, *World War II,* 368; *Montgomery Advertiser,* April 1, 1945.

67. Stokesbury, *World War II,* 369; Lamar Best, interview with the author, February 28, 1995.

68. Stokesbury, *World War II,* 371.

69. Millett and Maslowski, *For the Common Defense,* 463; *Montgomery Advertiser,* August 12, 1945.

70. Robert Lawrence, memorandum to the author, 1992.

71. Ibid.

72. Neal Howard to Mary Ellen Mathews, February 17, 1945; Fannie Lee Howard to Neal Howard, February 18, 1945, both in William Howard Collection.

73. Newton, "Death of an Alabama Soldier."

74. *Lightning,* pp. 124–141; Leslie Heaton to Nellie Howard, March 9, 1949, William Howard Collection.

75. Newton, "Death of an Alabama Soldier."

76. Ibid.

77. Ibid.

78. Ibid.

79. Fannie Lee Howard to Neal Howard, March 15, 1945; War Department, telegrams to William Howard, Sr., March 16 and 20, 1945, William Howard Collection.

80. Dorothy Van Sant to Fannie Lee Howard, n.d.; Mary Dannelly, to Fannie Lee Howard, n.d., both in William Howard Collection.

81. *Montgomery Advertiser,* February 9, March 14, 18, 25, April 22, May 1, 6, 1945.

82. *The Time-Life History of World War II,* 338–339; *Lightning,* 161–165.

83. Stokesbury, *World War II,* 358; Young, interview with the author, January 30, 1995.

84. Silas Nettles, interview with the author, September 20, 1994.

85. Ibid.

86. *Montgomery Advertiser,* May 6, 1945.

87. *Montgomery Advertiser,* June 24, 1945.

88. Ibid.

89. *Montgomery Advertiser,* April 25, 1945; Young, interview with the author, January 30, 1995.

90. Young, interview with the author, January 30, 1995.

91. *Montgomery Advertiser,* June 30, July 5, 1945.

92. *Alabama Journal,* April 12–13; *Montgomery Advertiser,* April 13–16; Ennels and Newton, *The Wisdom of Eagles,* 113.

93. Newton, "City Was War Weary."

94. Ibid.

95. Ibid. I quote p. 4F of the section of the *Advertiser* in which the article "City Was War Weary" appeared.

96. Newton, "City Was War Weary."

97. Ibid.

98. Ibid.; *Montgomery Advertiser,* May 9, 1945.

10. THE END OF THE WAR

1. *Montgomery Advertiser,* June 10, 1945.

2. *Montgomery Advertiser,* August 2, 1945.

3. *Montgomery Advertiser,* May 7, 1945.

4. *Montgomery Advertiser,* May 9, 1945.

5. Stokesbury, *World War II ,* 380; Cronenberg, *Forth to the Mighty Conflict,* 162; Newton, My Short Military Career.

6. *Montgomery Advertiser,* June 28, 1945.

7. *Montgomery Advertiser,* April 1, May 10–11, 16–17, June 3, 6, 9, 14, 1945.

8. *Montgomery Advertiser,* March 3, 25, May 4, 6, 10, 14, 16–19, 23, 25–26, 31, June 3, 12, 19–21, 27–28, July 1, 3–5, 1945.

9. *Montgomery Advertiser,* June 21, 1945.

10. *Montgomery Advertiser,* May 6, 22, June 5, July 13, 19, 23, 25, 1945.

11. *Montgomery Advertiser,* May 17, 23, 1945; Baldwin, Hill, and Matthews, interviews with the author, December 3, 1993.

12. Newton, My Short Military Career.

13. *Montgomery Advertiser,* June 3, 29, 1945; Maurer, *USAF Credits,* 106, 136, 185; Scott, "The Crommelin Brothers," 9–10.

14. Newton, My Short Military Career.

15. Ibid.

16. Ibid.

17. Ibid.; Mary Louise (Caton) Weed, audiotape, January 1992.

18. Silas "Brook" Nettles and Jean Severence Nettles, joint interview with the author, September 27, 1994.

19. Ibid.

20. Ibid.

21. Ibid.

22. *Montgomery Advertiser,* July 29, 1945

23. *Montgomery Advertiser,* May 18, June 30, July 16, August 12, 1945.

24. Eleanor ("Tobie") Tobias Hopper, telephone statement to the author, January 20, 1996.

25. *Montgomery Advertiser,* May 11, 13, 1945.

26. *Montgomery Advertiser,* June 17, 1945.

27. *Montgomery Advertiser,* December 17, 1944, August 12, 19, 1945.

28. *Montgomery Advertiser,* August 6, 1945; Newton, My Short Military Career.

29. *Montgomery Advertiser,* July 11, 18–20, 26, 1945.

30. *Montgomery Advertiser,* January 1, May 20, July 12, 1945.

31. *Montgomery Advertiser,* May 27, June 1–2, 1945.

32. *Montgomery Advertiser,* June 1, 4, 1945. Mayor Gunter's leadership in commercial aviation for Montgomery is described in Ennels and Newton, *The Wisdom of Eagles,* pp. 22–23, 28–30.

33. *Montgomery Advertiser,* June 17, July 4, 1945.

34. *Montgomery Advertiser,* May 9, 13, June 1, 1945.

35. *Montgomery Advertiser,* May 30, July 4–5, 29, 1945.

36. *Montgomery Advertiser,* April 17, 1944, June 11, 14, July 25, 28, September 9, 1945.

37. Burks, interview with the author, September 4, 1991.

38. Sawyer, interview with the author, September 10, 1991.

39. Ibid.

40. Ibid.

41. Ibid.

42. Spector, *Eagle Against the Sun,* 540; Aaron Harris, Jr., interviews, March 16 and 22, 1995.

43. Harris, interviews with the author, March 16 and 22, 1995.

44. Harris, interviews with the author, March 16 and 22, 1995.

45. Ralph Loeb, Jr., interview with the author, September 21, 1991.

46. Ibid.

47. Ibid.

48. *Montgomery Advertiser,* July 29, 1945.

49. Scott, "The Crommelin Brothers," 16.

50. *Montgomery Advertiser,* July 2, 29, August 5, 1945.

51. Allen and Polmar, *Code-Name Fail Safe,* 109–110, 152, 193, 203–208.

52. Stokesbury, *World War II,* 374.

53. *Montgomery Advertiser,* June 4, 1945.

54. Newton, "Word of War's End Spread Quickly."

55. Ibid.

56. Ibid.

57. Ibid.; Robert Lawrence, interview with the author, March 3, 1998.

58. Newton, "Word of War's End Spread Quickly." On the afternoon and early evening of August 14, I was picnicking on nearby Lake Jordan with Mary Louise Caton, Billy Crane, and Virginia Waits, the young woman (Lanier class of '43) whom Billy would soon marry. We did not join the downtown celebration.

59. Newton, "Word of War's End Spread Quickly."

60. Ibid. *Montgomery Advertiser,* August 15, 1945 (quoted).

61. Newton, "Word of War's End Spread Quickly."

62. Ibid.; *Montgomery Advertiser,* August 15, 1945 (quoted).

63. Newton, "Word of War's End Spread Quickly"; *Montgomery Advertiser,* August 15, 1945 (quoted).

64. Newton, "Word of War's End Spread Quickly"; *Montgomery Advertiser,* August 15, 1945 (quoted).

65. Newton, "Word of War's End Spread Quickly"; *Montgomery Advertiser,* August 15, 1945 (quoted).

66. *Montgomery Advertiser,* August 15, 18–19, 1945.

67. Newton, "Word of War's End Spread Quickly." The term "V-J Day" was rather broadly applied when the Japanese surrendered. The *Advertiser* used it in connection with the night of August 14–August 15 when the joyous celebration took place downtown. Most Montgomerians seem to have regarded this occasion as V-J Day. Governor Sparks gave state employees a day off work on August 15, and Truman gave federal employees the fifteenth and sixteenth off work, and so these days could be considered V-J Days. At Maxwell and Gunter the post commanders informed their assembled troops on August 17 that peace had formally come; the seventeenth was thus another V-J Day. The

U.S. government's official V-J Day was September 2, the day when the Japanese on the battleship *Missouri* signed the document of surrender.

68. Newton, My Short Military Career.

69. Sawyer, interview with the author, September 10, 1991; Loeb, interview with the author, September 21, 1991.

EPILOGUE

1. Morison, *The Oxford History of the American People,* 1053, 1056, 1064; Roberts, *A History of Europe,* 511–513, 519–520.

2. Bennett, *When Dreams Came True,* 2, 5; Morison, *The Oxford History of the American People,* 1051–1052. The *Advertiser* periodically listed the returnees and those discharged from September 1945 through the summer of 1946, although the paper could not record them all.

3. See the accounts of each one's return in this chapter.

4. Robert Lawrence, interview with the author, March 3, 1998; Lawrence, memorandum to the author, August 31, 1998.

5. Ralph Loeb's father died of a heart condition shortly before he left for the Pacific. My father died of a heart condition just after I returned from Europe. Both were in their fifties.

6. Lawrence, memorandum to the author, August 31, 1998.

7. Bobby Young, interview with the author, November 10, 1997; Young, memorandum to the author, August 27, 1998.

8. Young, memorandum to the author, August 27, 1998.

9. Marguerite Sherlock, interviews with the author, February 15 and August 18, 1998.

10. Sherlock, interview with the author, August 18, 1998; Lawrence, memorandum to the author, August 31, 1998.

11. Sherlock, interview with the author, August 18, 1998; Thomas, *Riveting and Rationing,* 121.

12. Young, memorandum to the author, August 27, 1998; Sherlock, interview with the author, August 18, 1998; Lawrence, memorandum to the author, August 31, 1998.

13. Ralph Loeb, interview with the author, September 9, 1994, and memorandum to the author, August 31, 1998.

14. Loeb, memorandum to the author, August 31, 1998. I collected my "52–20" from January to June 1946, when, with the essential aid of the G.I. Bill, I matriculated at the University of Missouri.

15. Lawrence, memorandum to the author, August 31, 1998; Young, memorandum to the author, August 27, 1998.

16. Sherlock, interview with the author, August 18, 1998; Aaron Harris, Jr., interview with the author, March 22, 1995.

17. Newton, My Short Military Career.

18. Billy Howard, personal communication, Montgomery, October 14, 1991; Catherine Cobb, interview with the author, September 13, 1998; Newton, "Death of an Alabama Soldier."

19. Billy Howard, personal communication, Montgomery, October 14, 1991; Catherine Cobb, interview with the author, September 13, 1998; Newton, "Death of an Alabama Soldier."

20. Dorothy Ghent, interview with the author, April 2, 1994; Margaret (Peggy Penton) Cravey, interview with the author, June 30, 1992.

21. Brook and Jean (Severence) Nettles, interview with the author, September 27, 1994; Crane, interview with the author, 1991; Minutes, MCC, meeting of September 1, 1945; Sawyer, interview with the author, September 10, 1991; Sawyer, memorandum to the author, August 27, 1998; Lawrence, memorandum to the author, August 31, 1998.

22. Bennett, *When Dreams Came True,* pp. 2–5.

23. Lawrence, memorandum to the author, August 31, 1998.

24. Bennett, *When Dreams Came True,* 2.

25. I kept in touch with these persons after the war with the exception of Marguerite Sherlock. See Sherlock, interview with the author, February 15, 1998.

26. Young, memorandum to the author, August 27, 1998.

27. Bennett, *When Dreams Came True,* n. 15, 325; Oliver, interview with the author, November 27, 1995.

28. Flynt, *Dixie's Forgotten People,* p. 94; Lawrence, memorandum to the author, August 31, 1998.

29. Lawrence, memorandum to the author, August 31, 1998; Loeb, memorandum to the author, August 31, 1998.

30. Lawrence, memorandum to the author, August 31, 1998.

31. Wampold, interview with the author, November 13, 1987. I lived in the South for much of the postwar era and observed the patterns of segregation.

32. Loeb, memorandum to the author, August 31, 1998.

33. Minutes, MCC, August 6, 1945, March 16, 30, May 14, June 6, August 28, 1945, June 11, 14, July 9, 16, August 6, 20, 1946. Regarding street improvements, see Minutes, MCC, August 1945–August 1946.

34. Silas ("Brook") Nettles, interview with the author, September 27, 1994.

Nettles was briefly a civilian after V-J Day, then became a regular officer in the U.S. Air Force. He retired as a full colonel.

35. Ennels and Newton, *The Wisdom of Eagles,* 117–124, 163.

36. Newton, "The Early History of Commercial Aviation in Montgomery."

37. Newton, "The Blue-Gray Game," 14.

38. *Montgomery Advertiser,* May 8, 1946; Thornton, "Challenge and Response," 464–467.

39. Nixon, interview with Randall Williams, n.d.; John Sawyer, memorandum to the author, Montgomery, August 27, 1998.

40. Thornton, "Challenge and Response," 470–472; Nixon, interview with Randall Williams, n.d.; *Montgomery Advertiser,* August 25, 1946.

41. Nixon, interview with Randall Williams, n.d.; Sawyer, memorandum to the author, August 27, 1998.

42. Burks, interview with the author, September 4, 1991.

43. Aaron Harris, Jr., interview with the author, March 22, 1995.

44. *Montgomery Advertiser,* May 5, 1946.

45. Ibid.

46. Regarding the end of segregation on Montgomery's municipal buses, see Thornton, "Challenge and Response."

Bibliography

PRIMARY SOURCES

ARCHIVES

Alabama Department of Archives and History, Montgomery
Alabama Governor Administrative Files. 1939–1943: Frank M. Dixon.
Alabama Governor Administrative Files. 1943–1945: Chauncey Sparks.
Alabama State Civilian Defense Program Administrative Files. 1941–1946.
Vera Ruth Millie (Gomillion) Prentiss Collection.
WSFA Radio, Montgomery. *Letter from Home.* 1943–1945.

U.S. Air Force Historical Research Agency, Maxwell Air Force Base, Alabama
Histories of Maxwell and Gunter Fields in World War II and supporting
    documents.
Letters, diaries, and other documents relating to World War II.

INTERVIEWS, MEMORANDA, AUTOBIOGRAPHICAL WRITINGS, AND TAPES

Allen, Lee N. Memorandum to the Author. September 29, 1995.
Anderson, Col. Hubert K. USAF (ret.), and Jeanne (Walker). Interview with
    the Author. October 25, 1996.
Baldwin, Betty. Interview with the Author. December 3, 1991.
Best, Lamar. Interview with the Author. February 28, 1995.
Borders, Mary Henrie (Harris). Interview with the Author. August 9, 1993.
Brown, Edward G. Interview with the Author. August 2, 1991.
Burks, Frederick D. Interview with the Author. July 7, 24, 31, September 4,
    1991.

Carr, Johnnie, J. Interview with the Author. April 25, 1995, August 19, 1997.

———. One Montgomery. Oral History Statement. September 15, 1998.

Cobb, Catherine (Kitty Johnson). Interview with the Author. November 13, 1998.

Crane, William. Interviews with the Author. Various dates, 1991.

Cravey, Margaret (Peggy Penton). Autobiographical writings. Manuscripts in the collection of Margaret Cravey, Montgomery.

———. Interviews with the Author. June 8, 1988, May 23, 1989, June 3, 8, 19, September 10, 1991, May 12, June 10, 30, 1992.

DeShields-Larson, Louise. Interviews with the Author. July 23, 1991, March 28, 1995.

Ghent, Dorothy. Interviews with the Author. October 27, 1991, April 2, 1994, February 1, 1995.

Harris, Aaron, Jr. Interview with the Author. March 16, 22, 1995.

Haynie, Loetta (Gardner). Interview with the Author. March 24, 1994.

Hill, Isabel (Dunn). Interview with the Author. December 3, 1991.

Holmes, Robert. Interview with the Author. December 3, 1995.

Hopper, Eleanor (Tobias). Statements Made in Telephone Conversations with the Author. October 5, 1995, and January 20, 1996.

Howard, William. Statement Made in Telephone Conversation with the Author, October 14, 1992.

Ireland, Pat (Caton). Interview with the Author. October 15, 1993.

Lawrence, Robert. Audiotape. 1942.

———. Interviews with the Author. November 4, 1995, March 3, 1998.

———. Memoranda to the Author. N.d., 1992, August 31, 1998.

Loeb, Ralph, Jr. Interviews with the Author. June 13, July 26, September 21, 1991, September 9, 1994.

———. Memorandum to the Author. August 31, 1998.

Loeb, Mrs. Ralph, Sr. Interview with the Author. February 2, 1988.

Matthews, Caroline "Dootsie" (Ball). Interview with the Author. December 3, 1991.

———. Note to the Author. February 15, 1995.

Neeley, Mary (Lett). Interview with the Author. August 4, 1992.

Neill, Algie (Hill). Interview with the Author. March 20, 1995.

Nettles, Jean (Severence). Interview with the Author. September 27, 1994.

Nettles, Silas S. ("Brook"). Interviews with the Author. August 30, September 20, 27, 1994.

Newton, Florence. Oral Statement to the Author. 1946.

Nixon, E. D. Interview with Randall Williams. N.d. In "Will the Circle Be Unbroken." Documentary radio history of the civil rights movement. Prepared by the Southern Regional Council, Atlanta, Ga., for the Public Broadcasting System, 1997.

Oliver, Thomas W. Interview with the Author. November 27, 1995.

Penn, Sadie (Gardner). Interviews with the Author. August 13, September 17, 1991, August 19, 1997.

Redden, Idessa (Williams). Interviews with the Author. August 18, 25, September 22, 1991.

Robinson, Paul. Interview with the Author. March 21, 1991.

Sawyer, John. Interviews with the Author. September 10, 1991, November 18, 1997.

————. Memorandum to the Author. August 27, 1998.

————. One Montgomery. Oral History Statement. September 15, 1998.

Sherlock, Marguerite. Interviews with the Author. June 21, 1991, February 5, August 18, 1998.

Shwarts, Kalman. Interview with the Author. August 1, 1999.

Smith, Mildred (Davies). Interview with the Author. January 29, 2000.

Sternenberg, Robert. Interview with the Author. August 9, 1999.

Stovall, John H. Interview with the Author. December 6, 1995.

Tankersley, Corrie (Hill). Interview with the Author. October 23, 1993.

Thornton, J. Mills, III. Interviews with the Author. July 27, 1992, June 22, 1995.

Wampole, Charles, Jr. Interview with the Author. November 13, 1987.

Weed, Mary Louise (Caton). Audiotape. January 1992.

————. Interviews with the Author. January 7, 12, November 8, 1994.

Wiggins, Sarah (Woolfolk). Memorandum to the Author. September 28, 1994.

Yelverton, Gerald P. Interview with the Author. May 12, 1992.

————. "Moonlight Serenade." Memorandum to the Author. June 1992.

Young, Robert A., Jr. Interview with the Author. November 10, 1997.

————. Memoranda to the Author. January 30, 1995, August 27, 1998.

LETTERS

Catherine ("Kitty" Johnson) Cobb Collection.
Margaret (Peggy Penton) Cravey Collection.
William Howard Collection.
Paul Robinson Collection.

Bese Stovall to John H. Stovall, July 29, 1944. Collection of Mr. and Mrs. John Stovall.

WSFA *Letter from Home.* No. 1, August 6, 1943–no. 126, December 28, 1945 (containing last letter). [Seven boxes of letters from service people responding to *Letter from Home.*]

NEWSPAPERS

Alabama Journal. 1939–1945.
Atlanta Daily World. January 3, 1944.
Baltimore Afro-American. September 11, 1943.
Chicago Tribune. August 22, 1942.
Montgomery Advertiser. 1939–1946.
[*Montgomery Advertiser*] "Alabama at the Front." December 14, 1941–March 17, 1946. ["Alabama at the Front" appeared in the paper's Sunday edition almost weekly during this period and included photographs, letters, letter fragments, diary excerpts, and portions of official documents such as interviews, orders, and the citations for decorations.]
Nashville Globe and Independent. November 13, 1942.
Pittsburg Courier. November 11, 1944.
Syracuse Herald-Journal. July 7, 1945.

OTHER

Carr, Johnnie J. USO Certificate. n.d. Collection of Mrs. Johnnie J. Carr.
Cravey, Margaret (Peggy Penton) Cravey. Paper presented at Architreats Program, Alabama Department of Archives and History, Montgomery. October 8, 1993.
Montgomery City Commission. Minutes. 1939–1946.
Montgomery City Directory. Montgomery, Ala.: R. L. Polk & Company, 1939–1946.
Montgomery County Board of Education. History of Black Schools in Montgomery. Montgomery, Ala.: Montgomery County Board of Education, n.d.
Montgomery County Probate Judge's Office. Tax Assessment Records. Books LG. 675, 684, 686, 691–692. Montgomery: Alabama Department of Archives and History.
Nettles, Jean (Severence). Excerpt from diary. August 26, n.d. [1939–1945].
Red Cross. Annual Report of Montgomery County Chapter. December 1, 1943–November 10, 1944.

SECONDARY SOURCES

ARTICLES

Allen, Lee N. "Auburn Fifty Years Ago." *Alabama Historical Association Newsletter* (March 1995): 8–9.

"An Auburn Knight Who Made It Big in the Big Time: Gerald P. Yelverton, AK '35–38." *Auburn Knights Association Newsletter,* September 15, 1944, pp. 3–4.

"A Night at the USO." *Alabama Magazine,* May 8, 1942, p. 12.

Ausfeld, Margaret Lynne, and Christine C. Neal. "The World of Kelly Fitzpatrick." *Alabama Heritage* (Summer 1996): 16–19.

Benton, Jeff. "Lanier's South Court Building Completed in 1929." *Montgomery Advertiser,* August 27, 1994.

Bibb, T. Clifford. "A Brief History of Alabama State University." *Montgomery County Historical Society Herald* 4 (October 1995): 9–11.

"Cadet Ball." *Alabama Magazine,* May 29, 1942, pp. 8–9.

Carter, Dibby. "Little Generals." *Montgomery Advertiser,* November 17 and December 15, 1940.

Crist, Sara. "An Army Camp Arises in a Peanut Grove." *Montgomery Advertiser,* December 15, 1940.

———. "Nazi Fear Stalks Refugees in Montgomery." *Montgomery Advertiser,* May 19, 1940.

———. "Southern Art Adjudged Best in Southern Homes." *Montgomery Advertiser,* November 17, 1940.

Ennels, Jerome, and Wesley Phillips Newton. "Then and Now: A Brief History of Maxwell Air Force Base." *Montgomery Advertiser,* August 5, 1993.

"Fine Folk: The Art of Bill Traylor." *American Way* 25 (February 15, 1992): 66–71.

McFarland, Stephen L., and Wesley Phillips Newton. "Turning Point." *Montgomery Advertiser,* March 4, 1994.

Manchester, William. "The Raggedy Ass Marines." In Mordecai Richter, ed., *Writers on World War II.* New York: Alfred A. Knopf, 1991.

Miller, Edward G. "Kesternich: Key Victory in the Hurtgen Campaign." *World War II* 11 (November 1996): 30–36.

Newton, Wesley Phillips. "Launching a Legend: Maxwell Field and Glenn Miller's Army Air Forces Band." *Alabama Review* 53, no. 4 (October 2000): 271–96.

———. "The Blue and Gray Game." *Montgomery Living.* November/December, 1998, pp. 11–14.

———. "City Was War Weary in '45." *Montgomery Advertiser.* May 7, 1995.

———. "The Death of an Alabama Soldier." Manuscript. Montgomery, Ala., n.d.

———. "The Early History of Commercial Aviation in Montgomery." Manuscript. Montgomery, Ala., n.d.

———. "Montgomery and Hollywood." *Montgomery County Historical Society Herald* 6 (July 1998): 4–7.

———. My Short Military Career. Untitled manuscript. Montgomery, Ala., n.d.

———. "News of Assault Brought Tears, Prayers." *Montgomery Advertiser,* June 6, 1994.

———."Soldier's Letters Tell of World War II." *Montgomery Advertiser,* December 11, 1994.

———. "Twister." *Montgomery County Historical Society Herald* 4 (July 1996): 8–9.

———. "Word of War's End Spread Quickly." *Montgomery Advertiser,* August 14, 1995.

Robbins, Chrys. "Blue-Gray Colonels." *Montgomery Living,* November/December 1998, pp. 17–18.

Robison, Clara Lull. "Dixie Art Colony Ends Eighth Successful Season." *Montgomery Advertiser,* August 25, 1940.

Scott, John B., Jr. "The Crommelin Brothers." *Alabama Heritage,* no. 46 (Fall 1997): 14.

Thornton, J. Mills, III. "Alabama Politics, J. Thomas Heflin, and the Expulsion Movement of 1929." In Sarah Woolfolk Wiggins, ed., *From Civil War to Civil Rights: Alabama, 1860–1960: An Anthology from the Alabama Review.* Tuscaloosa: University of Alabama Press, 1987.

———. "Challenge and Response in the Montgomery Bus Boycott of 1955–1956." In Sarah Woolfolk Wiggins, ed., *From Civil War to Civil Rights, 1860-1960: An Anthology from the Alabama Review.* Tuscaloosa: University of Alabama Press, 1987.

Williams, Lynn Barstis. "The Dixie Art Colony." *Alabama Heritage,* no. 41 (Summer 1996): 6–15.

BOOKS AND PAMPHLETS

Allen, Lee N. *The First 100 Years of Montgomery's First Baptist Church.*

Montgomery, Ala.: First Baptist Church, 1979.

Allen, Thomas B., and Norman Polmar. *Code-Name Fail Safe: The Secret Plan to Invade Japan—and Why Truman Dropped the Bomb.* New York: Simon and Schuster, 1995.

Ambrose, Stephen E. *D-Day, June 6, 1944: The Climactic Battle of World War II.* New York: Simon and Schuster, 1994.

Anderson, Robert Earle. *The Merchant Marine and the World Frontier.* New York: Cornell Maritime Press, 1945.

Banner, Lois. *Women in Modern America: A Brief History.* New York: Harcourt Brace Jovanovich, 1974.

Bells and Pomegranates. Montgomery, Ala.: Huntingdon College, 1943.

Bennett, Michael J. *When Dreams Came True: the G.I. Bill and the Making of Modern America.* Washington, D.C.: Brassey's, 1996.

Blum, John Morton. *V Was for Victory: Politics and American Culture During World War II.* New York: Harcourt Brace Jovanovich, 1976.

Branch, Taylor. *Parting the Waters: America in the King Years, 1954–63.* New York: Simon and Schuster, 1988.

Brooks, Michael. *Swing Time! The Fabulous Big Band Era, 1925–1955.* New York: Legacy Big Bands, 1993.

Carmen, Harry J., Harold C. Syrett, and Bernard W. Wishy. *A History of the American People,* vol. 2, *Since 1865.* New York: Alfred A. Knopf, 1965.

Carter, Kit C., and Robert Meuller, comp. *The Army Air Forces in World War II: Combat Chronology.* Washington, D.C.: Office of Air Force History, 1977.

Coleman, Lonnie. *Escape the Thunder.* New York: E. P. Dutton, 1944.

Connor, Tom. *Remember When. . . .* Montgomery, Ala.: Montgomery Advertiser, 1989.

Cronenberg, Allen T. *Forth to the Mighty Conflict: Alabama and World War II.* Tuscaloosa: University of Alabama Press, 1995.

Ellison, Rhoda Coleman. *History of Huntingdon College, 1854–1954.* Tuscaloosa: University of Alabama Press, 1954.

Ennels, Jerome A., and Wesley Phillips Newton. *The Wisdom of Eagles: A History of Maxwell Air Force Base.* Montgomery, Ala.: Black Belt Press, 1997.

Flynt, J. Wayne. *Dixie's Forgotten People: The South's PoorWhites.* Bloomington: Indiana University Press, 1979.

Ford, Daniel. *Claire Chennault and the American Volunteer Group.* Washington, D.C.: Smithsonian Institution Press, 1991.

Fussell, Paul. *Wartime: Understanding Behavior in the Second World War.* New York: Oxford University Press, 1989.

Goss, William A. "Air Defense of the Western Hemisphere." In *Plans and Early Operations, vol. 1, The Army Air Forces in World War II.* Chicago: University of Chicago Press, 1948.

Greenhaw, Wayne. *Montgomery: The Biography of a City.* Montgomery, Ala.: Montgomery Advertiser Company, 1993.

Hartmann, Susan M. *The Home Front and Beyond: American Women in the 1940s.* New York: G. K. Hall/Twayne, 1982.

History of the Catoma Street Church of Christ. Montgomery, Ala.: Catoma Street Church, 1973.

A History of Montgomery in Pictures. Montgomery, Ala.: Society of Pioneers of Montgomery, n.d.

Key, V. O., Jr. *Southern Politics in State and Nation.* New York: Alfred A. Knopf, 1949.

Kohn, Peter. *The Cradle.* New York: Vantage Press, 1969.

Lanier Oracle. 1943. Montgomery, Ala.: Sidney Lanier High School, 1943.

Lightning: The History of the Seventy-eighth Infantry Division. Washington, D.C.: Infantry Journal Press, 1947.

Lingeman, Richard R. *Don't You Know There's a War On? The Home Front, 1941–1945.* New York: Putnam, 1970.

MacDonald, Charles B. *A Time for Trumpets.* New York: William Morrow and Company, 1985.

McFarland, Stephen L., and Wesley Phillips Newton. *To Command the Sky: The Battle for Air Superiority over Germany, 1942–1944.* Washington, D.C.: Smithsonian Institution Press, 1991.

Mahoney, William J., Jr. *150 Years, 1824–1974: A Sesquicentennial History of the First Presbyterian Church, Montgomery, Alabama.* Montgomery, Ala.: Brown Printing Company, 1974.

Millett, Allen R., and Peter Maslowski. *For the Common Defense: A Military History of the United States of America.* New York: Free Press, 1984.

Morison, Samuel Eliot. *The Oxford History of the American People.* New York: Oxford University Press, 1965.

Morris, Richard B., ed. *The Encyclopedia of American History.* New York: Harper and Brothers, 1953.

Neeley, Mary Ann. *Montgomery: Capital City Corners.* Dover, N.H.: Arcadia Publishing, 1997.

Newton, Wesley Phillips, and Charles Troncale. *A History of the Church of St. Bede Venerable, 1925–1990.* Montgomery, Ala.: Church of St. Bede, 1990.

Paterson, Judith Hillman. *Sweet Mystery: A Book of Remembering.* New York: Farrar, Straus, and Giroux, 1996.

Polenberg, Richard. *One Nation Divisible.* New York: Penguin Books, 1980.

————. *War and Society: The United States, 1941–1945.* Philadelphia: J. B. Lippincott, 1972.

Roberts, J. M. *A History of Europe.* New York, Allen Lane, 1996.

Roer, Rhine, Ruhr. Berlin: Seventy-eighth Infantry Division, 1945. (Official history of the 310th Infantry.)

Rogers, William Warren, Robert David Ward, Leah Rawls Atkins, and Wayne Flynt. *Alabama: The History of a Deep South State.* Tuscaloosa, Ala.: University of Alabama Press: 1994.

Schulman, Bruce, J. *From Cotton Belt to Sun Belt: Federal Policy, Economic Development, and the Transformation of the South.* New York: Oxford University Press, 1991.

Sherry, Michael. *The Rise of American Air Power: The Creation of Armageddon.* New Haven: Yale University Press, 1987.

Simon, Hannah, ed. *The First 100 Years of Kahl Montgomery.* Montgomery, Ala.: Paragon Press, 1952.

Spector, Ronald H. *Eagle Against the Sun.* New York: Vintage Books, 1985.

Stokesbury, James L. *A Short History of Air Power.* New York: William Morrow, 1986.

————. *A Short History of World War II.* New York: William Morrow, 1980.

The Story of WSFA, NBC-Red, South Central. Peoria, Ill.: National Radio Personalities, 1941.

Thomas, Mary Martha. *Riveting and Rationing in Dixie: Alabama Women and the Second World War.* Tuscaloosa, Ala.: University of Alabama Press, 1987.

Time-Life History of World War II. New York: Barnes and Noble, 1995.

Tindall, George Burns. *The Emergence of the New South, 1913–1945.* Baton Rouge: Louisiana State University Press, 1967.

USAF Credits for the Destruction of Enemy Aircraft. USAF Historical Study No. 85. Montgomery, Ala.: Maxwell Air Force Base, Historical Research Agency, 1978.

Weinberg, Gerhard L. *A World at Arms: A Global History of World War II.* Cambridge: Cambridge University Press, 1994.

Index

About the Author

Wesley Phillips Newton, born and raised in Montgomery, was drafted into the army in 1943 at age eighteen and subsequently wounded and taken prisoner during the Battle of the Bulge. He received his bachelor's degree in English from the University of Missouri and his master's and Ph.D. in history from the University of Alabama. He is Professor Emeritus of History at Auburn University.